MongoDB Cookbook
Second Edition

Over 80 comprehensive recipes that will help you master
the art of using and administering MongoDB 3

Cyrus Dasadia

Amol Nayak

BIRMINGHAM - MUMBAI

MongoDB Cookbook
Second Edition

Copyright © 2016 Packt Publishing

First published: November 2014

Second Edition: January 2016

Production reference: 1060116

Published by Packt Publishing Ltd.
Livery Place
35 Livery Street
Birmingham B3 2PB, UK.

ISBN 978-1-78528-998-9

www.packtpub.com

Credits

Authors
Cyrus Dasadia

Amol Nayak

Reviewers
Christopher Dambamuromo

Laurence Putra Franslay

Jason Nichols

Commissioning Editor
Dipika Gaonkar

Acquisition Editor
Shaon Basu

Content Development Editor
Zeeyan Pinheiro

Technical Editor
Bharat Patil

Copy Editor
Tasneem Fatehi

Project Coordinator
Francina Pinto

Proofreader
Safis Editing

Indexer
Mariammal Chettiyar

Graphics
Disha Haria

Production Coordinator
Arvindkumar Gupta

Cover Work
Arvindkumar Gupta

About the Authors

Cyrus Dasadia always liked tinkering with open source projects since 1996. He has been working as a Linux system administrator and part-time programmer for over a decade. He works at InMobi, where he loves designing tools and platforms. His love for MongoDB started in 2013, when he was amazed by its ease of use and stability. Since then, almost all of his projects are written with MongoDB as the primary backend. Cyrus is also the creator of an open source alert management system called CitoEngine. He likes spending his spare time trying to reverse engineer software, playing computer games, or increasing his silliness quotient by watching reruns of Monty Python.

To my wife, Nilu, provider of unconditional love and support; recipient of bad jokes.

Amol Nayak is a MongoDB certified developer and has been working as a developer for over 8 years. He is currently employed with a leading financial data provider, working on cutting-edge technologies. He has used MongoDB as a database for various systems at his current and previous workplaces to support enormous data volumes. He is an open source enthusiast and supports it by contributing to open source frameworks and promoting them. He has made contributions to the Spring Integration project, and his contributions are the adapters for JPA, XQuery, MongoDB, Push notifications to mobile devices, and Amazon Web Services (AWS). He has also made some contributions to the Spring Data MongoDB project. Apart from technology, he is passionate about motor sports and is a race official at Buddh International Circuit, India, for various motor sports events. Earlier, he was the author of *Instant MongoDB, Packt Publishing*.

I would like to thank everyone at Packt Publishing who has been involved with this book. It started when Luke Presland from Packt Publishing approached me to author a book on Mongo. I was skeptical to take up the opportunity due to other commitments and tight deadlines, but if it wasn't for my mom, friends, and office colleagues who convinced me to take up the opportunity, I would not have written this book. The chapters and content covered was a lot, and I had a tough time keeping up with the timelines. A special thanks to Priyanka, Rebecca, Mary, and Joel with whom I interacted the most; they were very flexible to my changes in delivery timelines. A big thanks to Douglas Duncan and other reviewers of the book for reviewing the book closely and helping improve the quality of the content drastically. Finally, I would like to thank the other staff at Packt Publishing who were involved in the book's publishing process but haven't interacted with me.

About the Reviewers

Christopher Dambamuromo is a MongoDB evangelist who is an active contributor to StackOverflow on the MongoDB tag. Chris frequently engages the open source community and foster adoption of MongoDB. He helps engineering teams build scalable and performant applications in MongoDB. He also assesses the health, scalability, and capacity of distributed systems and advises engineering teams on the schema design, architecture, and deployment planning. He is a passionate and proficient C#/BI developer with more than 10 years of experience producing code to a consistently high standard. Chris has constantly been honing his skills in the technical aspects of software and business intelligence engineering (JavaScript, Node.js, HTML5, CSS3, Python, R, Java, ASP.NET MVC, C# Microsoft BI stack—MS SQL server, SSIS, SSRS, SSAS, SharePoint, and PowerPivot), data modeling, systems architecture, as well as business applications for BI solutions. He has an MSc degree in intelligent computer systems from the University of Glamorgan (UK), an MSc degree in mathematics and computing for finance from Swansea University, UK, and a BSc degree with honours in applied mathematics from the National University of Science and Technology, Zimbabwe. Chris is very fond of anything closely or remotely related to data and mathematics, and as long as it can be represented as a string of ones and zeros and then analyzed and visualized, you've got his attention! His GitHub handle is `http://github.com/chrisdamba` and can be found on StackOverflow as `http://stackoverflow.com/users/122005/chridam`.

Laurence Putra Franslay is a software engineer working in Singapore and runs the Singapore MongoDB user group. In his free time, he hacks away on random stuff and picks up new technologies. His key interests lie in security and distributed systems. For more information, view his profile at `http://geeksphere.net/`.

www.PacktPub.com

Support files, eBooks, discount offers, and more

For support files and downloads related to your book, please visit www.PacktPub.com.

Did you know that Packt offers eBook versions of every book published, with PDF and ePub files available? You can upgrade to the eBook version at www.PacktPub.com and as a print book customer, you are entitled to a discount on the eBook copy. Get in touch with us at service@packtpub.com for more details.

At www.PacktPub.com, you can also read a collection of free technical articles, sign up for a range of free newsletters and receive exclusive discounts and offers on Packt books and eBooks.

https://www2.packtpub.com/books/subscription/packtlib

Do you need instant solutions to your IT questions? PacktLib is Packt's online digital book library. Here, you can search, access, and read Packt's entire library of books.

Why Subscribe?

- ► Fully searchable across every book published by Packt
- ► Copy and paste, print, and bookmark content
- ► On demand and accessible via a web browser

Free Access for Packt account holders

If you have an account with Packt at www.PacktPub.com, you can use this to access PacktLib today and view 9 entirely free books. Simply use your login credentials for immediate access.

Table of Contents

Preface

MongoDB is a document-oriented, leading NoSQL database, which offers linear scalability, thus making it a good contender for high-volume, high-performance systems across all the business domains. It has an edge over the majority of NoSQL solutions for its ease of use, high performance, and rich features.

This book provides detailed recipes that describe how to use the different features of MongoDB. The recipes cover topics ranging from setting up MongoDB, knowing its programming language API, and monitoring and administration, to some advanced topics such as cloud deployment, integration with Hadoop, and some open source and proprietary tools for MongoDB. The recipe format presents the information in a concise, actionable form; this lets you refer to the recipe to address and know the details of just the use case in hand without going through the entire book.

What this book covers

Chapter 1, *Installing and Starting the Server*, is all about starting MongoDB. It will demonstrate how to start the server in the standalone mode, as a replica set, and as a shard, with the provided start up options from the command line or configuration file.

Chapter 2, *Command-line Operations and Indexes*, has simple recipes to perform CRUD operations in the Mongo shell and create various types of indexes in the shell.

Chapter 3, *Programming Language Drivers*, discusses about programming language APIs. Though Mongo supports a vast array of languages, we will look at how to use the drivers to connect to the MongoDB server from Java and Python programs only. This chapter also explores the MongoDB wire protocol used for communication between the server and programming language clients.

Chapter 4, *Administration*, contains many recipes for administration or your MongoDB deployment. This chapter covers a lot of frequently used administrative tasks such as viewing the stats of the collections and database, viewing and killing long-running operations and other replica sets, and sharding-related administration.

Chapter 5, Advanced Operations, is an extension of *Chapter 2, Command-line Operations and Indexes*. We will look at some of the slightly advanced features such as implementing server-side scripts, geospatial search, GridFS, full text search, and how to integrate MongoDB with an external full text search engine.

Chapter 6, Monitoring and Backups, tells you all about administration and some basic monitoring. However, MongoDB provides a state-of-the-art monitoring and real-time backup service, MongoDB Monitoring Service (MMS). In this chapter, we will look at some recipes around monitoring and backup using MMS.

Chapter 7, Deploying MongoDB on the Cloud, covers recipes that use MongoDB service providers for cloud deployment. We will set up our own MongoDB server on the AWS cloud as well as run MongoDB in Docker containers.

Chapter 8, Integration with Hadoop, covers recipes to integrate MongoDB with Hadoop to use the Hadoop MapReduce API in order to run MapReduce jobs on the data residing in MongoDB data files and write the results to them. We will also see how to use AWS EMR to run our MapReduce jobs on the cloud using Amazon's Hadoop cluster, EMR, with the mongo-hadoop connector.

Chapter 9, Open Source and Proprietary Tools, is about using frameworks and products built around MongoDB to improve a developer's productivity or about simplifying some of the day-to-day jobs using Mongo. Unless explicitly mentioned, the products/frameworks that we will be looking at in this chapter are open source.

Appendix, Concepts for Reference, gives you a bit of additional information on the write concern and read preference for reference.

What you need for this book

The version of MongoDB used to try out the recipes is 3.0.2. The recipes are good for version 2.6.*x* as well. In case of some special feature specific to version 2.6.*x*, it would be explicitly mentioned in the recipe. Unless explicitly mentioned, all commands should be executed on Ubuntu Linux.

The samples where Java programming was involved were tested and run on Java Version 1.7, and Python code was run using Python v2.7 (compatible with Python 3). For MongoDB drivers, you can choose to use the latest available version.

These are pretty common types of software, and their minimum versions are used across different recipes. All the recipes in this book will mention the required software to complete it and their respective versions. Some recipes need to be tested on a Windows system, while some on Linux.

Who this book is for

This book is designed for administrators and developers who are interested in knowing MongoDB and using it as a high-performance and scalable data storage. It is also for those who know the basics of MongoDB and would like to expand their knowledge. The audience of this book is expected to have at least some basic knowledge of MongoDB.

Conventions

In this book, you will find a number of styles of text that distinguish between different kinds of information. Here are some examples of these styles, and an explanation of their meaning.

In this book, you will find a number of text styles that distinguish between different kinds of information. Here are some examples of these styles and an explanation of their meaning.

Code words in text, database table names, folder names, filenames, file extensions, pathnames, dummy URLs, user input, and Twitter handles are shown as follows: "Create the `/data/mongo/db directory` (or any of your choice)."

A block of code is set as follows:

```
import com.mongodb.DB;
import com.mongodb.DBCollection;
import com.mongodb.DBObject;
import com.mongodb.MongoClient;
```

Any command-line input or output is written as follows:

```
$ sudo apt-get install default-jdk
```

New terms and **important words** are shown in bold. Words that you see on the screen, in menus or dialog boxes for example, appear in the text like this: "As we want to start a free micro instance, check the **Free tier only** checkbox on the left".

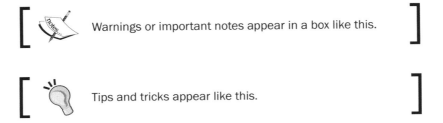

Warnings or important notes appear in a box like this.

Tips and tricks appear like this.

Reader feedback

Feedback from our readers is always welcome. Let us know what you think about this book—what you liked or may have disliked. Reader feedback is important for us to develop titles that you really get the most out of.

To send us general feedback, simply send an e-mail to feedback@packtpub.com, and mention the book title via the subject of your message.

If there is a topic that you have expertise in and you are interested in either writing or contributing to a book, see our author guide on www.packtpub.com/authors.

Customer support

Now that you are the proud owner of a Packt book, we have a number of things to help you to get the most from your purchase.

Downloading the example code

You can download the example code files for all Packt books you have purchased from your account at http://www.packtpub.com. If you purchased this book elsewhere, you can visit http://www.packtpub.com/support and register to have the files e-mailed directly to you.

Errata

Although we have taken every care to ensure the accuracy of our content, mistakes do happen. If you find a mistake in one of our books—maybe a mistake in the text or the code—we would be grateful if you would report this to us. By doing so, you can save other readers from frustration and help us improve subsequent versions of this book. If you find any errata, please report them by visiting http://www.packtpub.com/submit-errata, selecting your book, clicking on the **errata submission form** link, and entering the details of your errata. Once your errata are verified, your submission will be accepted and the errata will be uploaded on our website, or added to any list of existing errata, under the Errata section of that title. Any existing errata can be viewed by selecting your title from http://www.packtpub.com/support.

Piracy

Piracy of copyright material on the Internet is an ongoing problem across all media. At Packt, we take the protection of our copyright and licenses very seriously. If you come across any illegal copies of our works, in any form, on the Internet, please provide us with the location address or website name immediately so that we can pursue a remedy.

Please contact us at copyright@packtpub.com with a link to the suspected pirated material.

We appreciate your help in protecting our authors, and our ability to bring you valuable content.

Questions

You can contact us at questions@packtpub.com if you are having a problem with any aspect of the book, and we will do our best to address it.

1

Installing and Starting the Server

In this chapter, we will cover the following recipes:

- Installing single node MongoDB
- Starting a single node instance using the command-line options
- Installing single node MongoDB with options from the config file
- Connecting to a single node in the Mongo shell with JavaScript
- Connecting to a single node from a Java client
- Connecting to a single node from a Python client
- Starting multiple instances as part of a replica set
- Connecting to the replica set in the shell to query and insert data
- Connecting to the replica set to query and insert data from a Java client
- Connecting to the replica set to query and insert data using a Python client
- Starting a simple sharded environment of two shards
- Connecting to a shard in the shell and performing operations

Introduction

In this chapter, we will look at starting up the MongoDB server. Though it is a cakewalk to start the server with default settings for development purposes, there are numerous options available to fine-tune the start up behavior. We will start the server as a single node and then introduce various configuration options. We will conclude this chapter by setting up a simple replica set and running a sharded cluster. So, let's get started with installing and setting up the MongoDB server in the easiest way possible for simple development purposes.

Installing single node MongoDB

In this recipe, we will look at installing MongoDB in the standalone mode. This is the simplest and quickest way to start a MongoDB server, but it is seldom used for production use cases. However, this is the most common way to start the server for development purposes. In this recipe, we will start the server without looking at a lot of other startup options.

Getting ready

Well, assuming that we have downloaded the MongoDB binaries from the download site, extracted it, and have the resulting bin directory in the operating system's path variable. (This is not mandatory, but it really becomes convenient after doing so.) The binaries can be downloaded from http://www.mongodb.org/downloads after selecting your host operating system.

How to do it...

1. Create the directory, /data/mongo/db (or any of your choice). This will be our database directory, and it needs to have permission to write to it by the mongod (the mongo server process) process.

2. We will start the server from the console with the data directory, /data/mongo/db, as follows:

   ```
   > mongod --dbpath  /data/mongo/db
   ```

How it works...

If you see the following line on the console, you have successfully started the server:

```
[initandlisten] waiting for connections on port 27017
```

Starting a server can't get easier than this. Despite the simplicity in starting the server, there are a lot of configuration options that can be used to tune the behavior of the server on startup. Most of the default options are sensible and need not be changed. With the default values, the server should be listening to port `27017` for new connections, and the logs will be printed out to the standard output.

See also

There are times where we would like to configure some options on server startup. In the *Installing single node MongoDB* recipe, we will use some more start up options.

Starting a single node instance using command-line options

In this recipe, we will see how to start a standalone single node server with some command-line options. We will see an example where we want to do the following:

- Start the server listening to port `27000`
- Logs should be written to `/logs/mongo.log`
- The database directory is `/data/mongo/db`

As the server has been started for development purposes, we don't want to preallocate full-size database files. (We will soon see what this means.)

Getting ready

If you have already seen and executed the *Installing single node MongoDB* recipe, you need not do anything different. If all these prerequisites are met, we are good for this recipe.

How to do it...

1. The `/data/mongo/db` directory for the database and `/logs/` for the logs should be created and present on your filesystem with appropriate permissions to write to it.

2. Execute the following command:

```
> mongod --port 27000 --dbpath /data/mongo/db –logpath /logs/
mongo.log --smallfiles
```

How it works...

Ok, this wasn't too difficult and is similar to the previous recipe, but we have some additional command-line options this time around. MongoDB actually supports quite a few options at startup, and we will see a list of the most common and important ones in my opinion:

Option	Description
`--help` or `-h`	This is used to print the information of various start up options available.
`--config` or `-f`	This specifies the location of the configuration file that contains all the configuration options. We will see more on this option in a later recipe. It is just a convenient way of specifying the configurations in a file rather than on the command prompt; especially when the number of options specified is more. Using a separate configuration file shared across different MongoDB instances will also ensure that all the instances are running with identical configurations.
`--verbose` or `-v`	This makes the logs more verbose; we can put more v's to make the output even more verbose, for example, `-vvvvv`.
`--quiet`	This gives a quieter output; this is the opposite of verbose or the `-v` option. It will keep the logs less chatty and clean.
`--port`	This option is used if you are looking to start the server listening to some port other than the default `27017`. We would be frequently using this option whenever we are looking to start multiple mongo servers on the same machine, for example, `--port 27018` will start the server listening to port `27018` for new connections.
`--logpath`	This provides a path to a log file where the logs will be written. The value defaults to `STDOUT`. For example, `--logpath /logs/server.out` will use `/logs/server.out` as the log file for the server. Remember that the value provided should be a file and not a directory where the logs will be written.
`--logappend`	This option appends to the existing log file, if any. The default behavior is to rename the existing log file and then create a new file for the logs of the currently started mongo instance. Suppose that we have used the name of the log file as `server.out`, and on startup, the file exists, then by default this file will be renamed as `server.out.<timestamp>`, where `<timestamp>` is the current time. The time is GMT as against the local time. Let's assume that the current date is October 28th, 2013 and time is 12:02:15, then the file generated will have the following value as the timestamp: `2013-10-28T12-02-15`.

Option	Description
`--dbpath`	This provides you with the directory where a new database will be created or an existing database is present. The value defaults to `/data/db`. We will start the server using `/data /mongo/db` as the database directory. Note that the value should be a directory rather than the name of the file.
`--smallfiles`	This is used frequently for development purposes when we plan to start more than one mongo instance on our local machine. Mongo, on startup, creates a database file of size 64 MB (on 64-bit machines). This preallocation happens for performance reasons, and the file is created with zeros written to it to fill out space on the disk. Adding this option on startup creates a preallocated file of 16 MB only (again, on a 64-bit machine). This option also reduces the maximum size of the database and journal files. Avoid using this option for production deployments. Additionally, the file sizes double to a maximum of 2 GB by default. If the `--smallfile` option is chosen, it goes up to a maximum of 512 MB.
`--replSet`	This option is used to start the server as a member of the replica set. The value of this `arg` is the name of the replica set, for example, `--replSet repl1`. You will learn more on this option in a later recipe where we will start a simple mongo replica set.
`--configsvr`	This option is used to start the server as a configuration server. The role of the configuration server will be made clearer when we set up a simple sharded environment in a later recipe in this chapter.
`--shardsvr`	This informs the started mongod process that this server is being started as a shard server. By giving this option, the server also listens to port `27018` instead of the default `27017`. We will know more on this option when we start a simple sharded server.
`--oplogSize`	Oplog is the backbone of replication. It is a capped collection where the data being written to the primary instances is stored in order to be replicated to the secondary instances. This collection resides in a database named `local`. On initialization of the replica set, the disk space for oplog is preallocated, and the database file (for the local database) is filled with zeros as placeholders. The default value is 5% of the disk space, which should be good enough for most of the cases. The size of oplog is crucial because capped collections are of a fixed size and they discard the oldest documents in them on exceeding their size, thereby making space for new documents. Having a very small oplog size can result in data being discarded before being replicated to secondary nodes. A large oplog size can result in unnecessary disk space utilization and large duration for the replica set initialization. For development purposes, when we start multiple server processes on the same host, we might want to keep the oplog size to a minimum value, quickly initiate the replica set, and use minimum disk space.

Option	Description
`--storageEngine`	Starting with MongoDB 3.0, a new storage engine called Wired Tiger was introduced. The previous (default) storage engine is now called **mmapv1**. To start MongoDB with Wired Tiger instead of `mmapv1`, use the `wiredTiger` value with this option.
`--dirctoryperdb`	By default, MongoDB's database files are stored in a common directory (as provided in `--dbpath`). This option allows you to store each database in its own subdirectory in the aforementioned data directory. Having such granular control allows you to have separate disks for each database.

There's more...

For an exhaustive list of options that are available, use the `--help` or `-h` option. This list of options is not exhaustive, and we will see some more coming up in later recipes as and when we need them. In the next recipe, we will see how to use a configuration file instead of the command-line arguments.

See also

> ▸ *Single node installation of MongoDB with options from config file* for using configuration files to provide start up options

> ▸ *Starting multiple instances as part of a replica set* to start a replica set

> ▸ *Starting a simple sharded environment of two shards* to set up a sharded environment

Single node installation of MongoDB with options from the config file

As we can see, providing options from the command line does the work, but it starts getting awkward as soon as the number of options that we provide increase. We have a nice and clean alternative to provide the start up options from a configuration file rather than as command-line arguments.

Getting ready

If you have already executed the *Installing single node MongoDB* recipe, you need not do anything different as all the prerequisites of this recipe are the same.

How to do it...

The /data/mongo/db directory for the database and /logs/ for the logs should be created and present on your filesystem with the appropriate permissions to write to it and perform the following steps:

1. Create a configuration file that can have any arbitrary name. In our case, let's say that we create this in /conf/mongo.conf. We then edit the file and add the following lines to it:

    ```
    port = 27000
    dbpath = /data/mongo/db
    logpath = /logs/mongo.log
    smallfiles = true
    ```

2. Start the mongo server using the following command:

    ```
    > mongod --config  /config/mongo.conf
    ```

How it works...

All the command-line options that we discussed in the previous recipe, *Starting a single node instance using command-line options*, hold true. We are just providing them in a configuration file instead. If you have not visited the previous recipe, I would recommend you to do so as that is where we discussed some of the common command-line options. The properties are specified as <property name> = <value>. For all the properties that don't have values, for example, the smallfiles option, the value given is a Boolean value, true. If we need to have a verbose output, we would add v=true (or multiple v's to make it more verbose) to our configuration file. If you already know what the command-line option is, then it is pretty easy to guess what the value of the property is in the file. It is almost the same as the command-line option with just the hyphen removed.

Connecting to a single node in the Mongo shell with JavaScript

This recipe is about starting the mongo shell and connecting to a MongoDB server. Here we also demonstrate how to load JavaScript code in the shell. Though this is not always required, it is handy when we have a large block of JavaScript code with variables and functions with some business logic in them that is required to be executed from the shell frequently and we want these functions to be available in the shell always.

Getting ready

Although it is possible to run the mongo shell without connecting to the MongoDB server using `mongo --nodb`, we would rarely need to do so. To start a server on the localhost without much of a hassle, take a look at the first recipe, *Installing single node MongoDB*, and start the server.

How to do it...

1. First, we create a simple JavaScript file and call it `hello.js`. Type the following body in the `hello.js` file:

    ```
    function sayHello(name) {
      print('Hello ' + name + ', how are you?')
    }
    ```

2. Save this file at the location, `/mongo/scripts/hello.js`. (This can be saved at any other location too.)

3. On the command prompt, execute the following:

    ```
    > mongo --shell /mongo/scripts/hello.js
    ```

4. On executing this, we should see the following printed to our console:

    ```
    MongoDB shell version: 3.0.2
    connecting to: test
    >
    ```

5. Test the database that the shell is connected to by typing the following command:

    ```
    > db
    ```

    This should print out `test` to the console.

6. Now, type the following command in the shell:

    ```
    > sayHello('Fred')
    ```

7. You should get the following response:

    ```
    Hello Fred, how are you?
    ```

 Note: This book was written with MongoDB version 3.0.2. There is a good chance that you may be using a later version and hence see a different version number in the mongo shell.

How it works...

The JavaScript function that we executed here is of no practical use and is just used to demonstrate how a function can be preloaded on the startup of the shell. There could be multiple functions in the `.js` file containing valid JavaScript code—possibly some complex business logic.

On executing the `mongo` command without any arguments, we connect to the MongoDB server running on localhost and listen for new connections on the default port `27017`. Generally speaking, the format of the command is as follows:

```
mongo <options> <db address> <.js files>
```

In cases where there are no arguments passed to the mongo executable, it is equivalent to the passing of the `db address` as `localhost:27017/test`.

Let's look at some example values of the `db address` command-line option and its interpretation:

▶ `mydb`: This will connect to the server running on localhost and listen for a connection on port `27017`. The database connected will be `mydb`.

▶ `mongo.server.host/mydb`: This will connect to the server running on `mongo.server.host` and the default port `27017`. The database connected will be `mydb`.

▶ `mongo.server.host:27000/mydb`: This will connect to the server running on `mongo.server.host` and the port `27000`. The database connected will be `mydb`.

▶ `mongo.server.host:27000`: This will connect to the server running on `mongo.server.host` and the port `27000`. The database connected will be the default database test.

Now, there are quite a few options available on the mongo client too. We will see a few of them in the following table:

Option	Description
`--help` or `-h`	This shows help regarding the usage of various command-line options.
`--shell`	When the `.js` files are given as arguments, these scripts get executed and the mongo client will exit. Providing this option ensures that the shell remains running after the JavaScript files execute. All the functions and variables defined in these `.js` files are available in the shell on startup. As in the preceding case, the `sayHello` function defined in the JavaScript file is available in the shell for invocation.
`--port`	The specifies the port of the mongo server where the client needs to connect.
`--host`	This specifies the hostname of the mongo server where the client needs to connect. If the `db address` is provided with the hostname, port, and database, then both the `--host` and `--port` options need not be specified.

Option	Description
`--username` or `-u`	This is relevant when security is enabled for mongo. It is used to provide the username of the user to be logged in.
`--password` or `-p`	This option is relevant when security is enabled for mongo. It is used to provide the password of the user to be logged in.

Connecting to a single node using a Java client

This recipe is about setting up the Java client for MongoDB. You will repeatedly refer to this recipe while working on others, so read it very carefully.

Getting ready

The following are the prerequisites for this recipe:

- Java SDK 1.6 or above is recommended.
- Use the latest version of Maven available. Version 3.3.3 was the latest at the time of writing this book.
- MongoDB Java driver version 3.0.1 was the latest at the time of writing this book.
- Connectivity to the Internet to access the online maven repository or a local repository. Alternatively, you may choose an appropriate local repository accessible to you from your computer.
- The Mongo server is up and running on localhost and port `27017`. Take a look at the first recipe, *Installing single node MongoDB*, and start the server.

How to do it...

1. Install the latest version of JDK from `https://www.java.com/en/download/` if you don't already have it on your machine. We will not be going through the steps to install JDK in this recipe, but before moving on with the next step, JDK should be present.

2. Maven needs to be downloaded from `http://maven.apache.org/download.cgi`. We should see something similar to the following image on the download page. Choose the binaries in a `.tar.gz` or `.zip` format and download it. This recipe is executed on a machine running on the Windows platform and thus these steps are for installation on Windows.

Maven 3.3.3

This is the current stable version of Maven.

	Link	Checksum	Signature
Maven 3.3.3 (Binary tar.gz)	apache-maven-3.3.3-bin.tar.gz	apache-maven-3.3.3-bin.tar.gz.md5	apache-maven-3.3.3-bin.tar.gz.asc
Maven 3.3.3 (Binary zip)	apache-maven-3.3.3-bin.zip	apache-maven-3.3.3-bin.zip.md5	apache-maven-3.3.3-bin.zip.asc
Maven 3.3.3 (Source tar.gz)	apache-maven-3.3.3-src.tar.gz	apache-maven-3.3.3-src.tar.gz.md5	apache-maven-3.3.3-src.tar.gz.asc
Maven 3.3.3 (Source zip)	apache-maven-3.3.3-src.zip	apache-maven-3.3.3-src.zip.md5	apache-maven-3.3.3-src.zip.asc
Release Notes	3.3.3		
Release Reference Documentation	3.3.3		

---

3. Once the archive has been downloaded, we need to extract it and put the absolute path of the `bin` folder in the extracted archive in the operating system's path variable. Maven also needs the path of JDK to be set as the `JAVA_HOME` environment variable. Remember to set the root of your JDK as the value of this variable.

4. All we need to do now is type `mvn -version` on the command prompt, and if we see the output that begins with something as follows, we have successfully set up maven:

```
> mvn -version
```

5. At this stage, we have maven installed, and we are now ready to create our simple project to write our first Mongo client in Java. We start by creating a `project` folder. Let's say that we create a folder called `Mongo Java`. Then we create a folder structure, `src/main/java`, in this `project` folder. The root of the `project` folder then contains a file called `pom.xml`. Once this folder's creation is done, the folder structure should look as follows:

```
Mongo Java
+--src
|      +main
|            +java
|--pom.xml
```

6. We just have the project skeleton with us. We shall now add some content to the `pom.xml` file. Not much is needed for this. The following content is all we need in the `pom.xml` file:

```
<project>
  <modelVersion>4.0.0</modelVersion>
  <name>Mongo Java</name>
  <groupId>com.packtpub</groupId>
  <artifactId>mongo-cookbook-java</artifactId>
  <version>1.0</version>     <packaging>jar</packaging>
  <dependencies>
```

```
      <dependency>
        <groupId>org.mongodb</groupId>
        <artifactId>mongo-java-driver</artifactId>
        <version>3.0.1</version>
      </dependency>
    </dependencies>
</project>
```

7. We finally write our Java client that will be used to connect to the Mongo server and execute some very basic operations. The following is the Java class in the `src/main/java` location in the `com.packtpub.mongo.cookbook` package, and the name of the class is `FirstMongoClient`:

```java
package com.packtpub.mongo.cookbook;

import com.mongodb.BasicDBObject;
import com.mongodb.DB;
import com.mongodb.DBCollection;
import com.mongodb.DBObject;
import com.mongodb.MongoClient;

import java.net.UnknownHostException;
import java.util.List;

/**
 * Simple Mongo Java client
 *
 */
public class FirstMongoClient {

    /**
     * Main method for the First Mongo Client. Here we shall be
connecting to a mongo
     * instance running on localhost and port 27017.
     *
     * @param args
     */
    public static final void main(String[] args)
throws UnknownHostException {
        MongoClient client = new MongoClient("localhost", 27017);
        DB testDB = client.getDB("test");
        System.out.println("Dropping person collection in test
database");
        DBCollection collection = testDB.getCollection("person");
        collection.drop();
```

```
        System.out.println("Adding a person document in the person
collection of test database");
        DBObject person =
new BasicDBObject("name", "Fred").append("age", 30);
        collection.insert(person);
        System.out.println("Now finding a person using findOne");
        person = collection.findOne();
        if(person != null) {
            System.out.printf("Person found, name is %s and age is
%d\n", person.get("name"), person.get("age"));
        }
        List<String> databases = client.getDatabaseNames();
        System.out.println("Database names are");
        int i = 1;
        for(String database : databases) {
            System.out.println(i++ + ": " + database);
        }
    System.out.println("Closing client");
        client.close();
    }
}
```

8. It's now time to execute the preceding Java code. We will execute it using maven from the shell. You should be in the same directory as pom.xml of the project:

```
mvn compile exec:java -Dexec.mainClass=com.packtpub.mongo.
cookbook.FirstMongoClient
```

How it works...

These were quite a lot of steps to follow. Let's look at some of them in more detail. Everything up to step 6 is straightforward and doesn't need any explanation. Let's look at step 7 onwards.

The pom.xml file that we have here is pretty simple. We defined a dependency on mongo's Java driver. It relies on the online repository, repo.maven.apache.org, to resolve the artifacts. For a local repository, all we need to do is define the repositories and pluginRepositories tags in pom.xml. For more information on maven, refer to the maven documentation at http://maven.apache.org/guides/index.html.

For the Java class, the org.mongodb.MongoClient class is the backbone. We first instantiate it using one of its overloaded constructors giving the server's host and port. In this case, the hostname and port were not really needed as the values provided are the default values anyway, and the no-argument constructor would have worked well too. The following code snippet instantiates this client:

```
MongoClient client = new MongoClient("localhost", 27017);
```

The next step is to get the database, in this case, test using the getDB method. This is returned as an object of the com.mongodb.DB type. Note that this database might not exist, yet getDB will not throw any exception. Instead, the database will get created whenever we add a new document to the collection in this database. Similarly, getCollection on the DB object will return an object of the com.mongodb.DBCollection type representing the collection in the database. This too might not exist in the database and will get created on inserting the first document automatically.

The following two code snippets from our class show you how to get an instance of DB and DBCollection:

```
DB testDB = client.getDB("test");
DBCollection collection = testDB.getCollection("person");
```

Before we insert a document, we will drop the collection so that even upon multiple executions of the program, we will have just one document in the person collection. The collection is dropped using the drop() method on the DBCollection object's instance. Next, we create an instance of com.mongodb.DBObject. This is an object that represents the document to be inserted into the collection. The concrete class used here is BasicDBObject, which is a type of java.util.LinkedHashMap, where the key is String and the value is Object. The value can be another DBObject too, in which case, it is a document nested within another document. In our case, we have two keys, name and age, which are the field names in the document to be inserted and the values are of the String and Integer types, respectively. The append method of BasicDBObject adds a new key value pair to the BasicDBObject instance and returns the same instance, which allows us to chain the append method calls to add multiple key value pairs. This created DBObject is then inserted into the collection using the insert method. This is how we instantiated DBObject for the person collection and inserted it into the collection as follows:

```
DBObject person = new BasicDBObject("name", "Fred").append("age", 30);
collection.insert(person);
```

The findOne method on DBCollection is straightforward and returns one document from the collection. This version of findOne doesn't accept DBObject (which otherwise acts as a query executed before a document is selected and returned) as a parameter. This is synonymous to doing db.person.findOne() from the shell.

Finally, we simply invoke getDatabaseNames to get a list of databases' names in the server. At this point of time, we should at least be having test and the local database in the returned result. Once all the operations are complete, we close the client. The MongoClient class is thread-safe and generally one instance is used per application. To execute the program, we use the maven's exec plugin. On executing step 9, we should see the following lines toward the end in the console:

```
[INFO] [exec:java {execution: default-cli}]
--snip--
```

```
Dropping person collection in test database
Adding a person document in the person collection of test database
Now finding a person using findOne
Person found, name is Fred and age is 30
Database names are
1: local
2: test
INFO: Closed connection [connectionId{localValue:2, serverValue:2}] to
localhost:27017 because the pool has been closed.
[INFO] ---------------------------------------------------------------
------
[INFO] BUILD SUCCESSFUL
[INFO] ---------------------------------------------------------------
------
[INFO] Total time: 3 seconds
[INFO] Finished at: Tue May 12 07:33:00 UTC 2015
[INFO] Final Memory: 22M/53M
[INFO] ---------------------------------------------------------------
------
```

Connecting to a single node using a Python client

In this recipe, we will connect to a single MongoDB instance using the Python MongoDB driver called PyMongo. With Python's simple syntax and versatility clubbed together with MongoDB, many programmers find that this stack allows faster prototyping and reduced development cycles.

Getting ready

The following are the prerequisites for this recipe:

- ▶ Python 2.7.x (although the code is compatible with Python 3.x).
- ▶ PyMongo 3.0.1: Python MongoDB driver.
- ▶ Python package installer (pip).
- ▶ The Mongo server is up and running on localhost and port 27017. Take a look at the first recipe, *Installing single node MongoDB*, and start the server.

How to do it...

1. Depending on your operating system, install the pip utility, say, on the Ubuntu/Debian system. You can use the following command to install pip:

   ```
   > apt-get install python-pip
   ```

2. Install the latest PyMongo driver using pip:

   ```
   > pip install pymongo
   ```

3. Lastly, create a new file called `my_client.py` and type in the following code:

   ```python
   from __future__ import print_function
   import pymongo

   # Connect to server
   client = pymongo.MongoClient('localhost', 27017)

   # Select the database
   testdb = client.test

   # Drop collection
   print('Dropping collection person')
   testdb.person.drop()

   # Add a person
   print('Adding a person to collection person')
   employee = dict(name='Fred', age=30)
   testdb.person.insert(employee)

   # Fetch the first entry from collection
   person = testdb.person.find_one()
   if person:
       print('Name: %s, Age: %s' % (person['name'], person['age']))

   # Fetch list of all databases
   print('DB\'s present on the system:')
   for db in client.database_names():
       print('    %s' % db)


   # Close connection
   print('Closing client connection')
   client.close()
   ```

4. Run the script using the following command:

   ```
   > python my_client.py
   ```

How it works...

We start off by installing the Python MongoDB driver, pymongo, on the system with the help of the pip package manager. In the given Python code, we begin by importing `print_function` from the `__future__` module to allow compatibility with Python 3.x. Next, we import pymongo so that it can be used in the script.

We instantiate `pymongo.MongoClient()` with localhost and `27017` as the mongo server host and port, respectively. In pymongo, we can directly refer to the database and its collection by using the `<client>.<database_name>.<collection_name>` convention.

In our recipe, we used the client handler to select the database test simply by referring to `client.test`. This returns a database object even if the database does not exist. As a part of this recipe, we drop the collection by calling `testdb.person.drop()`, where `testdb` is a reference to `client.test` and `person` is a collection that we wish to drop. For this recipe, we are intentionally dropping the collection so that recurring runs will always yield one record in the collection.

Next, we instantiate a dictionary called `employee` with a few values such as name and age. We will now add this entry to our `person` collection using the `insert_one()` method.

As we now know that there is an entry in the person collection, we will fetch one document using the `find_one()` method. This method returns the first document in the collection, depending on the order of documents stored on the disk.

Following this, we also try to get the list of all the databases by calling the `get_databases()` method to the client. This method returns a list of database names present on the server. This method may come in handy when you are trying to assert the existence of a database on the server.

Finally, we close the client connection using the `close()` method.

Starting multiple instances as part of a replica set

In this recipe, we will look at starting multiple servers on the same host but as a cluster. Starting a single mongo server is enough for development purposes or non-mission-critical applications. For crucial production deployments, we need the availability to be high, where if one server instance fails, another instance takes over and the data remains available to query, insert, or update. Clustering is an advanced concept and we won't be doing justice by covering this whole concept in one recipe. Here, we will be touching the surface and going into more detail in other recipes in the administration section later in the book. In this recipe, we will start multiple mongo server processes on the same machine for the purpose of testing. In a production environment, they will be running on different machines (or virtual machines) in the same or even different data centers.

Let's see in brief what a replica set exactly is. As the name suggests, it is a set of servers that are replicas of each other in terms of data. Looking at how they are kept in sync with each other and other internals is something we will defer to some later recipes in the administration section, but one thing to remember is that write operations will happen only on one node, which is the primary one. All the querying also happens from the primary by default, though we may permit read operations on secondary instances explicitly. An important fact to remember is that replica sets are not meant to achieve scalability by distributing the read operations across various nodes in a replica set. Its sole objective is to ensure high availability.

Getting ready

Though not a prerequisite, taking a look at the *Starting a single node instance using command-line options* recipe will definitely make things easier just in case you are not aware of various command-line options and their significance while starting a mongo server. Additionally, the necessary binaries and setups as mentioned in the single server setup must be done before we continue with this recipe. Let's sum up on what we need to do.

We will start three mongod processes (mongo server instances) on our localhost.

We will create three data directories, /data/n1, /data/n2, and /data/n3 for Node1, Node2, and Node3, respectively. Similarly, we will redirect the logs to /logs/n1.log, /logs/n2.log, and /logs/n3.log. The following image will give you an idea on how the cluster would look:

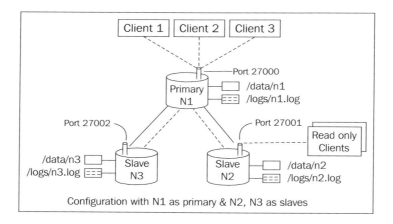

Configuration with N1 as primary & N2, N3 as slaves

How to do it...

Let's take a look at the steps in detail:

1. Create the `/data/n1`, `/data/n2`, `/data/n3`, and `/logs` directories for the data and logs of the three nodes respectively. On the Windows platform, you can choose the `c:\data\n1`, `c:\data\n2`, `c:\data\n3`, and `c:\logs\` directories or any other directory of your choice for the data and logs respectively. Ensure that these directories have appropriate write permissions for the mongo server to write the data and logs.

2. Start the three servers as follows. Users on the Windows platform need to skip the `--fork` option as it is not supported:

   ```
   $ mongod --replSet repSetTest --dbpath /data/n1 --logpath /logs/
   n1.log --port 27000 --smallfiles --oplogSize 128 --fork

   $ mongod --replSet repSetTest --dbpath /data/n2 --logpath /logs/
   n2.log --port 27001 --smallfiles --oplogSize 128 --fork

   $ mongod --replSet repSetTest --dbpath /data/n3 --logpath /logs/
   n3.log --port 27002 --smallfiles --oplogSize 128 -fork
   ```

3. Start the mongo shell and connect to any of the mongo servers running. In this case, we connect to the first one (listening to port `27000`). Execute the following command:

   ```
   $ mongo localhost:27000
   ```

4. Try to execute an insert operation from the mongo shell after connecting to it:

   ```
   > db.person.insert({name:'Fred', age:35})
   ```

   This operation should fail as the replica set has not been initialized yet. More information can be found in the *How it works...* section.

5. The next step is to start configuring the replica set. We start by preparing a JSON configuration in the shell as follows:

   ```
   cfg = {
     '_id':'repSetTest',
       'members':[
          {'_id':0, 'host': 'localhost:27000'},
          {'_id':1, 'host': 'localhost:27001'},
          {'_id':2, 'host': 'localhost:27002'}
       ]
   }
   ```

6. The last step is to initiate the replica set with the preceding configuration as follows:

   ```
   > rs.initiate(cfg)
   ```

7. Execute `rs.status()` after a few seconds on the shell to see the status. In a few seconds, one of them should become a primary and the remaining two should become secondary.

How it works...

We described the common options in the *Installing single node MongoDB* recipe with the command-line options recipe before and all these command-line options are described in detail.

As we are starting three independent mongod services, we have three dedicated database paths on the filesystem. Similarly, we have three separate log file locations for each of the processes. We then start three mongod processes with the database and log file path specified. As this setup is for test purposes and is started on the same machine, we use the `--smallfiles` and `--oplogSize` options. As these processes are running on the same host, we also choose the ports explicitly to avoid port conflicts. The ports that we chose here were 27000, 27001, and 27002. When we start the servers on different hosts, we may or may not choose a separate port. We can very well choose to use the default one whenever possible.

The `--fork` option demands some explanation. By choosing this option, we start the server as a background process from our operating system's shell and get the control back in the shell where we can then start more such mongod processes or perform other operations. In the absence of the `--fork` option, we cannot start more than one process per shell and would need to start three mongod processes in three separate shells.

If we take a look at the logs generated in the log directory, we should see the following lines in it:

```
[rsStart] replSet can't get local.system.replset config from self or any
seed (EMPTYCONFIG)

[rsStart] replSet info you may need to run replSetInitiate --
rs.initiate() in the shell -- if that is not already done
```

Though we started three mongod processes with the `--replSet` option, we still haven't configured them to work with each other as a replica set. This command-line option is just used to tell the server on startup that this process will be running as a part of a replica set. The name of the replica set is the same as the value of this option passed on the command prompt. This also explains why the insert operation executed on one of the nodes failed before the replica set was initialized. In mongo replica sets, there can be only one primary node where all the inserting and querying happens. In the image shown, the **N1** node is shown as the primary and listens to port **27000** for client connections. All the other nodes are slave/secondary instances, which sync themselves up with the primary and hence querying too is disabled on them by default. It is only when the primary goes down that one of the secondary takes over and becomes a primary node. However, it is possible to query the secondary for data as we have shown in the image; we will see how to query from a secondary instance in the next recipe.

Well, all that is left now is to configure the replica set by grouping the three processes that we started. This is done by first defining a JSON object as follows:

```
cfg = {
  '_id':'repSetTest',
    'members':[
       {'_id':0, 'host': 'localhost:27000'},
       {'_id':1, 'host': 'localhost:27001'},
       {'_id':2, 'host': 'localhost:27002'}
    ]
}
```

There are two fields, `_id` and `members`, for the unique ID of the replica set and an array of the hostnames and port numbers of the mongod server processes as part of this replica set, respectively. Using localhost to refer to the host is not a very good idea and is usually discouraged; however, in this case, as we started all the processes on the same machine, we are ok with it. It is preferred that you refer to the hosts by their hostnames even if they are running on localhost. Note that you cannot mix referring to the instances using localhost and hostnames both in the same configuration. It is either the hostname or localhost. To configure the replica set, we then connect to any one of the three running mongod processes; in this case, we connect to the first one and then execute the following from the shell:

```
> rs.initiate(cfg)
```

The `_id` field in the `cfg` object passed has a value that is the same as the value we gave to the `--replSet` option on the command prompt when we started the server processes. Not giving the same value would throw the following error:

```
{

    "ok" : 0,

    "errmsg" : "couldn't initiate : set name does not match the set
name host Amol-PC:27000 expects"

}
```

If all goes well and the initiate call is successful, we should see something similar to the following JSON response on the shell:

```
{"ok" : 1}
```

In a few seconds, you should see a different prompt for the shell that we executed this command from. It should now become a primary or secondary. The following is an example of the shell connected to a primary member of the replica set:

```
repSetTest:PRIMARY>
```

Executing `rs.status()` should give us some stats on the replica set's status, which we will explore in depth in a recipe later in the book in the administration section. For now, the `stateStr` field is important and contains the PRIMARY, SECONDARY, and other texts.

There's more...

Look at the *Connecting to the replica set in the shell to query and insert data* recipe to perform more operations from the shell after connecting to a replica set. Replication isn't as simple as we saw here. See the administration section for more advanced recipes on replication.

See also

If you are looking to convert a standalone instance to a replica set, then the instance with the data needs to become a primary first, and then empty secondary instances will be added to which the data will be synchronized. Refer to the following URL on how to perform this operation:

```
http://docs.mongodb.org/manual/tutorial/convert-standalone-to-replica-set/
```

Connecting to the replica set in the shell to query and insert data

In the previous recipe, we started a replica set of three mongod processes. In this recipe, we will work with this setup by connecting to it using the mongo client application, perform queries, insert data, and take a look at some of the interesting aspects of a replica set from a client's perspective.

Getting ready

The prerequisite for this recipe is that the replica set should be set up and running. Refer to the previous recipe, *Starting multiple instances as part of a replica set*, for details on how to start the replica set.

How to do it...

1. We will start two shells here, one for PRIMARY and one for SECONDARY. Execute the following command on the command prompt:

    ```
    > mongo localhost:27000
    ```

2. The prompt of the shell tells us whether the server to which we have connected is PRIMARY or SECONDARY. It should show the replica set's name followed by a :, followed by the server state. In this case, if the replica set is initialized, up, and running, we should see either repSetTest:PRIMARY> or repSetTest:SECONDARY>.

3. Suppose that the first server we connected to is a secondary, we need to find the primary. Execute the `rs.status()` command in the shell and look out for the `stateStr` field. This should give us the primary server. Use the mongo shell to connect to this server.

4. At this point, we should be having two shells running, one connected to a primary and another connected to a secondary.

5. In the shell connected to the primary node, execute the following insert:

```
repSetTest:PRIMARY> db.replTest.insert({_id:1, value:'abc'})
```

6. There is nothing special about this. We just inserted a small document in a collection that we will use for the replication test.

7. By executing the following query on the primary, we should get the following result:

```
repSetTest:PRIMARY> db.replTest.findOne()
{ "_id" : 1, "value" : "abc" }
```

8. So far, so good. Now, we will go to the shell that is connected to the SECONDARY node and execute the following:

```
repSetTest:SECONDARY> db.replTest.findOne()
```

On doing this, we should see the following error on the console:

```
{ "$err" : "not master and slaveOk=false", "code" : 13435 }
```

9. Now execute the following on the console:

```
repSetTest:SECONDARY>  rs.slaveOk(true)
```

10. Execute the query that we executed in step 7 again on the shell. This should now get the results as follows:

```
repSetTest:SECONDARY>db.replTest.findOne()
{ "_id" : 1, "value" : "abc" }
```

11. Execute the following insert on the secondary node; it should not succeed with the following message:

```
repSetTest:SECONDARY> db.replTest.insert({_id:1, value:'abc'})
not master
```

How it works...

We have done a lot of things in this recipe, and we will try to throw some light on some of the important concepts to remember.

We basically connect to a primary and secondary node from the shell and perform (I would say, try to perform) selects and inserts. The architecture of a Mongo replica set is made of one primary (just one, no more, no less) and multiple secondary nodes. All writes happen on the PRIMARY only. Note that replication is not a mechanism to distribute the read request load that enables scaling the system. Its primary intent is to ensure high availability of data. By default, we are not permitted to read data from the secondary nodes. In step 6, we simply insert data from the primary node and then execute a query to get the document that we inserted. This is straightforward and nothing related to clustering here. Just note that we inserted the document from the primary and then queried it back.

In the next step, we execute the same query but this time, from the secondary's shell. By default, querying is not enabled on the SECONDARY. There might be a small lag in replicating the data possibly due to heavy data volumes to be replicated, network latency, or hardware capacity to name a few of the causes, and thus, querying on the secondary might not reflect the latest inserts or updates made on the primary. However, if we are ok with it and can live with the slight lag in the data being replicated, all we need to do is enable querying on the SECONDARY node explicitly by just executing one command, rs.slaveOk() or rs.slaveOk(true). Once this is done, we are free to execute queries on the secondary nodes too.

Finally, we try to insert the data into a collection of the slave node. Under no circumstances is this permitted, regardless of whether we have done rs.slaveOk(). When rs.slaveOk() is invoked, it just permits the data to be queried from the SECONDARY node. All write operations still have to go to the primary and then flow down to the secondary. The internals of replication will be covered in a different recipe in the administration section.

See also

The next recipe, *Connecting to the replica set to query and insert data from a Java client*, is about connecting to a replica set from a Java client.

Connecting to the replica set to query and insert data from a Java client

In this recipe, we will demonstrate how to connect to a replica set from a Java client and how the client would automatically failover to another node in the replica set, should a primary node fail.

Getting ready

We need to take a look at the *Connecting to the single node using a Java client* recipe as it contains all the prerequisites and steps to set up maven and other dependencies. As we are dealing with a Java client for replica sets, a replica set must be up and running. Refer to the *Starting multiple instances as part of a replica set* recipe for details on how to start the replica set.

How to do it...

1. Write/copy the following piece of code: (This Java class is also available for download from the Packt website.)

```java
package com.packtpub.mongo.cookbook;

import com.mongodb.BasicDBObject;
import com.mongodb.DB;
import com.mongodb.DBCollection;
import com.mongodb.DBObject;
import com.mongodb.MongoClient;
import com.mongodb.ServerAddress;

import java.util.Arrays;

/**
 *
 */
public class ReplicaSetMongoClient {

  /**
   * Main method for the test client connecting to the
     replica set.
   * @param args
   */
  public static final void main(String[] args) throws
    Exception {
    MongoClient client = new MongoClient(
      Arrays.asList(
        new ServerAddress("localhost", 27000),
          new ServerAddress("localhost", 27001),
            new ServerAddress("localhost", 27002)
      )
    );
    DB testDB = client.getDB("test");
```

```java
System.out.println("Dropping replTest collection");
DBCollection collection =
  testDB.getCollection("replTest");
collection.drop();
DBObject object = new BasicDBObject("_id",
  1).append("value", "abc");
System.out.println("Adding a test document to replica
  set");
collection.insert(object);
System.out.println("Retrieving document from the
  collection, this one comes from primary node");
DBObject doc = collection.findOne();
showDocumentDetails(doc);
System.out.println("Now Retrieving documents in a loop
  from the collection.");
System.out.println("Stop the primary instance after few
  iterations ");
for(int i = 0 ; i < 10; i++) {
  try {
    doc = collection.findOne();
    showDocumentDetails(doc);
  }
  catch (Exception e) {
    //Ignoring or log a message
  }
  Thread.sleep(5000);
  }
}

/**
*
* @param obj
*/
private static void showDocumentDetails(DBObject obj) {
  System.out.printf("_id: %d, value is %s\n",
    obj.get("_id"), obj.get("value"));
  }
}
```

2. Connect to any of the nodes in the replica set, say to `localhost:27000`, and execute `rs.status()` from the shell. Take a note of the primary instance in the replica set and connect to it from the shell if `localhost:27000` is not a primary. Here, switch to the administrator database as follows:

repSetTest:PRIMARY>use admin

3. We now execute the preceding program from the operating system shell as follows:

```
$ mvn compile exec:java -Dexec.mainClass=com.packtpub.mongo.
cookbook.ReplicaSetMongoClient
```

4. Shut down the primary instance by executing the following on the mongo shell that is connected to the primary:

```
repSetTest:PRIMARY> db.shutdownServer()
```

5. Watch the output on the console where the com.packtpub.mongo.cookbook.ReplicaSetMongoClient class is executed using maven.

How it works...

An interesting thing to observe is how we instantiate the MongoClient instance. It is done as follows:

```
MongoClient client = new MongoClient(Arrays.asList(
  new ServerAddress("localhost", 27000),
    new ServerAddress("localhost", 27001),
      new ServerAddress("localhost", 27002)));
```

The constructor takes a list of com.mongodb.ServerAddress. This class has a lot of overloaded constructors but we choose to use the one that takes the hostname and then port. What we have done is provided all the server details in a replica set as a list. We haven't mentioned what is the PRIMARY node and what are the SECONDARY nodes. MongoClient is intelligent enough to figure this out and connect to the appropriate instance. The list of servers provided is called the seed list. It need not contain an entire set of servers in a replica set though the objective is to provide as much as we can. MongoClient will figure out all the server details from the provided subset. For example, if the replica set is of five nodes but we provide only three servers, it works fine. On connecting with the provided replica set servers, the client will query them to get the replica set metadata and figure out the rest of the provided servers in the replica set. In the preceding case, we instantiated the client with three instances in the replica set. If the replica set was to have five members, then instantiating the client with just three of them is still good enough and the remaining two instances will be automatically discovered.

Next, we start the client from the command prompt using maven. Once the client is running in the loop, we bring down the primary instance to find one document. We should see something as the following output to the console:

```
_id: 1, value is abc
Now Retrieving documents in a loop from the collection.
Stop the primary instance manually after few iterations
_id: 1, value is abc
```

```
_id: 1, value is abc
Nov 03, 2013 5:21:57 PM com.mongodb.ConnectionStatus$UpdatableNode update
WARNING: Server seen down: Amol-PC/192.168.1.171:27002
java.net.SocketException: Software caused connection abort: recv failed
        at java.net.SocketInputStream.socketRead0(Native Method)
        at java.net.SocketInputStream.read(SocketInputStream.java:150)
        ...
WARNING: Primary switching from Amol-PC/192.168.1.171:27002 to Amol-
PC/192.168.1.171:27001
_id: 1, value is abc
```

As we can see, the query in the loop was interrupted when the primary node went down. However, the client switched to the new primary seamlessly. Well, nearly seamlessly, as the client might have to catch an exception and retry the operation after a predetermined interval has elapsed.

Connecting to the replica set to query and insert data using a Python client

In this recipe, we will demonstrate how to connect to a replica set using a Python client and how the client would automatically failover to another node in the replica set, should a primary node fail.

Getting ready

Refer to the *Connecting to the single node using a Python client* recipe as it describes how to set up and install PyMongo, the Python driver for MongoDB. Additionally, a replica set must be up and running. Refer to the *Starting multiple instances as part of a replica set* recipe for details on how to start the replica set.

How to do it...

1. Write/copy the following piece of code to `replicaset_client.py`: (This script is also available for download from the Packt website.)

    ```python
    from __future__ import print_function
    import pymongo
    import time

    # Instantiate MongoClient with a list of server addresses
    ```

```
client = pymongo.MongoClient(['localhost:27002',
'localhost:27001', 'localhost:27000'], replicaSet='repSetTest')

# Select the collection and drop it before using
collection = client.test.repTest
collection.drop()

#insert a record in
collection.insert_one(dict(name='Foo', age='30'))

for x in range(5):
    try:
        print('Fetching record: %s' % collection.find_one())
    except Exception as e:
        print('Could not connect to primary')
    time.sleep(3)
```

2. Connect to any of the nodes in the replica set, say to `localhost:27000`, and execute `rs.status()` from the shell. Take a note of the primary instance in the replica set and connect to it from the shell, if `localhost:27000` is not a primary. Here, switch to the administrator database as follows:

   > **repSetTest:PRIMARY>use admin**

3. We now execute the preceding script from the operating system shell as follows:

   $ **python replicaset_client.py**

4. Shut down the primary instance by executing the following on the mongo shell that is connected to the primary:

   > **repSetTest:PRIMARY> db.shutdownServer()**

5. Watch the output on the console where the Python script is executed.

How it works...

You will notice that, in this script, we instantiated the mongo client by giving a list of hosts instead of a single host. As of version 3.0, the pymongo driver's `MongoClient()` class can accept either a list of hosts or a single host during initialization and deprecate `MongoReplicaSetClient()`. The client will attempt to connect to the first host in the list, and if successful, will be able to determine the other nodes in the replica set. We are also passing the `replicaSet='repSetTest'` parameter exclusively, ensuring that the client checks whether the connected node is a part of this replica set.

Once connected, we perform normal database operations such as selecting the test database, dropping the `repTest` collection, and inserting a single document into the collection.

Following this, we enter a conditional for loop, iterating five times. Each time, we fetch the record, display it, and sleep for three seconds. While the script is in this loop, we shut down the primary node in the replica set as mentioned in step 4. We should see an output similar to this:

```
Fetching record: {u'age': u'30', u'_id': ObjectId('5558bfaa0640fd1923fce
1a1'), u'name': u'Foo'}

Fetching record: {u'age': u'30', u'_id': ObjectId('5558bfaa0640fd1923fce
1a1'), u'name': u'Foo'}

Fetching record: {u'age': u'30', u'_id': ObjectId('5558bfaa0640fd1923fce
1a1'), u'name': u'Foo'}

Could not connect to primary

Fetching record: {u'age': u'30', u'_id': ObjectId('5558bfaa0640fd1923fce
1a1'), u'name': u'Foo'}
```

In the preceding output, the client gets disconnected from the primary node midway. However, very soon, a new primary node is selected by the remaining nodes and the mongo client is able to resume the connection.

Starting a simple sharded environment of two shards

In this recipe, we will set up a simple sharded setup made up of two data shards. There will be no replication configured as this is the most basic shard setup to demonstrate the concept. We won't be getting deep into the internals of sharding, which we will explore more in the administration section.

Here is a bit of theory before we proceed. Scalability and availability are two important cornerstones to build any mission-critical application. Availability is something that was taken care of by the replica sets, which we discussed in previous recipes in this chapter. Let's look at scalability now. Simply put, scalability is the ease with which the system can cope with increasing data and request load. Consider an e-commerce platform. On regular days, the number of hits to the site and load is fairly modest and the system's response times and error rates are minimal. (This is subjective.) Now, consider the days where the system load becomes twice, thrice, or even more than that of an average day's load, say on Thanksgiving day, Christmas, and so on. If the platform is able to deliver similar levels of service on these high load days as on any other day, the system is said to have scaled up well to the sudden increase in the number of requests.

Now, consider an archiving application that needs to store the details of all the requests that hit a particular website over the past decade. For each request hitting the website, we create a new record in the underlying data store. Suppose that each record is of 250 bytes with an average load of three million requests per day, we will cross 1 TB of the data mark in about five years. This data would be used for various analytics purposes and might be frequently queried. The query performance should not be drastically affected when the data size increases. If the system is able to cope with this increasing data volume and still give decent performance comparable to performance on low data volumes, the system is said to have scaled up well.

Now that we have seen in brief what scalability is, let me tell you that sharding is a mechanism that lets a system scale to increasing demands. The crux lies in the fact that the entire data is partitioned into smaller segments and distributed across various nodes called shards. Suppose that we have a total of 10 million documents in a mongo collection. If we shard this collection across 10 shards, then we will ideally have *10,000,000/10 = 1,000,000* documents on each shard. At a given point of time, only one document will reside on one shard (which by itself will be a replica set in a production system). However, there is some magic involved that keeps this concept hidden from the developer who is querying the collection and who gets one unified view of the collection irrespective of the number of shards. Based on the query, it is mongo that decides which shard to query for the data and returns the entire result set. With this background, let's set up a simple shard and take a closer look at it.

Getting ready

Apart from the MongoDB server already installed, no prerequisites are there from a software perspective. We will be creating two data directories, one for each shard. There will be a directory for the data and one for logs.

How to do it...

1. We start by creating directories for the logs and data. Create the following directories, `/data/s1/db`, `/data/s2/db`, and `/logs`. On Windows, we can have `c:\data\s1\db` and so on for the data and log directories. There is also a configuration server that is used in the sharded environment to store some metadata. We will use `/data/con1/db` as the data directory for the configuration server.

2. Start the following mongod processes, one for each of the two shards, one for the configuration database, and one mongos process. For the Windows platform, skip the `--fork` parameter as it is not supported.

```
$ mongod --shardsvr --dbpath /data/s1/db --port 27000 --logpath /logs/s1.log --smallfiles --oplogSize 128 --fork

$ mongod --shardsvr --dbpath /data/s2/db --port 27001 --logpath /logs/s2.log --smallfiles --oplogSize 128 --fork
```

```
$ mongod --configsvr --dbpath  /data/con1/db --port 25000
--logpath  /logs/config.log --fork
$ mongos --configdb localhost:25000 --logpath  /logs/mongos.log
--fork
```

3. From the command prompt, execute the following command. This should show a mongos prompt as follows:

```
$ mongo
MongoDB shell version: 3.0.2
connecting to: test
mongos>
```

4. Finally, we set up the shard. From the mongos shell, execute the following two commands:

```
mongos> sh.addShard("localhost:27000")
mongos> sh.addShard("localhost:27001")
```

5. On each addition of a shard, we should get an ok reply. The following JSON message should be seen giving the unique ID for each shard added:

```
{ "shardAdded" : "shard0000", "ok" : 1 }
```

 We used localhost everywhere to refer to the locally running servers. It is not a recommended approach and is discouraged. The better approach would be to use hostnames even if they are local processes.

How it works...

Let's see what all we did in the process. We created three directories for data (two for the shards and one for the configuration database) and one directory for logs. We can have a shell script or batch file to create the directories as well. In fact, in large production deployments, setting up shards manually is not only time-consuming but also error-prone.

Downloading the example code

You can download the example code files for all Packt books you have purchased from your account at http://www.packtpub.com. If you purchased this book elsewhere, you can visit http://www.packtpub.com/support and register to have the files e-mailed directly to you.

Let's try to get a picture of what exactly we have done and are trying to achieve. The following is an image of the shard setup that we just did:

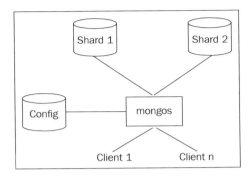

If we look at the preceding image and the servers started in step 2, we have shard servers that would store the actual data in the collections. These were the first two of the four processes that we started listening to ports 27000 and 27001. Next, we started a configuration server that is seen on the left side in this image. It is the third server of the four servers started in step 2 and it listens to port 25000 for the incoming connections. The sole purpose of this database is to maintain the metadata about the shard servers. Ideally, only the mongos process or drivers connect to this server for the shard details/metadata and the shard key information. We will see what a shard key is in the next recipe, where we play around a sharded collection and see the shards that we have created in action.

Finally, we have a mongos process. This is a lightweight process that doesn't do any persistence of data and just accepts connections from clients. This is the layer that acts as a gatekeeper and abstracts the client from the concept of shards. For now, we can view it as basically a router that consults the configuration server and takes the decision to route the client's query to the appropriate shard server for execution. It then aggregates the result from various shards if applicable and returns the result to the client. It is safe to say that no client connects directly to the configuration or shard servers; in fact, no one ideally should connect to these processes directly except for some administration operations. Clients simply connect to the mongos process and execute their queries and insert or update operations.

Just starting the shard server, configuration server, and mongos process doesn't create a sharded environment. On starting up the mongos process, we provided it with the details of the configuration server. What about the two shards that would be storing the actual data? However, the two mongod processes started as shard servers are not yet declared anywhere as shard servers in the configuration. This is exactly what we do in the final step by invoking `sh.addShard()` for both the shard servers. The mongos process is provided with the configuration server's details on startup. Adding shards from the shell stores this metadata about the shards in the configuration database, and the mongos processes then would be querying this config database for the shard's information. On executing all the steps of the recipe, we have an operational shard as follows:

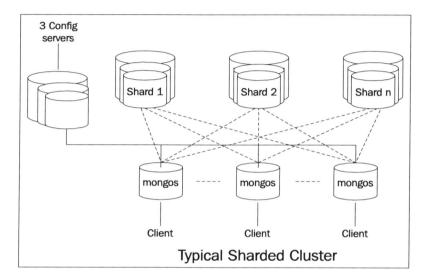

Before we conclude, the shard that we have set up here is far from ideal and not how it would be done in a production environment. The preceding image gives us an idea of how a typical shard would be in a production environment. The number of shards would not be two but many more. Additionally, each shard will be a replica set to ensure high availability. There would be three configuration servers to ensure availability of the configuration servers as well. Similarly, there will be any number of mongos processes created for a shard listening for client connections. In some cases, it might even be started on a client application's server.

There's more...

What good is a shard unless we put it to action and see what happens from the shell on inserting and querying the data? In the next recipe, we will make use of the shard setup here, add some data, and see it in action.

Connecting to a shard in the shell and performing operations

In this recipe, we will connect to a shard from a command prompt, see how to shard a collection, and observe the data splitting in action on some test data.

Getting ready

Obviously, we need a sharded mongo server setup up and running. See the previous recipe, *Starting a simple sharded environment of two shards*, for more details on how to set up a simple shard. The mongos process, as in the previous recipe, should be listening to port number 27017. We have got some names in a JavaScript file called names.js. This file needs to be downloaded from the Packt website and kept on the local filesystem. The file contains a variable called names and the value is an array with some JSON documents as the values, each one representing a person. The contents look as follows:

```
names = [
  {name:'James Smith', age:30},
  {name:'Robert Johnson', age:22},
...
]
```

How to do it...

1. Start the mongo shell and connect to the default port on localhost as follows. This will ensure that the names will be available in the current shell:

   ```
   mongo --shell names.js
   MongoDB shell version: 3.0.2
   connecting to: test
   mongos>
   ```

2. Switch to the database that would be used to test the sharding; we call it shardDB:

   ```
   mongos> use shardDB
   ```

3. Enable sharding at the database level as follows:

   ```
   mongos> sh.enableSharding("shardDB")
   ```

4. Shard a collection called person as follows:

   ```
   mongos>sh.shardCollection("shardDB.person", {name: "hashed"},
   false)
   ```

5. Add the test data to the sharded collection:

```
mongos> for(i = 1; i <= 300000 ; i++) {
... person = names[Math.round(Math.random() * 100) % 20]
... doc = {_id:i, name:person.name, age:person.age}
... db.person.insert(doc)
}
```

6. Execute the following to get a query plan and the number of documents on each shard:

```
mongos> db.person.getShardDistribution()
```

How it works...

This recipe demands some explanation. We downloaded a JavaScript file that defines an array of 20 people. Each element of the array is a JSON object with the `name` and `age` attributes. We start the shell connecting to the mongos process loaded with this JavaScript file. We then switch to `shardDB`, which we use for the purpose of sharding.

For a collection to be sharded, the database in which it will be created needs to be enabled for the sharding first. We do this using `sh.enableSharding()`.

The next step is to enable the collection to be sharded. By default, all the data will be kept on one shard and not split across different shards. Think about it; how will Mongo be able to split the data meaningfully? The whole intention is to split it meaningfully and as evenly as possible so that whenever we query based on the shard key, Mongo would easily be able to determine which shard(s) to query. If a query doesn't contain the shard key, the execution of the query will happen on all the shards and the data would then be collated by the mongos process before returning it to the client. Thus, choosing the right shard key is very crucial.

Let's now see how to shard the collection. We do this by invoking `sh.shardCollection("shardDB.person", {name: "hashed"}, false)`. There are three parameters here:

- The fully qualified name of the collection in the `<db name>.<collection name>` format is the first parameter of the `shardCollection` method.

- The second parameter is the field name to shard on in the collection. This is the field that would be used to split the documents on the shards. One of the requirements of a good shard key is that it should have high cardinality. (The number of possible values should be high.) In our test data, the name value has very low cardinality and thus is not a good choice as a shard key. We hash this key when using this as a shard key. We do so by mentioning the key as `{name: "hashed"}`.

> ▶ The last parameter specifies whether the value used as the shard key is unique or not. The name field is definitely not unique and thus it will be false. If the field was, say, the person's social security number, it could have been set as true. Additionally, SSN is a good choice for a shard key due to its high cardinality. Remember that the shard key has to be present for the query to be efficient.

The last step is to see the execution plan for the finding of all the data. The intent of this operation is to see how the data is being split across two shards. With 300,000 documents, we expect something around 150,000 documents on each shard. However, from the distribution statistics, we can observe that `shard0000` has `1,49,715` documents whereas `shard0001` has `150285`:

```
Shard shard0000 at localhost:27000
 data : 15.99MiB docs : 149715 chunks : 2
 estimated data per chunk : 7.99MiB
 estimated docs per chunk : 74857


Shard shard0001 at localhost:27001
 data : 16.05MiB docs : 150285 chunks : 2
 estimated data per chunk : 8.02MiB
 estimated docs per chunk : 75142


Totals
 data : 32.04MiB docs : 300000 chunks : 4
 Shard shard0000 contains 49.9% data, 49.9% docs in cluster, avg obj size
on shard : 112B
 Shard shard0001 contains 50.09% data, 50.09% docs in cluster, avg obj
size on shard : 112B
```

There are a couple of additional suggestions that I would recommend you to do.

Connect to the individual shard from the mongo shell and execute queries on the person collection. See that the counts in these collections are similar to what we see in the preceding plan. Additionally, one can find out that no document exists on both the shards at the same time.

We discussed in brief about how cardinality affects the way the data is split across shards. Let's do a simple exercise. We first drop the person collection and execute the shardCollection operation again but, this time, with the `{name: 1}` shard key instead of `{name: "hashed"}`. This ensures that the shard key is not hashed and stored as is. Now, load the data using the JavaScript function we used earlier in step number 5, and then execute the `explain()` command on the collection once the data is loaded. Observe how the data is now split (or not) across the shards.

There's more...

A lot of questions must now be coming up such as what are the best practices? What are some tips and tricks? How is the sharding thing pulled off by MongoDB behind the scenes in a way that is transparent to the end user?

This recipe here only explained the basics. In the administration section, all such questions will be answered.

2

Command-line
Operations and Indexes

In this chapter, we will cover the following topics:

- ▸ Creating test data
- ▸ Performing simple querying, projections, and pagination from the Mongo shell
- ▸ Updating and deleting data from the shell
- ▸ Creating an index and viewing plans of queries
- ▸ Creating a background and foreground index in the shell
- ▸ Creating and understanding sparse indexes
- ▸ Expiring documents after a fixed interval using the TTL index
- ▸ Expiring documents at a given time using the TTL index

Introduction

In this chapter we will be performing simple queries using the mongo shell. Later in the chapter, we will have a detailed look at commonly used MongoDB indexes.

Creating test data

This recipe is about creating test data for some of the recipes in this chapter and also for the later chapters in this book. We will demonstrate how to load a CSV file in a mongo database using the mongo import utility. This is a basic recipe, and if the reader is aware of the data import utility; they can just download the CSV file from the Packt website (`pincodes.csv`), load it in the collection by themselves, and skip the rest of the recipe. We will use the default database, `test`, and the collection will be named `postalCodes`.

Getting ready

The data used here is for postcodes in India. Download the `pincodes.csv` file from the Packt website. The file is a CSV file with 39,732 records; it should create 39,732 documents on successful import. We need to have the Mongo server up and running. Refer to the *Installing single node MongoDB* recipe from *Chapter 1, Installing and Starting the Server* for instructions on how to start the server. The server should begin listening for connections on the default port, `27017`.

How to do it...

1. Execute the following command from the shell with the file to be imported in the current directory:

    ```
    $ mongoimport --type csv -d test -c postalCodes --headerline
    --drop pincodes.csv
    ```

2. Start the mongo shell by typing in `mongo` on the command prompt.

3. In the shell, execute the following command:

    ```
    > db.postalCodes.count()
    ```

How it works...

Assuming that the server is up and running, the CSV file has been downloaded and is kept in a local directory where we execute the import utility with the file in the current directory. Let's look at the options given in the `mongoimport` utility and their meanings:

Command-line option	Description
`--type`	This specifies that the type of the input file is CSV. It defaults to JSON; another possible value being TSV.
`-d`	This is the target database in which the data will be loaded.
`-c`	This is the collection in the previously mentioned database in which the data will be loaded.
`--headerline`	This is relevant only in case of TSV or CSV files. It indicates that the first line of the file is the header. The same names would be used as the name of the fields in the document.
`--drop`	Drop the collection before importing data.

The final value on the command prompt after all the options are given is the name of the file, `pincodes.csv`.

If the import goes through successfully, you should see something similar to the following printed to the console:

```
2015-05-19T06:51:54.131+0000       connected to: localhost
2015-05-19T06:51:54.132+0000       dropping: test.postalCodes
2015-05-19T06:51:54.810+0000       imported 39732 documents
```

Finally, we start the mongo shell and find the count of the documents in the collection; it should indeed be 39,732 as seen in the preceding import log.

 The postal code data has been taken from `https://github.com/kishorek/India-Codes/`. This data is not taken from an official source and might not be accurate as it is being compiled manually for free public use.

See also

The *Performing simple querying, projections, and pagination from Mongo shell* recipe is about executing some basic queries on the data imported.

Performing simple querying, projections, and pagination from Mongo shell

In this recipe, we will get our hands dirty with a bit of querying to select documents from the test data that we set up in our previous recipe, *Creating test data*. There is nothing extravagant in this recipe and someone who is well versed with the query language basics can skip this recipe. Others who aren't too comfortable with basic querying or those who want to get a small refresher can continue to read the next section of the recipe. Additionally, this recipe is intended to get a feel of the test data setup from the previous recipe.

Getting ready

To execute simple queries, we need to have a server up and running. A simple single node is what we need. Refer to the *Installing single node MongoDB* recipe from *Chapter 1, Installing and Starting the Server* for instructions on how to start the server. The data that we would be operating on needs to be imported in the database. The steps to import the data are given in the previous recipe, *Creating test data*. You also need to start the mongo shell and connect to the server running on the localhost. Once these prerequisites are complete, we are good to go.

How to do it...

1. Let's first find a count of the documents in the collection:

   ```
   > db.postalCodes.count()
   ```

2. Let's find just one document from the `postalCodes` collection as follows:

   ```
   > db.postalCodes.findOne()
   ```

3. Now, we find multiple documents in the collection as follows:

   ```
   > db.postalCodes.find().pretty()
   ```

4. The preceding query retrieves all the keys of the first 20 documents and displays them on the shell. At the end of the result, you will notice a line that says `Type "it"` `for more`. By typing `"it"`, the mongo shell will iterate over the resulting cursor. Let's do a couple of things now; we will just display the `city`, `state`, and `pincode` fields. Additionally, we want to display the documents numbered 91 to 100 in the collection. Let's see how we do this:

   ```
   > db.postalCodes.find({}, {_id:0, city:1, state:1, pincode:1}).
   skip(90).limit(10)
   ```

5. Let's move a step ahead and write a slightly complex query where we find the top 10 cities in the state of Gujarat sorted by the name of the city, and, similar to the last query, we just select `city`, `state`, and the `pincode` field:

   ```
   > db.postalCodes.find({state:'Gujarat'},{_id:0, city:1, state:1,
   pincode:1}).sort({city:1}).limit(10)
   ```

How it works...

This recipe is pretty simple and allows us to get a feel for the test data that we set up in the previous recipe. Nevertheless, as with other recipes, I do owe you all some explanation for what we did here.

We first found the count of the documents in the collection using `db.postalCodes.count()` and it should give us 39,732 documents. This should be in sync with the logs that we saw while importing the data in the postal codes collection. We next queried for one document from the collection using `findOne`. This method returns the first document in the result set of the query. In absence of a query or sort order, as in this case, it will be the first document in the collection sorted by its natural order.

Next, we perform `find` rather than `findOne`. The difference between both of them is that the `find` operation returns an iterator for the result set, which we can use to traverse through the results of the find operation, whereas `findOne` returns a document. Adding a pretty method call to the `find` operation will print the result in a pretty or formatted way.

Note that the `pretty` method makes sense and works only with `find` and not with `findOne`. This is because the return value of `findOne` is a document and there is no `pretty` operation on the returned document.

We will now execute the following query on the mongo shell:

```
> db.postalCodes.find({}, {_id:0, city:1, state:1, pincode:1}).skip(90).
limit(10)
```

Here, we pass two parameters to the `find` method:

- The first one is { }, which is the query to select the documents, and, in this case, we ask mongo to select all the documents.
- The second parameter is the set of fields that we want in the result documents also known as **projection**. Remember that the `_id` field is present by default unless we explicitly say `_id:0`. For all the other fields, we need to say `<field_name>:1` or `<field_name>:true`. The find portion with projections is the same as saying `select field1, field2 from table` in a relational world, and not specifying the fields to be selected in the find is saying `select * from table` in a relational world.

Moving on, we just need to look at what `skip` and `limit` do:

- The `skip` function skips the given number of documents from the result set all the way up to the end document
- The `limit` function then limits the result to the given number of documents

Let's see what this all means with an example. By doing `.skip(90).limit(10)`, we say that we want to skip the first `90` documents from the result set and start returning from the 91st document. The limit, however, says that we will be returning only `10` documents from the 91st document.

Now, there are some border conditions that we need to know here. What if skip is being provided with a value more than the total number of documents in the collection? Well, in this case, no documents will be returned. Additionally, if the number provided to the limit function is more than the actual number of documents remaining in the collection, then the number of documents returned will be the same as the remaining documents in the collection and no exception will be thrown in either cases.

Updating and deleting data from the shell

This again will be a simple recipe that will be looking at executing deletes and updates on a test collection. We won't be dealing with the same test data that we imported as we don't want to update/delete any of that, but instead, we will work on a test collection created for this recipe only.

Getting ready

For this recipe, we will create a collection called `updAndDelTest`. We will require the server to be up and running. Refer to the *Installing single node MongoDB* recipe from *Chapter 1, Installing and Starting the Server* for instructions on how to start the server. Start the shell with the `UpdAndDelTest.js` script loaded. This script will be available on the Packt website for download. To know how to start the shell with a script preloaded, refer to the *Connecting to a single node in the Mongo shell with JavaScript* recipe in *Chapter 1, Installing and Starting the Server*.

How to do it...

1. Start the MongoDB shell and preload the script:

    ```
    $ mongo --shell updAndDelTest.js
    ```

2. With the shell started and script loaded, execute the following in the shell:

    ```
    > prepareTestData()
    ```

3. If all goes well, you should see `Inserted 20 documents in updAndDelTest` printed to the console:

4. To get a feel of the collection, let's query it as follows:

    ```
    > db.updAndDelTest.find({}, {_id:0})
    ```

5. We should see that for each value of x as 1 and 2, we have y incrementing from 1 to 10 for each value of x.

6. We will first update some documents and observe the results. Execute the following update:

    ```
    > db.updAndDelTest.update({x:1}, {$set:{y:0}})
    ```

7. Execute the following `find` command and observe the results; we should get 10 documents. For each of them, note the value of y.

    ```
    > db.updAndDelTest.find({x:1}, {_id:0})
    ```

8. We shall now execute the following update:

    ```
    > db.updAndDelTest.update({x:1}, {$set:{y:0}}, {multi:true})
    ```

9. Executing the query given in step 6 again to view the updated documents. It will show the same documents that we saw earlier. Take a note of the values of y again and compare them to the results that we saw when we executed this query last time before executing the update given in step 7.

10. We will now see how delete works. We will again choose the documents where x is 1 for the deletion test. Let's delete all the documents where x is 1 from the collection:

    ```
    > db.updAndDelTest.remove({x:1})
    ```

11. Execute the following `find` command and observe the results. We will not get any results. It seems that the `remove` operation has removed all the documents with x as 1.

```
> db.updAndDelTest.find({x:1}, {_id:0})
```

 When you are in the mongo shell and you want to see the source code of a function, simply type in the function name without the parenthesis. For example, in this recipe, we can view the code of our custom function by typing the function name, `prepareTestData`, without the parenthesis, and press *Enter*.

How it works...

First, we set up the data that we will use for the updating and deleting `test`. We have already seen the data and know what it is. An interesting thing to observe is that when we execute an update such as `db.updAndDelTest.update({x:1}, {$set:{y:0}})`, it only updates the first document that matches the query provided as the first parameter. This is something we will observe when we query the collection after this update. The update function has the following format `db.<collection name>.update(query, update object, {upsert: <boolean>, multi:<boolean>})`.

We will see what upsert is in the later recipes. The multi parameter is set to `false` by default. This means that multiple documents will not be updated by the `update` method; only the first matching document will be updated. However, when we do `db.updAndDelTest.update({x:1}, {$set:{y:0}}, {multi:true})` with multi set to `true`, all the documents in the collection that match the given query are updated. This is something that we can verify after querying the collection.

Removals, on the other hand, behave differently. By default, the `remove` operation deletes all the documents that match the provided query. However, if we want to delete only one document, we explicitly pass the second parameter as `true`.

 The default behavior of update and remove is different. An `update` call, by default, updates only the *first* matching document, whereas `remove` deletes *all* the documents matching the query.

Creating index and viewing plans of queries

In this recipe, we will look at querying the data, analyzing its performance by explaining the query plan, and then optimizing it by creating indexes.

Getting ready

For the creation of indexes, we need to have a server up and running. A simple single node is what we need. Refer to the *Installing single node MongoDB* recipe from *Chapter 1, Installing and Starting the Server* for instructions on how to start the server. The data that we will operate on needs to be imported in the database. The steps to import the data are given in the previous recipe, *Creating test data*. Once this prerequisite is complete, we are good to go.

How to do it...

We are trying to write a query that would find us all the zip codes in a given state.

1. Execute the following query to view the plan of this query:

   ```
   > db.postalCodes.find({state:'Maharashtra'}).
   explain('executionStats')
   ```

   Take a note of the following fields: `stage`, `nReturned`, `totalDocsExamined`, `docsExamined`, and `executionTimeMillis` in the result of the explain plan operation.

2. Let's again execute the same query, but this time, we limit the results to 100 results only:

   ```
   > db.postalCodes.find({state:'Maharashtra'}).limit(100).explain()
   ```

3. Take a note of the following fields: `nReturned`, `totalDocsExamined`, `docsExamined`, and `executionTimeMillis` in the result.

4. We now create an index on the `state` and `pincode` fields as follows:

   ```
   > db.postalCodes.createIndex({state:1, pincode:1})
   ```

5. Execute the following query:

   ```
   > db.postalCodes.find({state:'Maharashtra'}).explain()
   ```

   Take a note of the following fields: `stage`, `nReturned`, `totalDocsExamined`, `docsExamined`, and `executionTimeMillis` in the result.

6. As we want the pincodes only, we modify the query as follows and view its plan:

   ```
   > db.postalCodes.find({state:'Maharashtra'}, {pincode:1, _id:0}).
   explain()
   ```

   Take a note of the following fields: `stage`, `nReturned`, `totalDocsExamined`, `docsExamined`, and `executionTimeMillis` in the result.

How it works...

There is a lot to explain here. We will first discuss what we just did and how to analyze the stats. Next, we will discuss some points to be kept in mind for the index creation and some caveats.

Analyzing the plan

Okay, let's look at the first step and analyze the output that we executed:

```
db.postalCodes.find({state:'Maharashtra'}).explain()
```

The output on my machine is as follows: (I am skipping the nonrelevant fields for now.)

```
{
        "stage" : "COLLSCAN",
...
        "nReturned" : 6446,
        "totalDocsExamined " : 39732,
            ...
    "docsExamined" : 39732,
            ...

        "executionTimeMillis" : 12,
    ...
    }
```

The value of the `stage` field in the result is COLLSCAN, which means that a full collection scan (all the documents scanned one after another) has happened in order to search the matching documents in the entire collection. The nReturned value is 6446, which is the number of results that matched the query. The `totalDocsExamined` and docsExamined field have values of 39,732, which is the number of documents in the collection scanned to retrieve the results. This is the also the total number of documents present in the collection and all were scanned for the result. Finally, executionTimeMillis is the number of milliseconds taken to retrieve the result.

Improving the query execution time

So far, the query doesn't look too good in terms of performance and there is great scope for improvement. To demonstrate how the limit applied to the query affects the query plan, we can find the query plan again without the index but with the limit clause as follows:

```
> db.postalCodes.find({state:'Maharashtra'}).limit(100).explain()

{
```

```
    "stage" : "COLLSCAN",
    ...

    "nReturned" : 100,
    "totalDocsExamined" : 19951,


    ...
    "docsExamined" : 19951,
    ...

    "executionTimeMillis" : 8,
    ...

}
```

The query plan this time around is interesting. Though we still haven't created an index, we do see an improvement in the time that the query took for execution and the number of objects scanned to retrieve the results. This is due to the fact that mongo ignores the scanning of the remaining documents once the number of documents specified in the `limit` function has been reached. We can thus conclude that it is recommended that you use the `limit` function to limit your number of results where the maximum number of documents accessed is known up front. This may give better query performance. The word `may` is important as, in the absence of an index, the collection might still be completely scanned if the number of matches is not met.

Improvement using indexes

Moving on, we then create a compound index on the state and pincode field. The order of the index is ascending in this case (as the value is one) and is not significant unless we plan to execute a multi-key sorting. This is a deciding factor as to whether the result can be sorted using an index only or mongo needs to sort it in memory later on before returning the results. As far as the plan of the query is concerned, we can see that there is a significant improvement:

```
{
"executionStages" : {
      "stage" : "FETCH",
...
"inputStage" : {
      "stage" : "IXSCAN",
...

      "nReturned" : 6446,
      "totalDocsExamined" : 6446,
```

```
        "docsExamined" : 6446,

    ...

        "executionTimeMillis" : 4,

...

}
```

The `inputStage` field now has the `IXSCAN` value, which shows that the index is indeed used now. The number of results stays, as expected, the same at `6446`. The number of objects scanned in the index and the documents scanned in the collection has now reduced to the same number of documents as in the result. This is because we have now used an index that gives us the starting document to scan, and only then, the required number of documents are scanned. This is similar to using the book's index to find a word or scanning the entire book to search for the word. As expected, the time in `executionTimeMillis` has reduced as well.

Improvement using covered indexes

This leaves us with one field, `executionStages`, which is `FETCH`, and we will see what this means. To know what this value is, we need to look briefly at how indexes operate.

Indexes store a subset of fields of the original document in the collection. The fields present in the index are the same as those that the index is created on. The fields, however, are kept sorted in the index in an order specified during the index creation. Apart from the fields, there is an additional value stored in the index that acts as a pointer to the original document in the collection. Thus, whenever the user executes a query, the index is consulted to get a set of matches if the query contains fields that an index is present on. The pointer, stored with the index entries matching the query, is then used to make another IO operation to fetch the complete document from the collection, which is then returned to the user.

The value of `executionStages`, which is `FETCH`, indicates that the data requested by the user in the query is not entirely present in the index, but an additional IO operation is needed to retrieve the entire document from the collection following the pointer from the index. If the value is present in the index itself, an additional operation to retrieve the document from the collection would not be necessary and the data from the index would be returned. This is called a covered index, and the value of `executionStages`, in this case, would be `IXSCAN`.

In our case, we just needed the pincodes. So, why not use projection in our queries to retrieve just what we need? This would also make the index covered as the index entry just has the state's name and pincode, and the required data can be served completely without retrieving the original document from the collection. The plan of the query in this case is interesting too.

Execute the following command:

```
db.postalCodes.find({state:'Maharashtra'}, {pincode:1, _id:0}).explain()
```

This gives us the following plan:

```
{
"executionStages" : {
      "stage" : "PROJECTION",
...

"inputStage" : {
       "stage" : "IXSCAN",
...

       "nReturned" : 6446,
       "totalDocsExamined" : 0,
    "totalKeysExamined": 6446
  "executionTimeMillis" : 4,

...

}
```

The value of the `totalDocsExamined` and `executionStage: PROJECTION` fields is something to observe. As expected, the data that we requested in the projection can be served from the index alone. In this case, we scanned 6446 entries in the index and thus, the `totalKeysExamined` value is `6446`.

As the entire result was fetched from the index, our query did not fetch any documents from the collection. Hence, the value of `totalDocsExamined` is `0`.

As this collection is small, we do not see a significant difference in the execution time of the query. This will be more evident on larger collections. Making use of indexes is great and gives us a good performance. Making use of covered index gives us an even better performance.

The explain results feature of MongoDB has had a major overhaul in version 3.0. I would suggest spending a few minutes going through its documentation at `http://docs.mongodb.org/manual/reference/explain-results/`.

Another thing to remember is that if your document has a lot of fields, try and use projection to retrieve only the number of fields we need. The `_id` field is retrieved every time by default. Unless we plan to use it, set `_id:0` to not retrieve it if it is not a part of the index. Executing a covered query is the most efficient way to query a collection.

Some caveats of index creations

We will now see some pitfalls in index creation and some facts when an array field is used in the index.

Some of the operators that do not use the index efficiently are the `$where`, `$nin`, and `$exists` operators. Whenever these operators are used in the query, one should bear in mind that a possible performance bottleneck might occur when the data size increases.

Similarly, the `$in` operator must be preferred over the `$or` operator as both can be used to achieve more or less the same result. As an exercise, try to find the pincodes in the state of Maharashtra and Gujarat in the `postalCodes` collection. Write two queries: one using `$or` and one using the `$in` operator. Explain the plan for both these queries.

What happens when an array field is used in the index?

Mongo creates an index entry for each element present in the array field of a document. So, if there are 10 elements in an array in a document, there will be 10 index entries, one for each element in the array. However, there is a constraint while creating indexes containing array fields. When creating indexes using multiple fields, no more than one field can be of a type array, and this is done to prevent a possible explosion in the number of indexes on adding even a single element to the array used in the index. If we think of it carefully, an index entry is created for each element in the array. If multiple fields of the type array were allowed to be a part of an index, then we would have a large number of entries in the index, which would be a product of the length of these array fields. For example, a document added with two array fields, each of length 10, would add 100 entries to the index if it is allowed to create one index using these two array fields.

This should be good enough, for now, to scratch the surfaces of a plain, vanilla index. We will see more options and types in the following few recipes.

Creating a background and foreground index in the shell

In our previous recipe, we looked at how to analyze the queries, how to decide what index needs to be created, and how to create indexes. This, by itself, is straightforward and looks reasonably simple. However, for large collections, things start getting worse as the index creation time is large. The objective of this recipe is to throw some light on these concepts and avoid these pitfalls while creating indexes, especially on large collections.

Getting ready

For the creation of indexes, we need to have a server up and running. A simple single node is what we need. Refer to the *Installing single node MongoDB* recipe from *Chapter 1, Installing and Starting the Server* for instructions on how to start the server.

Start connecting two shells to the server by just typing `mongo` from the operating system shell. Both of them will, by default, connect to the `test` database.

Our test data for zip codes is too small to demonstrate the problem faced in index creation on large collections. We need to have more data and thus, we will start by creating some data to simulate the problems during index creation. The data has no practical meaning but is good enough to test the concepts. Copy the following piece in one of the started shells and execute: (It is a pretty easy snippet to type out.)

```
for(i = 0; i < 5000000 ; i++) {
  doc = {}
  doc._id = i
  doc.value = 'Some text with no meaning and number ' + i + ' in
    between'
  db.indexTest.insert(doc)
}
```

A document in this collection will look something as follows:

```
{ _id:0, value:"Some text with no meaning and number 0 in between" }
```

The execution will take quite a lot of time, so we need to be patient. Once the execution is over, we are all set for the action.

> If you are keen to know what the current number of documents loaded in the collection is, keep evaluating the following from the second shell periodically:
> ```
> db.indexTest.count()
> ```

How to do it...

1. Create an index on the `value` field of the document as follows:

    ```
    > db.indexTest.createIndex({value:1})
    ```

2. While the index creation is in progress, which should take quite some time, switch over to the second console and execute the following:

    ```
    > db.indexTest.findOne()
    ```

3. Both the index creation shell and the one where we executed `findOne` will be blocked and the prompt will not be shown on both of them until the index creation is complete.

4. Now, this was foreground index creation by default. We want to see the behavior in background index creation. Drop the created index as follows:

```
> db.indexTest.dropIndex({value:1})
```

5. Create the index again, but this time in background, as follows:

```
> db.indexTest.createIndex({value:1}, {background:true})
```

6. In the second mongo shell, execute `findOne` as follows:

```
> db.indexTest.findOne()
```

7. This should return one document, which is unlike the first instance, where the operation was blocked until the index creation completed in the foreground.

8. In the second shell, repeatedly execute the following explain operation with a four-to-five second interval between each explain plan invocation until the index creation process is complete:

```
> db.indexTest.find({value:"Some text with no meaning and number 0
in between"}).explain()
```

How it works...

Let's now analyze what we just did. We created about five million documents with no practical importance, but we are just looking to get some data that will take a significant amount of time to build the index.

An index can be built in two ways, in the foreground and background. In either case, the shell doesn't show the prompt until the `createIndex` operation has been completed and will block all operations until the index is created. To illustrate the difference between a foreground and background index creation, we executed a second mongo shell.

We first created the index in the foreground, which is the default behavior. This index building didn't allow us to query the collection (from the second shell) until the index was constructed. The `findOne` operation is blocked until the entire index was built (from the first shell) before returning the result. On other hand, the index that was built in the background didn't block the `findOne` operation. If you want to try inserting new documents into the collection while the index building is on, this should work very well. Feel free to drop the index and recreate it in the background, while simultaneously inserting a document into the `indexTest` collection, and you will notice that it works smoothly.

Well, what is the difference between the two approaches and why not always build the index in the background? Apart from an extra parameter, `{background:true}` (which can also be `{background:1}`) passed as a second parameter to the `createIndex` call, there are few differences. The index creation process in the background will be slightly slower than the index created in the foreground. Furthermore, internally—though not relevant to the end user—the index created in the foreground will be more compact than the one created in the background.

Other than this, there will be no significant difference. In fact, if a system is running and an index needs to be created while it is serving the end users (not recommended, but a situation can come up at times that demands index creation in a live system), then creating an index in the background is the only way you can do it. There are other strategies to perform such administrative activities, which we will see in some recipes in the administration section.

To make things worse for foreground index creation, the lock acquired by mongo during index creation is not at the collection level but is at the database level. To explain what this means, we will have to drop the index on the `indexTest` collection and perform the following small exercise:

1. Start by creating the index in the foreground from the shell by executing the following command:

   ```
   > db.indexTest.createIndex({value:1})
   ```

2. Now, insert a document into the person collection, which may or may not exist at this point in the test database, as follows:

   ```
   > db.person.insert({name:'Amol'})
   ```

We will see that this insert operation in the person collection will be blocked while index creation on the `indexTest` collection is in process. However, if this insert operation was done on a collection in a different database during the index building, it would execute normally without blocking. (You can try this out as well.) This clearly shows that the lock is acquired at the database level and not at the collection or global level.

Prior to version 2.2 of mongo, locks were at the global level, which is at the mongod process level, and not at the database level as we saw previously. You need to remember this fact when dealing with a distribution of mongo older than version 2.2.

Creating and understanding sparse indexes

Schemaless design is one of the fundamental features of Mongo. This allows documents in a collection to have disparate fields, with some fields present in some documents and absent in others. In other words, these fields might be sparse, which might have already given you a clue on what sparse indexes are. In this recipe, we will create some random test data and see how sparse indexes behave against a normal index. We shall see the advantages and one major pitfall of using a sparse index.

Getting ready

For this recipe, we need to create a collection called `sparseTest`. We will require a server to be up and running. Refer to the *Installing single node MongoDB* recipe from *Chapter 1, Installing and Starting the Server* for instructions on how to start the server. Start the shell with the `SparseIndexData.js` script loaded. This script is available on the Packt website for download. To know how to start the shell with a script preloaded, refer to the *Connecting to a single node in the Mongo shell with JavaScript* recipe in *Chapter 1, Installing and Starting the Server*.

How to do it...

1. Load the data in the collection by invoking the following. This should import 100 documents in the `sparseTest` collection.

   ```
   > createSparseIndexData()
   ```

2. Now, take a look at the data by executing the following query, taking note of the y field in the top few results:

   ```
   > db.sparseTest.find({}, {_id:0})
   ```

3. We can see that the y field is absent, or it is unique if it is present. Let's then execute the following query:

   ```
   > db.sparseTest.find({y:{$ne:2}}, {_id:0}).limit(15)
   ```

4. Take a note of the result; it contains both the documents that match the condition as well as fields that do not contain the given field, y.

5. As the value of y seems unique, let's create a new unique index on the y field as follows:

   ```
   > db.sparseTest.createIndex({y:1}, {unique:1})
   ```

   This throws an error complaining that the value is not unique and the offending value is the null value.

6. We will fix this by making this index sparse as follows:

```
> db.sparseTest.createIndex({y:1}, {unique:1, sparse:1})
```

7. This should fix our problem. To confirm that the index got created, execute the following on the shell:

```
> db.sparseTest.getIndexes()
```

This should show two indexes, the default one on `_id` and the one that we just created in the preceding step.

8. Now, execute the query that we executed earlier in step 3 again and see the result.

9. Look at the result and compare it with what we saw before the index was created. Re-execute the query but with the following hint forcing a full collection scan:

```
>db.sparseTest.find({y:{$ne:2}},{_id:0}).limit(15).
hint({$natural:1})
```

10. Observe the result.

How it works...

These were a lot of steps that we just performed. We will now dig deeper and explain the internals and reasoning for the weird behavior that we see while querying the collection that used sparse indexes.

The test data that we created using the JavaScript method just created documents with a key, x, whose value is a number starting from one, all the way up to 100. The value of y is set only when x is a multiple of three—its value is a running number as well, starting from one and should go up to a maximum of 33 when x is `99`.

We then execute a query and see the following result:

```
> db.sparseTest.find({y:{$ne:2}}, {_id:0}).limit(15)
{ "x" : 1 }
{ "x" : 2 }
{ "x" : 3, "y" : 1 }
{ "x" : 4 }
{ "x" : 5 }
{ "x" : 7 }
{ "x" : 8 }
{ "x" : 9, "y" : 3 }
{ "x" : 10 }
{ "x" : 11 }
```

```
{ "x" : 12, "y" : 4 }
{ "x" : 13 }
{ "x" : 14 }
{ "x" : 15, "y" : 5 }
{ "x" : 16 }
```

The value where `y` is 2 is missing in the result and this is what we intended. Note that the documents where `y` isn't present are still seen in the result. We now plan to create an index on the `y` field. As the field is either not present or has a value that is unique, it seems natural that a unique index should work.

Internally, indexes add an entry in the index by default, even if the field is absent in the original document in the collection. The value going in the index will, however, be null. This means that there will be the same number of entries in the index as the number of documents in the collection. For a unique index, the value (including the null values) should be unique across the collection, which explains why we got an exception during index creation where the field is sparse (not present in all the documents).

A solution for this problem is making the index sparse, and all we did was add `sparse:1` to the options along with `unique:1`. This does not put an entry in the index if the field doesn't exist in the document. Thus, the index will now contain fewer entries. It will only contain those entries where the field is present in the document. This not only makes the index smaller, making it easy to fit in the memory, but also solves our problem of adding a unique constraint. The last thing that we want is an index of a collection with millions of documents to have millions of entries, where only a few hundred have some values defined.

Though we can see that creating a sparse index did make the index efficient, it introduced a new problem where some query results were not consistent. The same query that we executed earlier yields different results. See the following output:

```
> db.sparseTest.find({y:{$ne:2}}, {_id:0}).hint({y:1}).limit(15)
{ "x" : 3, "y" : 1 }
{ "x" : 9, "y" : 3 }
{ "x" : 12, "y" : 4 }
{ "x" : 15, "y" : 5 }
{ "x" : 18, "y" : 6 }
{ "x" : 21, "y" : 7 }
{ "x" : 24, "y" : 8 }
{ "x" : 27, "y" : 9 }
{ "x" : 30, "y" : 10 }
{ "x" : 33, "y" : 11 }
{ "x" : 36, "y" : 12 }
```

```
{ "x" : 39, "y" : 13 }
{ "x" : 42, "y" : 14 }
{ "x" : 45, "y" : 15 }
{ "x" : 48, "y" : 16 }
```

Why did this happen? The answer lies in the query plan for this query. Execute the following to view the plan of this query:

```
>db.sparseTest.find({y:{$ne:2}}, {_id:0}). hint({y:1}).limit(15).
explain()
```

This plan shows that it used the index to fetch the matching results. As this is a sparse index, all the documents that didn't have the `y` field are not present in it and they didn't show up in the result, though they should have. This is a pitfall that we need to be careful of when querying a collection with a sparse index and the query happens to use the index. It will yield unexpected results. One solution is to force a full collection scan, where we provide the query analyzer a hint using the `hint` function. Hints are used to force query analyzers to use a user-specified index. Though this is not recommended usually as you really need to know what you are doing, this is one of the scenarios where this is really needed. So, how do we force a full table scan? All we do is provide `{$natural:1}` in the `hint` function. A natural ordering of a collection is the order that it is stored in on the disk for a particular collection. This `hint` forces a full table scan and now we get the results as before. The query performance will, however, degrade for large collections as it is now using a full table scan.

If the field is present in a lot of documents (There is no formal cutoff for what is a *lot*; it can be 50% for some or 75% for others.) and not really sparse, then making the index sparse doesn't make much sense apart from when we want to make it unique.

 If two documents have a null value for the same field, unique index creation will fail, and creating it as a sparse index will not help either.

Expiring documents after a fixed interval using the TTL index

One of the interesting features in Mongo is automatically expiring data in the collection after a predetermined amount of time. This is a very useful tool when we want to purge some data older than a particular timeframe. For a relational database, it is not common for folks to set up a batch job that runs every night to perform this operation.

With the TTL feature of Mongo, you need not worry about this as the database takes care of it out of the box. Let's see how we can achieve this.

Getting ready

Let's create data in Mongo that we want to play with using the TTL indexes. We will create a collection called `ttlTest` for this purpose. We will require a server to be up and running. Refer to the *Installing single node MongoDB* recipe from *Chapter 1, Installing and Starting the Server* for instructions on how to start the server. Start the shell with the `TTLData.js` script loaded. This script is available on the Packt website for download. To know how to start the shell with a script preloaded, refer to the *Connecting to a single node in the Mongo shell with JavaScript* recipe from *Chapter 1, Installing and Starting the Server*.

How to do it...

1. Assuming that the server has started and the script provided is loaded on the shell, invoke the following method from the mongo shell:

    ```
    > addTTLTestData()
    ```

2. Create a TTL index on the `createDate` field as follows:

    ```
    > db.ttlTest.createIndex({createDate:1}, {expireAfterSeconds:300})
    ```

3. Now, query the collection as follows:

    ```
    > db.ttlTest.find()
    ```

4. This should give us three documents. Repeat the process and execute the `find` query in approximately 30-40 seconds repeatedly to see the three documents getting deleted until the entire collection has zero documents left in it.

How it works...

Let's start by opening the `TTLData.js` file and see what is going on inside it. The code is pretty simple and it just gets the current date using new `Date()`. It then creates three documents with `createDate` that were four, three, and two minutes behind the current time for the three documents. So, on the execution of the `addTTLTestData()` method in this script, we have three documents in the `ttlTest` collection with each having a difference of one minute in their creation time.

The next step is the core of the TTL feature: the creation of the TTL index. It is similar to the creation of any other index using the `createIndex` method, except that it also accepts a second parameter that is a JSON object. These two parameters are as follows:

- ▸ The first parameter is `{createDate:1}`; this will tell mongo to create an index on the `createDate` field, and the order of the index is ascending as the value is `1` (`-1` would have been descending).

- ▸ The second parameter, `{expireAfterSeconds:300}`, is what makes this index a TTL index, and it tells Mongo to automatically expire the documents after 300 seconds (five minutes).

Okay, but five minutes since when? Is it the time they were inserted in the collection or some other timestamp? In this case, it considers the `createTime` field as the base because this was the field that we created the index on.

This now raises a question: if a field is being used as a base for the computation of time, there has to be some restriction on its type. It just doesn't make sense to create a TTL index, as we created previously, on a `char` field holding, say, the name of a person.

Yes; as we guessed, the type of the field can be of a BSON type date or an array of dates. What will happen in the case where an array has multiple dates? What will be considered in that case?

It turns out that Mongo uses a minimum of dates available in the array. Try this scenario out as an exercise.

Put two dates separated by about five minutes from each other in a document against the field name, `updateField`, and then create a TTL index on this field to expire the document after 10 minutes (600 seconds). Query the collection and see when the document gets deleted from the collection. It should get deleted after roughly 10 minutes have elapsed after the minimum time value present in the `updateField` array.

Apart from the constraint for the type of field, there are a few more constraints:

- ▸ If a field already has an index on it, you cannot create a TTL index. As the `_id` field of the collection already has an index by default, it effectively means that you cannot create a TTL index on the `_id` field.

- ▸ A TTL index cannot be a compound index involving multiple fields.

- ▸ If a field doesn't exist, it will never expire. (That's pretty logical, I guess.)

- ▸ It cannot be created on capped collections. In case you are not aware of capped collections, they are special collections in Mongo with a size limit on them with a FIFO insertion order and delete old documents to make place for new documents, if needed.

TTL indexes are supported only on the Mongo version 2.2 and above. Note that the document will not be deleted at exactly the given time in the field. The cycle will be of a granularity of one minute, which will delete all the documents eligible for deletion since the last time the cycle was run.

See also

A use case might not demand deleting all the documents after a fixed interval has elapsed. What if we want to customize the point until a document stays in the collection? This too can be achieved, which is what will be demonstrated in the next recipe, *Expiring documents at a given time using the TTL index*.

Expiring documents at a given time using the TTL index

In the previous recipe, *Expiring documents after a fixed interval using the TTL index*, we have seen how documents can expire after a fixed time period. However, there can be some cases where we might want to have documents expiring at different times. This is not what we saw in the previous recipe. In this recipe, we will see how we can specify the time that the document can expire and it might be different for different documents.

Getting ready

For this recipe, we will create a collection called `ttlTest2`. We will require a server to be up and running. Refer to the *Installing single node MongoDB* recipe from *Chapter 1, Installing and Starting the Server* for instructions on how to start the server. Start the shell with the `TTLData.js` script loaded. This script is available on the Packt website for download. To know how to start the shell with a script preloaded, refer to the *Connecting to a single node in the Mongo shell with JavaScript* recipe in *Chapter 1, Installing and Starting the Server*.

How to do it...

1. Load the required data in the collection using the `addTTLTestData2` method. Execute the following on the mongo shell:

    ```
    > addTTLTestData2()
    ```

2. Now, create the TTL index on the `ttlTest2` collection as follows:

    ```
    > db.ttlTest2.createIndex({expiryDate :1}, {expireAfterSeconds:0})
    ```

3. Execute the following `find` query to view the three documents in the collection:

   ```
   > db.ttlTest2.find()
   ```

4. Now, after approximately four, five, and seven minutes, see that the documents with the IDs two, one, and three get deleted, respectively.

How it works...

Let's start by opening the `TTLData.js` file and see what is going on inside it. Our method of interest for this recipe is `addTTLTestData2`. This method simply creates three documents in the `tllTest2` collection with `_id` of 1, 2, and 3 with their `exipryDate` fields set to 5, 4, and 7 minutes after the current time, respectively. Note that this field has a future date, unlike the date given in the previous recipe, where it was a creation date.

Next, we create an index: `db.ttlTest2.createIndex({expiryDate :1}, {expireAfterSeconds:0})`. This is different from the way we created the index for the previous recipe, where the `expireAfterSeconds` field of the object was set to a non-zero value. This is how the value of the `expireAfterSeconds` attribute is interpreted. If the value is non-zero, then this is the time in seconds that has elapsed after a base time when the document will be deleted from the collection by Mongo. This base time is the value held in the field that the index is created on (`createTime`, as in the previous recipe). If this value is zero, then the date value that the index is created on (`expiryDate`, in this case) will be the time when the document will expire.

To conclude, TTL indexes work well if you want to delete the document upon expiry. There are quite a lot of cases where we might want to move the document to an archive collection, where the archived collection might be created based on, say, the year and month. In any such scenarios, a TTL index is not helpful and we might have to write an external job ourselves that does this work. Such a job could also read the collection for a range of documents, add them to the target collection, and delete them from the source collection. The folks at MongoDB have already planned to release a feature that addresses this issue.

See also

In this and the previous recipe, we looked at TTL indexes and how to use them. However, what if, after creating a TTL index, we want to modify the TTL value? This is possible using the `collMod` option. See more on this option in the administration section.

3
Programming Language Drivers

In this chapter, we will cover the following recipes:

- ▶ Executing query and insert operations with PyMongo
- ▶ Executing update and delete operations using PyMongo
- ▶ Implementing aggregation in Mongo using PyMongo
- ▶ Executing MapReduce in Mongo using PyMongo
- ▶ Executing query and insert operations using a Java client
- ▶ Executing update and delete operations using a Java client
- ▶ Implementing aggregation in Mongo using a Java client
- ▶ Executing MapReduce in Mongo using a Java client

Introduction

So far, we have executed the majority of operations in the shell using Mongo. The Mongo shell is a great tool for administrators to perform administrative tasks and for developers who would like to quickly test things by querying the data before coding the logic in the application. However, how do we write application code that will allow us to query, insert, update, and delete (among other things) the data in MongoDB? There has to be a library for the programming language that we write our application in. We should be able to instantiate something or invoke methods from the program to perform some operations on the remote Mongo process.

How would this happen unless there is some bridge that understands the protocol of communication with the remote server and is able to transmit the operation over the wire that we require in order to execute on the Mongo server process and get the result back to the client. This bridge, simply put, is called the **driver**, also referred to as client libraries. Drivers form the backbone of Mongo's programming language interface; in their absence, it would have been the responsibility of the application to communicate with the Mongo server using a low-level protocol that the server understands. This would have been a lot of work, not only to develop, but also to test and maintain. Though the communication protocol is standard, there cannot be one implementation that works for all the languages. A variety of programming languages need to have their own implementations exposing similar sets of programming interfaces to all the languages. The core concepts of client APIs, which we will see in this chapter, holds good for all the languages.

> Mongo has support for all major programming and is supported by MongoDB Inc. There is even a huge array of programming languages supported by the community. You can take a look at the various platforms supported by Mongo by visiting `http://docs.mongodb.org/ecosystem/drivers/community-supported-drivers/`.

Executing query and insert operations with PyMongo

This recipe is all about executing basic query and `insert` operations using PyMongo. This is similar to what we did with the Mongo shell earlier in the book.

Getting ready

To execute simple queries, we need to have a server up and running. A simple single node is what we need. Refer to the *Installing single node MongoDB* recipe from *Chapter 1, Installing and Starting the Server* for instructions on how to start the server. The data that we will be operating on needs to be imported in the database. The steps to import the data are given in the *Creating test data* recipe from *Chapter 2, Command-line Operations and Indexes*. Python 2.7, or higher, has to be present on the host operating system along with MongoDB's Python client, PyMongo. Look at the earlier recipe, *Connecting to a single node using a Python client*, in *Chapter 1, Installing and Starting the Server* on how to install PyMongo for your host operating system. Additionally, in this recipe, we will execute `insert` operations and provide a write concern to use.

How to do it...

Let's start with querying for Mongo in the Python shell. This will be identical to what we do in the mongo shell except that this is in the Python programming language, as opposed to the JavaScript that we have in the mongo shell. We can use the basics that we will see here to write big production systems that run on Python and use mongo as a data store.

Let's begin by starting the Python shell from the operating system's command prompt. All these steps are independent of the host operating system. Perform the following steps:

1. Type the following in the shell and the Python shell should start:

   ```
   $ python
   Python 2.7.6 (default, Mar 22 2014, 22:59:56)
   [GCC 4.8.2] on linux2
   Type "help", "copyright", "credits" or "license" for more
   information.
   >>>
   ```

2. Then, import the pymongo package and create the client as follows:

   ```
   >>> import pymongo
   >>> client = pymongo.MongoClient('localhost', 27017)
   ```
   The following is an alternative way to connect
   ```
   >>> client = pymongo.MongoClient('mongodb://localhost:27017')
   ```

3. This works well and achieves the same result. Now that we have the client, our next step is to get the database that we will be performing the operations on. This is unlike some of the programming languages where we have a getDatabase() method to get an instance of the database. We will get a reference to the database object that we will be performing the operations on, test in this case. We will do this in the following way:

   ```
   >>> db = client.test
   ```
   Another alternative is
   ```
   >>> db = client['test']
   ```

4. We will query the postalCodes collection. We will limit our results to 10 items.

   ```
   >>> postCodes = db.postalCodes.find().limit(10)
   ```

5. Iterate over the results. Watch out for the indentation of the print after the for statement. The following fragment should print 10 documents as returned:

   ```
   >>> for postCode in postCodes:
     print 'City: ', postCode['city'], ', State: ',
   postCode['state'], ', Pin Code: ', postCode['pincode']
   ```

6. To find one document, execute the following:

```
>>> postCode = db.postalCodes.find_one()
```

7. Print the `state` and `city` of the returned result as follows:

```
>>> print 'City: ', postCode['city'], ', State: ',
postCode['state'], ', Pin Code: ', postCode['pincode']
```

8. Let's query top 10 cities in the state of Gujarat sorted by the name of the city and, additionally, we just select the `city`, `state`, and `pincode`. Execute the following query in the Python shell:

```
>>> cursor = db.postalCodes.find({'state':'Gujarat'}, {'_
id':0, 'city':1, 'state':1, 'pincode':1}).sort('city', pymongo.
ASCENDING).limit(10)
```

The preceding cursor's results can be printed in the same way that we printed the results in step 5.

9. Let's sort the data that we query. We want to sort in a descending order of state and then by ascending order of the city. We will write the query as follows:

```
>>> city = db.postalCodes.find().sort([('state', pymongo.
DESCENDING),('city',pymongo.ASCENDING)]).limit(5)
```

10. Iterating through this cursor should print out five results to the console. Refer to step 5 on how we iterate over a cursor returned to print the results.

11. So, we have played a bit to find documents and covered the basic operations in Python as far as the querying of MongoDB is concerned. Now, let's see a bit about the `insert` operation. We will use a test collection to perform these operations and not disturb our postal codes test data. We will use a `pymongoTest` collection for this purpose and add documents in a loop to it as follows:

```
>>> for i in range(1, 21):
    db.pymongoTest.insert_one({'i':i})
```

12. The `insert` can take a list of dictionary objects and perform a bulk insert. So now, something similar to the following `insert` is perfectly valid:

```
>>> db.pythonTest.insert_many([{'name':'John'}, {'name':'Mark'}])
```

Any guesses on the return value? In case of a single document insert, the return value is the value of `_id` for the newly created document. In this case, it is a list of IDs.

How it works...

In step 2, we instantiate the client and get the reference to the `MongoClient` object that will be used to access the database. There are a couple of ways to get this reference. The first option is more convenient, unless your database name has some special character, such as a hyphen (-). For example, if the name is `db-test`, we would have no option other than to use the `[]` operator to access the database. Using either of the alternatives, we now have an object for the test database in the `db` variable. After we get the `client` and `db` instances in Python, we query to find the top 10 documents in the natural order from the collection in step 3. The syntax is identical to how this query would have been executed in the shell. Step 4 simply prints out the results, 10 of them in this case. Generally, if you need instant help on a particular class using the class name or an instance of this class from the Python interpreter, simply perform `dir(<class_name>)` or `dir(<object of a class>)`, which gives you a list of attributes and functions defined in the module passed. For example, `dir('pymongo.MongoClient')` or `dir(client)`, where the client is the variable holding reference to an instance of `pymongo.MongoClient`, can be used to get the list of all the supported attributes and functions. The `help` function is more informative, prints out the module's documentation, and is a great source of reference just in case you need instant help. Try typing `help('pymongo.MongoClient')` or `help(client)`.

In steps 3 and 4, we query the `postalCodes` collection, limit the result to the top 10 results, and print them. The returned object is of a type `pymongo.cursor.Cursor` class. The next step gets just one document from the collection using the `find_one()` function. This is synonymous to the `findOne()` method on the collection invoked in the shell. The value returned by this function is an inbuilt object, `dict`.

In step 6, we execute another `find` to query the data. In step 8, we pass two Python dicts. The first dict is the query, similar to the query parameter we use in mongo shell. The second dictionary is used to provide the fields to be returned in the result. A value, one, for a field indicates that the value is to be selected and returned in the result. This is synonymous with the `select` statement in a relational database with a few sets of columns provided explicitly to be selected. The `_id` field is selected by default unless it is explicitly set to zero in the selector `dict` object. The selector provided here is `{'_id':0, 'city':1, 'state':1, 'pincode':1}`, which selects the city, state, and pincode and suppresses the `_id` field. We have a sort method as well. This method has two formats as follows:

```
sort(sort_field, sort_direction)
sort([(sort_field, sort_direction)...(sort_field, sort_direction)])
```

The first one is used when we want to sort by one field only. The second representation accepts a list of pairs of the sort field and sort directions and is used when we want to sort by multiple fields. We used the first form in the query in step 8 and the second format in our query in step 9 as we sort first by the state `name` and then, by `city`.

If we look at the way we invoke `sort`, it is invoked on the `Cursor` instance. Similarly, the `limit` function is also on the `Cursor` class. The evaluation is lazy and deferred until the iteration is performed in order to retrieve the results from the cursor. Until this point of time, the `Cursor` object is not evaluated on the server.

In step 11, we insert a document 20 times in a collection. Each insert, as we can see in the Python shell, will return a generated `_id` field. In terms of the syntax of insert, it is exactly identical to the operation that we perform in the shell. The parameter passed for the insert is an object of type `dict`.

In step 12, we pass a list of documents to insert in the collection. This is referred to as a bulk insert operation, which inserts multiple documents in a single call to the server. The return value in this case is a list of IDs, one for each document inserted, and the order is the same as those passed in the input list. However, as MongoDB doesn't support transactions, each insert will be independent of each other, and a failure of one insert doesn't roll back the entire operation automatically.

Adding the functionality of inserting multiple documents demanded another parameter for the behavior. When one of the inserts in the list given fails, should the remaining inserts continue or the insertion stop as soon as the first error is encountered? The name of the parameter to control this behavior is `continue_on_error` and its default value is `False`, that is, stop as soon as the first error is encountered. If this value is `True` and multiple errors occur during insertion, only the latest error will be available, and hence the default option with `False` as the value is sensible. Let's look at a couple of examples. In the Python shell, execute the following:

```
>>> db.contOnError.drop()
>>> db.contOnError.insert([{'_id':1}, {'_id':1}, {'_id':2}, {'_id':2}])
>>> db.contOnError.count()
```

The count that we will get is 1, which is for the first document with the `_id` field as 1. The moment another document with the same value of the `_id` field is found, 1 in this case, an error is thrown and the bulk insert stops. Now execute the following `insert` operation:

```
>>> db.contOnError.drop()
>>> db.contOnError.insert([{'_id':1}, {'_id':1}, {'_id':2}, {'_id':2}],
continue_on_error=True)
>>> db.contOnError.count()
```

Here, we have passed an additional parameter, `continue_on_error`, whose value is `True`. What this does is ensures that the `insert` operation will continue with the next document even if an intermediate `insert` operation fails. The second insert with `_id:1` fails, yet the next insert goes through before another insert with `_id:2` fails (as one document with this `_id` is already present). Additionally, the error reported is for the last failure, the one with `_id:2`.

See also

The next recipe, *Executing update and delete operations using PyMongo*, picks up where this leaves off and introduces the update, remove, and atomic find operations.

Executing update and delete operations using PyMongo

In the previous recipe, we saw how to execute `find` and `insert` operations in MongoDB using PyMongo. In this recipe, we will see how update and delete work in Python. We will also see what atomic find and update/delete is and how to execute them. We then conclude by revisiting find operations and looking at some interesting functions of the `cursor` object.

Getting ready

If you have already seen and completed the previous recipe, you are all set to go. If not, it is recommended that you first complete that recipe before going ahead with this one. Additionally, if you are not sure what read preference and write concern are, refer to the two recipes, *Read preference for querying* and *Write concern and its significance*, in *Appendix, Concepts for Reference* of the book.

Before we get started, let's define a small function that iterates through the cursor and shows the results of a cursor on the console. We will use this function whenever we want to display the results of a query on the `pymongoTests` collection. The following is the function body:

```
>>> def showResults(cursor):
        if cursor.count() != 0:
            for e in cursor:
                print e
        else:
            print 'No documents found'
```

You can refer to steps 1 and 2 in the previous recipe on how to create a connection to the MongoDB server and the `db` object that is used to perform CRUD operations on this database. Additionally, refer to step 8 in the previous recipe on how to insert the required test data in the `pymongoTest` collection. You can confirm the data in this collection by executing the following in the Python shell once the data is present:

```
>>> showResults(db.pymongoTest.find())
```

For a part of the recipe, one is also expected to know how to start a replica set instance. Refer to the *Starting multiple instances as part of a replica set* and *Connecting to the replica set in the shell to query and insert data* recipes in the first chapter for more details on a replica set and how to start one.

How to do it...

We will begin by running the following commands in the Python shell:

1. We will set a field named gtTen specified with a Boolean value True if the i field has a value greater than 10. Let's execute the following update:

   ```
   >>>result = db.pymongoTest.update_one({'i':{'$gt':10}},
   {'$set':{'gtTen':True}})
   >>> print result.raw_result
   {u'n': 1, u'nModified': 0, u'ok': 1, 'updatedExisting': True}
   ```

2. Query the collection, view its data by executing the following, and check the data that got updated:

   ```
   >>> showResults(db.pymongoTest.find())
   ```

3. The results displayed confirm that only one document got updated. We will now execute the same update again, but this time around, we will update all the documents that match the provided query. Execute the following update in the Python shell. Note that this update is identical to the one we performed in step 1 except for the additional parameter called multi whose value is given as True. Note the value of n in the response, which is 10 this time.

   ```
   >>> result = db.pymongoTest.update_many({'i':{'$gt':10}},{'$set':{
   'gtTen':True}})
   print result.raw_result
   {u'n': 10, u'nModified': 9, u'ok': 1, 'updatedExisting': True}
   ```

4. Execute the operation that we did in step 2 again to view the contents in the pymongoTest collection and verify the documents that got updated.

5. Let's look at how upsert operations can be performed. Upserts are updates plus inserts, and they update a document if one exists, just as an update would do, or else they insert a new document. We will look at an example. Consider the following update on a document that doesn't exist in the collection:

   ```
   >>> db.pymongoTest.update_one({'i':21},{'$set':{'gtTen':True}})
   ```

6. The update here will not update anything and will return the number of updated documents as zero. However, consider that we want to update a document if it exists, or else insert a new document and apply the update to it atomically, then we perform an `upsert` operation. In this case, the `upsert` operation is executed as follows. Note that the return result mentions `upsert`, `ObjectId` of the newly inserted document, and the `updatedExisting` value, which is `False`:

```
>>>result = db.pymongoTest.update_one({'i':21},{'$set':{'gtTen':Tr
ue}}, upsert=True)
>>> print result.raw_result
{u'n': 1,
 u'nModified': 0,
 u'ok': 1,
 'updatedExisting': False,
 u'upserted': ObjectId('557bd3a618292418c38b046d')}
```

7. Let's see how to delete documents from the collection using the `remove` method:

```
>>>result = db.pymongoTest.delete_one({'i':21})
>>> print result.raw_result
{u'n': 1, u'ok': 1}
```

8. If we look at the value of `n` in the preceding response, we can see that it is `1`. This means that one document has been removed.

9. To remove multiple documents from the collection, we use the `delete_many` method:

```
>>>result = db.pymongoTest.delete_many({'i':{'$gt': 10}})
>>> print result.raw_result
{u'n': 10, u'ok': 1}
```

10. We will look at the find and modify operations now. We can look at these operations as a way to find a document and update/remove it, and both of these operations are performed atomically. Once the operation is performed, the document returned is either the one before or after the update operation was done. (In case of `remove`, there will be no document after the operation.) In the absence of this operation, we cannot guarantee atomicity where multiple client connections could be performing a similar operation on the same document. The following is an example of how to perform this find and modify operation in Python:

```
>>> db.pymongoTest.find_one_and_update({'i':20},
{'$set':{'inWords':'Twenty'}})
{u'_id': ObjectId('557bdb070640fd0a0a935c22'), u'i': 20}
```

The previous result shows us that the resulting document returned is the one before the update was applied.

11. Execute the following `find` method to query and view the document that we updated in the last step. The resulting document would contain the newly added in the `Words` field:

```
>>> db.pymongoTest.find_one({'i':20})
{u'i': 20, u'_id': ObjectId('557bdb070640fd0a0a935c22'),
u'inWords': u'Twenty'}
```

12. We will execute the `find` and `modify` operation again, but this time around, we return the updated document rather than the document before the update that we saw in step 9. Execute the following in the Python shell:

```
>>> db.pymongoTest.find_one_and_update({'i':19}, {'$set':{'inWords
':'Nineteen'}}, new=True)
{u'_id': ObjectId('557bdb070640fd0a0a935c21'), u'i': 19,
u'inWords': u'Nineteen'}
```

13. We saw how to use queries with PyMongo in the previous recipe. Here, we will continue with the query operation. We saw how the `sort` and `limit` functions were chained to the find operation. The prototype of the call on the `postalCodes` collection is as follows:

```
db.postalCode.find(..).limit(..).sort(..)
```

14. There is an alternate way to achieve this same result. Execute the following query in the Python shell:

```
>>>cursor = db.postalCodes.find({'state':'Gujarat'}, {'_id':0,
'city':1, 'state':1, 'pincode':1}, limit=10, sort=[('city',
pymongo.ASCENDING)])
```

15. Print the preceding cursor using the `showResult` function already defined.

How it works...

Let's look at what all we did in this recipe; we started with updating the documents in a collection in step 1. The update operation, however, updates only the first matching document by default and the rest of the matching documents are not updated. In step 2, we added a parameter called `multi` with a value `True` to update multiple documents as part of the same update operation. Note that all these documents are not updated atomically as part of one transaction. Looking at the update done in the Python shell, we see a striking resemblance to what we would have done in the Mongo shell. If we want to name the arguments of the update operation, the names of the parameter are called `spec` and `document` for the document provided as a query to be used in order to select the documents to update and the update document, respectively. For instance, the following update is valid:

```
>>> db.pymongoTest.update_one(spec={'i':{'$gt':10}},document=
{'$set':{'gtTen':True}})
```

In step 6, we did an `upsert` (update plus insert) operation. All we had was an additional parameter, `upsert`, with a value, `True`. However, what exactly happens in the case of an upsert? Mongo tries to update the document matching the provided condition, and if it finds one, then this would be a regular update. However, in this case (`upsert` in step 6), the document was not found. The server inserted the document given as the spec (the first parameter) parameter in the collection and then applied the update to it with both these operations taking place atomically.

In steps 7 and 9, we saw the `remove` operation. The first variant accepted a query and the matching document was removed. The second variant, in step 9, removes all the matching documents.

In steps 10 to 12, we executed the `find` and `modify` operations. The gist of these operations is pretty straightforward. What we didn't mention was the `find_one_and_replace()` method, which, as the name suggests, can be used to search a document and completely replace it with another.

All the operations that we saw in this recipe were for a client connected to a standalone instance. If you are connected to a replica set, the client is instantiated in a different way. We are also aware of the fact that we are not allowed to query the secondary nodes for data by default. We need to explicitly do `rs.slaveOk()` in the mongo shell connected to a secondary node to query it. It is done in a similar way in a Python client as well. If we are connected to a secondary node, we cannot query it by default, but the way in which we specify that we are ok to query on a secondary node is slightly different. Starting with PyMongo 3.0, we can now pass `ReadPreference` when initiating `MongoClient`. This is primarily because, starting with PyMongo 3.0, `pymongo.MongoClient()` is the only way to connect to a standalone instance, replica set, or sharded cluster. The available read preferences are PRIMARY, SECONDARY, PRIMARY_PREFERRED, SECONDARY_PREFERRED, and NEAREST.

```
>> client = pymongo.MongoClient('localhost', 27017, readPreference='secon
daryPreferred')
>> print cl.read_preference
SecondaryPreferred(tag_sets=None)
```

In addition to the client, PyMongo also allows you to have read preferences set at the database or collection level.

By default, `read_preference` for a client initialized without an explicit read preference is PRIMARY (with value zero). However, if we now get the database object from the client initialized previously, the read preference will be NEAREST (with value 4).

```
>>> db = client.test
>>> db.read_preference
Primary()
>>>
```

Setting the read preference is as simple as doing the following:

```
>>>db = client.get_database('test', read_preference=ReadPreference.
SECONDARY)
```

Again, as the read preference gets inherited from the client to the database object, it gets inherited from the database object to the collection object. This would be used as the default value for all the queries executed against this collection unless the read preference is specified explicitly in the `find` operation.

Thus, `db.pymongoTest.find_one()` will have a cursor that uses the read preference as SECONDARY (as we have just set it previously to SECONDARY at the database object level).

We will now wrap up the basic operations from a Python driver by trying to do some common operations that we do in a mongo shell such as getting all the database names, getting a list of collections in a database, and creating an index on a collection.

In the shell, we do show `dbs` to show all the database names in the mongo instance connected. From the Python client, we do the following on the client instance:

```
>>> client.database_names()
[u'local', u'test']
```

Similarly, to see the list of collections, we do show collections in the mongo shell; in Python, all we do on the database object is as follows:

```
>>> db.collection_names()
[u'system.indexes', u'writeConcernTest', u'pymongoTest']
```

Now for the `index` operations; we first see what all indexes are present in the `pymongoTest` collection. Execute the following in the Python shell to view the indexes on a collection:

```
>>> db.pymongoTest.index_information()
{u'_id_': {u'key': [(u'_id', 1)], u'ns': u'test.pymongoTest', u'v': 1}}
```

We now will create an index on key x, which is sorted in an ascending order on the `pymongoTest` collection as follows:

```
>>>from pymongo import IndexModel, ASCENDING
>>> myindex = IndexModel([("x", ASCENDING)], name='Index_on_X')
>>>db.pymongoTest.create_indexes([myindex])
  ['Index_on_X']
```

We can again list the indexes to confirm the creation of the index:

```
>>> db.pymongoTest.index_information()
{u'Index_on_X': {u'key': [(u'x', 1)], u'ns': u'test.pymongoTest', u'v':
1},
  u'_id_': {u'key': [(u'_id', 1)], u'ns': u'test.pymongoTest', u'v': 1}}
```

We can see that the index has been created. Removing the index is also simple as follows:

```
db.pymongoTest.drop_index('Index_on_X')
```

Another parameter called `CursorType.TAILABLE` is used to denote that the cursor returned by `find` is a tailable cursor. Explaining what tailable cursors and giving more details is not in the scope of this recipe and will be explained in the recipe named *Creating and tailing a capped collection cursors in MongoDB* in *Chapter 5, Advanced Operations.*

Implementing aggregation in Mongo using PyMongo

We have already seen PyMongo using Python's client interface for Mongo in previous recipes. In this recipe, we will use the postal codes collection and run an aggregation example using PyMongo. The intention of this recipe is not to explain aggregation but to show how aggregation can be implemented using PyMongo. In this recipe, we will aggregate the data based on the state names and get the top five state names by the number of documents that they appear in. We will make use of the $project, $group, $sort, and $limit operators for the process.

Getting ready

To execute the aggregation operation, we need to have a server up and running. A simple single node is what we need. Refer to the *Installing single node MongoDB* recipe from *Chapter 1, Installing and Starting the Server* for instructions on how to start the server. The data that we will operate on needs to be imported in the database. The steps to import the data are mentioned in the *Creating test data* recipe in *Chapter 2, Command-line Operations and Indexes*. Additionally, refer to the *Connecting to a single node using a Python client* recipe in *Chapter 1, Installing and Starting the Server* on how to install PyMongo for your host operating system. As this is a way to implement aggregation in Python, it is assumed that the reader is aware of the aggregation framework in MongoDB.

How to do it...

1. Open the Python terminal by typing the following on the command prompt:

   ```
   $ Python
   ```

2. Once the Python shell opens, import pymongo as follows:

   ```
   >>> import pymongo
   ```

3. Create an instance of MongoClient as follows:

   ```
   >>> client = pymongo.MongoClient('mongodb://localhost:27017')
   ```

4. Get the test database's object as follows:

   ```
   >>> db = client.test
   ```

5. Now, we execute the aggregation operation on the postalCodes collection as follows:

   ```
   result = db.postalCodes.aggregate(
       [
           {'$project':{'state':1, '_id':0}},
           {'$group':{'_id':'$state', 'count':{'$sum':1}}},
           {'$sort':{'count':-1}},
   ```

```
                {'$limit':5}
        ]
    )
```

6. Type the following to view the results:

```
>>>for r in result:
print r
{u'count': 6446, u'_id': u'Maharashtra'}
{u'count': 4684, u'_id': u'Kerala'}
{u'count': 3784, u'_id': u'Tamil Nadu'}
{u'count': 3550, u'_id': u'Andhra Pradesh'}
{u'count': 3204, u'_id': u'Karnataka'}
```

How it works...

The steps are pretty straightforward. We have connected to the database running on localhost and created a database object. The aggregation operation that we invoked on the collection using the aggregate function is very similar to how we would invoke aggregation in the shell. The object in the return value, `result`, is a cursor, which returns an object of type `dict` on iteration. This `dict` contains two keys, each with the name of the state and count of the number of their occurrence. In step 6, we are simply iterating over the cursor (result) to fetch each result.

Executing MapReduce in Mongo using PyMongo

In our previous recipe, *Implementing aggregation in Mongo using PyMongo*, we saw how to execute aggregation operations in Mongo using PyMongo. In this recipe, we will work on the same use case as we did for the aggregation operation but we will use MapReduce. The intent is to aggregate the data based on the state names and get the top five state names by the number of documents that they appear in.

Programming language drivers provide us with an interface to invoke the map reduce jobs written in JavaScript on the server.

Getting ready

To execute the map reduce operations, we need to have a server up and running. A simple single node is what we need. Refer to the *Installing single node MongoDB* recipe from *Chapter 1, Installing and Starting the Server* for instructions on how to start the server. The data that we will operate on needs to be imported in the database. The steps to import the data are mentioned in the *Creating test data* recipe in *Chapter 2, Command-line Operations and Indexes*. Additionally, refer to the *Connecting to a single node using Python client* recipe in *Chapter 1, Installing and Starting the Server* on how to install PyMongo for your host operating system.

How to do it...

1. Open the Python terminal by typing the following on the command prompt:

   ```
   >>>python
   ```

2. Once the Python shell opens, import the bson package as follows:

   ```
   >>> import bson
   ```

3. Import the pymongo package as follows:

   ```
   >>> import pymongo
   ```

4. Create an of MongoClient as follows:

   ```
   >>> client = pymongo.MongoClient('mongodb://localhost:27017')
   ```

5. Get the test database's object as follows:

   ```
   >>> db = client.test
   ```

6. Write the following mapper function:

   ```
   >>>  mapper = bson.Code('''function() {emit(this.state, 1)}''')
   ```

7. Write the following reducer function:

   ```
   >>>  reducer = bson.Code('''function(key, values){return Array.
   sum(values)}''')
   ```

8. Invoke map reduce; the result will be sent to the pymr_out collection:

   ```
   >>>  db.postalCodes.map_reduce(map=mapper, reduce=reducer,
   out='pymr_out')
   ```

9. Verify the result as follows:

   ```
   >>>  c = db.pymr_out.find(sort=[('value', pymongo.DESCENDING)],
   limit=5)
   >>> for elem in c:
   ```

```
...     print elem
...
{u'_id': u'Maharashtra', u'value': 6446.0}
{u'_id': u'Kerala', u'value': 4684.0}
{u'_id': u'Tamil Nadu', u'value': 3784.0}
{u'_id': u'Andhra Pradesh', u'value': 3550.0}
{u'_id': u'Karnataka', u'value': 3204.0}
>>>
```

How it works...

Apart from the regular import for pymongo, here we import the bson package as well. This is where we have the Code class; it is the Python object that we use for the JavaScript map and reduce functions. It is instantiated by passing the JavaScript function body as a constructor argument.

Once two instances of the Code class are instantiated, one for map and the other for reduce, all we do is invoke the map_reduce function on the collection. In this case, we passed three parameters: two Code instances for the map and reduce functions with parameter names map and reduce, respectively and one string value used to provide the name of the output collection that the results are written to.

We won't be explaining the map reduce JavaScript functions here but it is pretty simple, and all it does is emit keys as the names of the states and values that are the number of times the particular state name occurs. This result document with the key used, the state's name as the _id field, and another field called value that is the sum of the times the particular state's name given in the _id field appears in the collection is added to the output collection, pymr_out. For example, in the entire collection, the state Maharashtra appeared 6446 times, thus the document for the state of Maharashtra is {u'_id': u'Maharashtra', u'value': 6446.0}. To verify that the result is correct, you can execute the following query in the mongo shell and see that the result is indeed 6446:

```
> db.postalCodes.count({state:'Maharashtra'})
6446
```

We are still not done as the requirement is to find the top five states by their occurrence in the collection; we still have just the states and their occurrences, so the final step is to sort the documents by the value field, which is the number of times the state's name occurred in descending order and limit the result to five documents.

See also

Refer to *Chapter 8, Integration with Hadoop* for different recipes on executing map reduce jobs in MongoDB using the Hadoop connector. This allows us to write the `map` and `reduce` functions in languages such as Java, Python, and so on.

Executing query and insert operations using a Java client

In this recipe, we will look at executing the query and `insert` operations using the Java client for MongoDB. Unlike the Python programming language, Java code snippets cannot be executed from an interactive interpreter, and thus we will be having some unit test cases already implemented, whose relevant code snippets will be shown and explained.

Getting ready

For this recipe, we will start a standalone instance. Refer to the *Installing single node MongoDB* recipe from *Chapter 1, Installing and Starting the Server* for instructions on how to start the server.

The next step is to download the Java project, `mongo-cookbook-javadriver`, from the Packt website. This recipe uses a JUnit test case to test out various features of the Java client. In this whole process, we will use some of the most common API calls and thus learn to use them.

How to do it...

To execute the test case, one can either import the project in an IDE-like Eclipse and execute the test case or execute the test case from the command prompt using Maven.

The test case that we will execute for this recipe is `com.packtpub.mongo.cookbook.MongoDriverQueryAndInsertTest`.

1. If you are using an IDE, open this test class and execute it as a JUnit test case.

2. If you are planning to use Maven to execute this test case, go to the command prompt, change the directory at the root of the project, and execute the following to execute this single test case:

```
$ mvn -Dtest=com.packtpub.mongo.cookbook.
MongoDriverQueryAndInsertTest test
```

Everything should get executed fine and the test case should succeed if the Java SDK and Maven are properly set up and the MongoDB server is up and running and listening to port `27017` for the incoming connections.

How it works...

We will now open the test class that we executed and see some of the important API calls in the `test` method. The super class of our `test` class is `com.packtpub.mongo.cookbook.AbstractMongoTest`.

We start by looking at the `getClient` method in this class. The `client` instance that has been created is an instance of the `com.mongodb.MongoClient type`. There are several overloaded constructors for this class; however, we use the following to instantiate the client:

```
MongoClient client = new MongoClient("localhost:27017");
```

Another method to look at is `getJavaDriverTestDatabase` in the same abstract class that gets us the database instance. This instance is synonymous to the implicit variable db in the shell. Here in Java, this class is an instance of the `com.mongodb.DB` type. We get an instance of this `DB` class by invoking the `getDB()` method on the client instance. In our case, we want the `DB` instance for the `javaDriverTest` database, which we get as follows:

```
getClient().getDB("javaDriverTest");
```

Once we get the instance of `com.mongodb.DB`, we use it to get the instance of `com.mongodb.DBCollection`, which would be used to perform various operations—`find` and `insert`—on the collection. The `getJavaTestCollection` method in the abstract test class returns one instance of `DBCollection`. We get an instance of this class for the `javaTest` collection by invoking the `getCollection()` method on `com.mongodb.DB` as follows:

```
getJavaDriverTestDatabase().getCollection("javaTest")
```

Once we get an instance of `DBCollection`, we are now ready to perform the operations on it. In the scope of this recipe, it is limited to the `find` and `insert` operations.

Now, we open the main test case class, `com.packtpub.mongo.cookbook.MongoDriverQueryAndInsertTest`. Open this class in an IDE or a text editor. We will look at the methods in this class. The first method that we will look at is `findOneDocument`. Here, the line of our interest is the one that queries for the document with the value of `_id` as 3: `collection.findOne(new BasicDBObject("_id", 3))`.

This method returns an instance of `com.mongodb.DBObject`, which is a key value map returning the fields of a document as a key and the value of this corresponding key. For instance, to get the value of `_id` from the returned `DBObject` instance, we invoke `result.get("_id")` on the returned result.

Our next method to inspect is `getDocumentsFromTestCollection`. This test case executes a `find` operation on the collection and gets all the documents in it. The `collection.find()` call executes the `find` operation on the instance of `DBCollection`. The return value of the `find` operation is `com.mongodb.DBCursor`. An important point to note is that invoking the `find` operation itself doesn't execute the query but just returns the instance of `DBCursor`. This is an inexpensive operation that doesn't consume server-side resources. The actual query gets executed on the server side only when the `hasNext` or `next` method is invoked on the `DBCursor` instance. The `hasNext()` method is used to check if there are more results and the `next()` method is used to navigate to the next `DBObject` instance in the result. An example usage of the `DBCursor` instance returned to iterate through the results is as follows:

```
while(cursor.hasNext()) {
  DBObject object = cursor.next();
  //Some operation on the returned object to get the fields and
  //values in the document
}
```

We now look at two methods, `withLimitAndSkip` and `withQueryProjectionAndSort`. These methods show us how to sort, limit the number of results, and skip a number of initial results. As we can see, the sort, limit, and skip methods are chained to each other:

```
DBCursor cursor = collection
        .find(null)
        .sort(new BasicDBObject("_id", -1))
        .limit(2)
        .skip(1);
```

All these methods return an instance of `DBCursor` itself, which allows us to chain the calls. These methods are defined in the `DBCursor` class, which changes certain states according to the operation that they perform in the instance and has return this at the end of the method to return the same instance.

Remember that the actual operation is invoked on the server only on invoking the `hasNext` or `next` method on `DBCursor`. Invoking any method such as `sort`, `limit`, and `skip` after the execution of the query on the server will throw `java.lang.IllegalStateException`.

We used two variants of the `find` method. One accepts one parameter for the query to be executed and one accepts two parameters—the first one for the query and the second is another `DBObject`, which is used for projection that will return only a selected set of fields from the document in the result.

For instance, the following query from the `withQueryProjectionAndSort` method of the test case selects all the documents as the first argument as `null` and the returned `DBCursor` will have documents containing just one field called `value`:

```
DBCursor cursor = collection
        .find(null, new BasicDBObject("value", 1).append("_id", 0))
        .sort(new BasicDBObject("_id", 1));
```

The `_id` field is to be explicitly set to `0`, or else it will be returned by default.

Finally, we look at two more methods in the test case, `insertDataTest` and `insertTestDataWithWriteConcern`. We use a couple of variants of the `insert` method in these two methods. All `insert` methods are invoked on the `DBCollection` instance and return an instance, `com.mongodb.WriteResult`. The result can be used to get the error that occurred during the write operation by invoking the `getLastError()` method, the number of documents inserted using the `getN()` method, and the write concern for the operation among the few operations. Refer to the Javadoc of the MongoDB API for more detail on the methods. The two insert operations that we did are as follows:

```
collection.insert(new BasicDBObject("value", "Hello World"));

collection.insert(new BasicDBObject("value", "Hello World"),
WriteConcern.JOURNALED);
```

Both of these accept a `DBObject` instance for the document to be inserted as the first parameter. The second method allows us to provide the write concern to be used for the `write` operation. There are `insert` methods in the `DBCollection` class that allow bulk insert as well. Refer to the Javadocs for more details on various overloaded versions of the `insert` method.

See also...

The Javadocs for the current version of the MongoDB driver can be found at `https://api.mongodb.org/java/current/`.

Executing update and delete operations using a Java client

In the previous recipe, we saw how to execute `find` and `insert` operations in MongoDB using the Java client; in this recipe, we will see how updates and deletes work in the Java client.

Getting ready

For this recipe, we will start a standalone instance. Refer to the *Installing single node MongoDB* recipe from *Chapter 1, Installing and Starting the Server* for instructions on how to start the server.

The next step is to download the Java project, `mongo-cookbook-javadriver`, from the Packt website. This recipe uses a JUnit test case to test out various features of the Java client. In this whole process, we will use some of the most common API calls and thus learn to use them.

How to do it...

To execute the test case, one can either import the project in an IDE-like Eclipse and execute the test case or execute test case from the command prompt using Maven.

The test case that we are going to execute for this recipe is `com.packtpub.mongo.cookbook.MongoDriverUpdateAndDeleteTest`.

1. If you are using an IDE, open this test class and execute it as a JUnit test case.

2. If you are planning to use Maven to execute this test case, go to the command prompt, change the directory at the root of the project, and execute the following to execute this single test case:

   ```
   $ mvn -Dtest=com.packtpub.mongo.cookbook.
   MongoDriverUpdateAndDeleteTest test
   ```

Everything should get executed fine if the Java SDK and Maven are properly set up and the MongoDB server is up and running and listening to port `27017` for the incoming connections.

How it works...

We created a test data for the recipes using a `setupUpdateTestData()` method. Here, we simply put documents in the `javaTest` collection in the `javaDriverTest` database. We add 20 documents to this collection with the value of `i` ranging from 1 to 20. This test data is used in different test case methods to create test data.

Let's now take a look at the methods in this class. We will first look at `basicUpdateTest()`. In this method, we first create the test data and then execute the following update:

```
collection.update(
  new BasicDBObject("i", new BasicDBObject("$gt", 10)),
  new BasicDBObject("$set", new BasicDBObject("gtTen", true)));
```

The update method here takes two arguments. The first is the query that would be used to select the eligible documents for the update, and the second parameter is the actual update. The first parameter looks confusing due to nested BasicDBObject instances; however, it is the `{'i' : {'$gt' : 10}}` condition and the second parameter is the update, `{'$set' : {'gtTen' : true}}`. The result of the update is an instance of com.mongodb.WriteResult. The instance of WriteResult tells us the number of documents that got updated and gets the error that occurred while executing the write operation and write concern used for the update. Refer to the Javadocs of the WriteConcern class for more details. This update only updates the first matching document by default only if multiple documents match the query.

The next method that we will look at is multiUpdateTest, which will update all the matching documents for the given query instead of the first matching document. The method that we used is updateMulti on the collection instance. The updateMulti method is a convenient way to update multiple documents. The following is the call that we make to update multiple documents:

```
collection.updateMulti(new BasicDBObject("i",
    new BasicDBObject("$gt", 10)),
    new BasicDBObject("$set", new BasicDBObject("gtTen", true)));
```

The next operation that we did was to remove documents. The test case method to remove documents is deleteTest(). The documents are removed as follows:

```
collection.remove(new BasicDBObject(
    "i", new BasicDBObject("$gt", 10)),
    WriteConcern.JOURNALED);
```

We have two parameters here. The first is the query for which the matching documents will be removed from the collection. Note that all matching documents will be removed by default unlike update, where only the first matching document will be removed by default. The second parameter is the write concern to be used for the remove operation.

Note that when the server is started on a 32-bit machine, journaling is disabled by default. When you use Write Concern on such machines, it may cause the operation to fail with the following exception:

```
com.mongodb.CommandFailureException: { "serverUsed" :
"localhost/127.0.0.1:27017" , "connectionId" : 5 , "n" : 0 , "badGLE" :
{ "getlasterror" : 1 , "j" : true} , "ok" : 0.0 , "errmsg" : "cannot use
'j' option when a host does not have journaling enabled" , "code" : 2}
```

This would require the server to be started with the --journal option. On 64-bit machines, this is not necessary as journaling is enabled by default.

We will look at the findAndModify operation next. The test case method to perform this operation is findAndModifyTest. The following lines of code are used to perform this operation:

```
DBObject old = collection.findAndModify(
    new BasicDBObject("i", 10),
    new BasicDBObject("i", 100));
```

The operation is the query that will find the matching documents and then update them. The return type of the operation is an instance of DBObject before the update is applied. One important feature of the findAndModify operation is that the find and update operations are performed atomically.

The preceding method is a simple version of the findAndModify operation. There is an overloaded version of this method with the following signature:

DBObject findAndModify(DBObject query, DBObject fields, DBObject sort,boolean remove, DBObject update, boolean returnNew, boolean upsert)

Let's see what these parameters are in the following table:

Parameter	Description
query	This is the query that is used to query the document, which is the one that gets updated/deleted.
fields	The find method supports the projection of fields that need to be selected in the result document(s) selected. The parameter here does the same job of selecting the fixed set of fields from the resulting document.
sort	If you haven't noticed already, let me tell you that the method can perform this atomic operation on only one document and also return one document. This sort function can be used in cases where the query selects multiple documents and only the first gets chosen for the operation. The sort function is applied on the result before picking up the first document to update.
remove	This is a Boolean flag that indicates whether to remove or update the document. If this value is true, the document will be removed.
update	Unlike the preceding attribute, this is not a Boolean value but a DBObject instance that will tell what the update needs to be. Note that the remove Boolean flag gets precedence over this parameter; if the remove attribute is true, the update will not happen even if one is provided.
returnNew	The find operation returns a document, but which one? The one before the update was executed or the one after the update gets executed? This Boolean flag, when given as true, returns the document after the update is executed.
upsert	This is a Boolean flag again that executes upsert when true. It is relevant only when the intended operation is update.

There are more overloaded methods of this operation. Refer to the Javadocs of `com.mongodb.DBCollection` for more methods. The `findAndModify` method that we used ultimately invokes the method we discussed with the fields and sort parameters as null with the remaining parameters, `remove`, `returnNew`, and `upsert` being `false`.

Finally, we look at the query builder support in MongoDB's Java API.

All the queries in mongo are `DBObject` instances with possibly more nested `DBObject` instances in them. Things are simple for small queries, but they start getting ugly for more complicated queries. Consider a relatively simple query where we want to query for documents with `i > 10` and `i < 15`. The mongo query for this is `{$and:[{i:{$gt:10}}, {i:{$lt:15}}]}`. Writing this in Java would mean using `BasicDBObject` instances, which is even painful and looks as follows:

```
DBObject query = new BasicDBObject("$and",
  new BasicDBObject[] {
    new BasicDBObject("i", new BasicDBObject("$gt", 10)),
    new BasicDBObject("i", new BasicDBObject("$lt", 15))
  });
```

Thankfully, however, there is a class called `com.mongodb.QueryBuilder`, which is a utility class to build the complex queries. The preceding query is built using a query builder as follows:

```
DBObject query = QueryBuilder.start("i").greaterThan(10).and("i").
lessThan(15).get();
```

This is less error prone when writing a query and easy to read as well. There are a lot of methods in the `com.mongodb.QueryBuilder` class and I would encourage you to go through the Javadocs of this class. The basic idea is to start construction using the `start` method and the key. We then chain the method calls to add different conditions, and when the addition of various conditions is done, the query is constructed using the `get()` method, which returns `DBObject`. Refer to the `queryBuilderSample` method in the test class for a sample usage of query builder support of the MongoDB Java API.

See also

There are some more operations using the GridFS and geospatial indexes. We will see how to use them in the Java application with a small sample in the advanced query chapter. Refer to *Chapter 5, Advanced Operations* for such recipes.

The Javadocs for the current version of the MongoDB driver can be found at `https://api.mongodb.org/java/current/`.

Implementing aggregation in Mongo using a Java client

The intention of this recipe is not to explain aggregation but to show you how aggregation can be implemented using the Java client from a Java program. In this recipe, we will aggregate the data based on the state names and get the top five state names by the number of documents that they appear in. We will use the `$project`, `$group`, `$sort`, and `$limit` operators for the process.

Getting ready

The test class used for this recipe is `com.packtpub.mongo.cookbook.MongoAggregationTest`. To execute the aggregation operations, we need to have a server up and running. A simple single node is what we need. Refer to the *Installing single node MongoDB* recipe from *Chapter 1, Installing and Starting the Server* for instructions on how to start the server. The data that we will operate on needs to be imported in the database. The steps to import the data are given in the *Creating test data* recipe in *Chapter 2, Command-line Operations and Indexes*. The next step is to download the Java project, `mongo-cookbook-javadriver`, from the Packt website. Though Maven can be used to execute the test case, it is convenient to import the project in an IDE and execute the test case class. It is assumed that you are familiar with the Java programming language and comfortable using the IDE that the project will be imported to.

How to do it...

To execute the test case, one can either import the project in an IDE-like Eclipse and execute the test case or execute the test case from the command prompt using Maven.

1. If you are using an IDE, open the test class and execute it as a JUnit test case.
2. If you are planning to use Maven to execute this test case, go to the command prompt, change the directory at the root of the project, and execute the following to execute this single test case:

```
$ mvn -Dtest=com.packtpub.mongo.cookbook.MongoAggregationTesttest
```

Everything should get executed fine if the Java SDK and Maven are properly set up and the MongoDB server is up and running and listening to port `27017` for the incoming connections.

How it works...

The method used for the aggregation functionality is `aggregationTest()` in our test class. The aggregation operation is performed on MongoDB from a Java client using the `aggregate()` method defined in the `DBCollection` class. The method has the following signature:

```
AggregationOutput aggregate(firstOp, additionalOps)
```

Only the first argument is mandatory, which forms the first operation in the pipeline. The second argument is a `varagrs` argument (variable number of arguments with zero or more values), which allows more pipeline operators. All these arguments are of the `com.mongodb.DBObject` type. In case any exception occurs in the execution of the aggregation command, the aggregation operation will throw `com.mongodb.MongoException` with the cause of the exception.

The return type, `com.mongodb.AggregationOutput`, is used to get the result of the aggregation operation. From a developer's perspective, we are more interested in the `results` field of this instance, which can be accessed using the `results()` method of the returned object. The `results()` method returns an object of type, `Iterable<DBObject>`, which one can iterate to get the results of the aggregation.

Let's look at how we implemented the aggregation pipeline in our test class:

```
AggregationOutput output = collection.aggregate(
    //{'$project':{'state':1, '_id':0}},
    new BasicDBObject("$project", new BasicDBObject("state",
1).append("_id", 0)),
    //{'$group':{'_id':'$state', 'count':{'$sum':1}}}
    new BasicDBObject("$group", new BasicDBObject("_id", "$state")
      .append("count", new BasicDBObject("$sum", 1))),
    //{'$sort':{'count':-1}}
    new BasicDBObject("$sort", new BasicDBObject("count", -1)),
    //{'$limit':5}
    new BasicDBObject("$limit", 5)
);
```

There are four steps in the pipeline in the following order: a `$project` operation, followed by `$group`, `$sort`, and then `$limit`.

The last two operations look inefficient where we sort all and then just take the top five elements. In such scenarios, the MongoDB server is intelligent enough to consider the limit operation while sorting, where only the top five results need to be maintained rather than sorting all the results.

For version 2.6 of MongoDB, the aggregation result can return a cursor. Though the preceding code is still valid, the `AggregationResult` object is no longer the only way to get the results of the operation. We can use `com.mongodb.Cursor` that can be used to iterate the results. Additionally, the preceding format is now deprecated in favor of the format that accepts a list of pipeline operators rather than `varargs` for the operators. Refer to the Javadocs of the `com.mongodb.DBCollection` class and look at the various overloaded `aggregate()` methods.

Executing MapReduce in Mongo using a Java client

In our previous recipe, *Implementing aggregation in Mongo using a Java client*, we saw how to execute aggregation operations in Mongo using the Java client. In this recipe, we will work on the same use case as we did for the aggregation operation but We will use MapReduce. The intent is to aggregate the data based on the state names and get the top five state names by the number of documents that they appear in.

If somebody is not aware of how to write MapReduce code for Mongo from a programming language client and is seeing it for the first time, you might be surprised to see how it is actually done. You might have imagined that you would be writing the `map` and `reduce` function in the programming language that you are writing the code in, Java in this case, and then using it to execute the map reduce. However, we need to bear in mind that the MapReduce jobs run on the mongo servers and they execute JavaScript functions. Hence, irrespective of the programming language driver, the map reduce functions are written in JavaScript. The programming language drivers just act as a means of letting us invoke and execute the map reduce functions (written in JavaScript) on the server.

Getting ready

The test class used for this recipe is `com.packtpub.mongo.cookbook.MongoMapReduceTest`. To execute the map reduce operations, we need to have a server up and running. A simple single node is what we need. Refer to the *Installing single node MongoDB* recipe from *Chapter 1, Installing and Starting the Server* for instructions on how to start the server. The data that we will operate on needs to be imported in the database. The steps to import the data are given in the *Creating test data* recipe in *Chapter 2, Command-line Operations and Indexes*. The next step is to download the Java project, `mongo-cookbook-javadriver`, from the Packt website. Though Maven can be used to execute the test case, it is convenient to import the project in an IDE and execute the test case class. It is assumed that you are familiar with the Java programming language and comfortable using the IDE that the project will be imported to.

How to do it...

To execute the test case, one can either import the project in an IDE-like Eclipse and execute the test case or execute the test case from the command prompt using Maven.

1. If you are using an IDE, open the test class and execute it as a JUnit test case.

2. If you are planning to use Maven to execute this test case, go to the command prompt, change the directory at the root of the project, and execute the following to execute this single test case:

```
$ mvn -Dtest=com.packtpub.mongo.cookbook.MongoMapReduceTesttest
```

Everything should get executed fine if the Java SDK and Maven are properly set up and the MongoDB server is up and running and listening to port `27017` for the incoming connections.

How it works...

The test case method for our map reduce test is `mapReduceTest()`.

Map reduce operations can be done in Mongo from a Java client using the `mapReduce()` method defined in the `DBCollection` class. There are a lot of overloaded versions, and you can refer to the Javadocs of the `com.mongodb.DBCollection` class for more details on the various flavors of this method. The one that we used is `collection.mapReduce(mapper, reducer, output collection, query)`.

The method accepts the following four parameters:

▶   The `mapper` function is of type String and a JavaScript code that would be executed on the mongo database server

▶   The `reducer` function is of type String and a JavaScript code that would be executed on the mongo database server

▶   The name of the collection that the output of the map reduce execution will be written to

▶   The query that will be executed by the server and the result of this query will be the input to the map reduce job execution

As the assumption is that the reader is well-versed with the map reduce operations in the shell, we won't explain the map reduce JavaScript functions that we used in the test case method. All it does is emit keys as the names of the states and values, which are the number of times the particular state name occurs. This result is added to the output collection, `javaMROutput`, in this case. For example, in the entire collection, the state `Maharashtra` appears `6446` times; thus, the document for the state of `Maharashtra` is `{'_id':` `'Maharashtra', 'value': 6446}`. To confirm that this is the true value or not, you can execute the following query in the mongo shell and see that the result is indeed `6446`:

```
> db.postalCodes.count({state:'Maharashtra'})
6446
```

We are still not done as the requirement is to find the top five states by their occurrence in the collection; we still have just the states and their occurrences, so the final step is to sort the documents by the `value` field, which is the number of times the state's name occurs in descending order, and limit the result to five documents.

See also

Refer to *Chapter 8*, *Integration with Hadoop* for different recipes on executing Map Reduce jobs in MongoDB using the Hadoop connector. This allows us to write the `Map` and `Reduce` functions in languages such as Java, Python, and so on.

4
Administration

In this chapter, we will see the following recipes related to MongoDB administration:

- ▶ Renaming a collection
- ▶ Viewing collection stats
- ▶ Viewing database stats
- ▶ Manually padding a document
- ▶ The mongostat and mongotop utilities
- ▶ Getting current executing operations and killing them
- ▶ Using profiler to profile operations
- ▶ Setting up users in Mongo
- ▶ Interprocess security in Mongo
- ▶ Modifying collection behavior using the collMod command
- ▶ Setting up MongoDB as a Windows service
- ▶ Replica set configurations
- ▶ Stepping down as primary from the replica set
- ▶ Exploring the local database of a replica set
- ▶ Understanding and analyzing oplogs
- ▶ Building tagged Replica sets
- ▶ Configuring the default shard for non-sharded collections
- ▶ Manual split and migration of chunks
- ▶ Domain-driven sharding using tags
- ▶ Exploring the config database in a sharded setup

Introduction

In this chapter we will cover some of the tools and practices for administering MongoDB. The following recipes will help you collect statistics from your database, administer user access, analyze oplogs and look into some aspects of working with replica sets.

Renaming a collection

Have you ever come across a scenario where you have named a table in a relational database and at a later point of time felt that the name could have been better? Or perhaps the organization you work for was late in realizing that the table names are really getting messy and enforce some standards on the names? Relational databases do have some proprietary ways to rename the tables and a database admin would do that for you.

This raises a question though. In Mongo world, where collections are synonymous to tables, is there a way to rename a collection to some other name after it is created? In this recipe, we will explore this feature of Mongo where we rename an existing collection with some data in it.

Getting ready

We would need to run a MongoDB instance to perform this collection renaming experiment. Refer to the recipe *Installing single node MongoDB* in *Chapter 1, Installing and Starting the Server* for information on how to start the server. The operations we will perform would be from mongo shell.

How to do it...

1. Once the server is started and assuming it is listening for client connections on default port `27017`, execute the following command to connect to it from the shell:

   ```
   > mongo
   ```

2. Once connected, using the default test database. Let's create a collection with some test data. The collection we will use is named:

   `sloppyNamedCollection.`
   ```
   > for(i = 0 ; i < 10 ; i++) { db.sloppyNamedCollection.
   insert({'i':i}) };
   ```

3. The test data will now be created (we may verify the data by querying the collection `sloppyNamedCollection`).

4. Rename the collection `neatNamedCollection` as follows:

   ```
   > db.sloppyNamedCollection.renameCollection('neatNamedCollection')
   { "ok" : 1 }
   ```

5. Verify that the collection `sloppyNamedCollection` is no longer present by executing:

    ```
    > show collections
    ```

6. Finally, query the `neatNamedCollection` collection to verify that the data originally in `sloppyNamedCollection` is indeed present in it. Simply execute the following on the mongo shell:

    ```
    > db.neatNamedCollection.find()
    ```

How it works...

Renaming a collection is pretty simple. It is accomplished with the `renameCollection` method, which takes two arguments. Generally, the function signature is as follows:

```
> db.<collection to rename>.renameCollection('<target name of the
collection>', <drop target if exists>)
```

The first argument is the name to which the collection is to be renamed.

The second parameter that we didn't use is a Boolean value that tells the command whether to drop the target collection if it exists. This value defaults to false, which means do not drop the target but give an error. This is a sensible default, otherwise the results would be ghastly if we accidently gave a collection name that exists and didn't wish to drop it. However, if you know what you are doing and want the target to be dropped while renaming the collection, pass the second parameter as true. The name of this parameter is `dropTarget`. In our case, the call would have been:

```
> db.sloppyNamedCollection.renameCollection('neatNamedCollection', true)
```

As an exercise, try creating the `sloppyNamedCollection` again and rename it without the second parameter (or false as the value). You should see mongo complaining that the target namespace exists. Then, again rename with the second parameter as true, and now the renaming operation executes successfully.

Note that the rename operation will keep the original and the newly renamed collection in the same database. This `renameCollection` method is not enough to move/rename the collection across another database. In such cases, we need to run the `renameCollection` command that looks like this:

```
> db.runCommand({ renameCollection: "<source_namespace>", to: "<target_
namespace>", dropTarget: <true|false> });
```

Suppose we want to rename the collection `sloppyNamedCollection` to `neatNamedCollection` as well as move it from `test` database to `newDatabase`, we can do so by executing the following command. Note the switch `dropTarget: true` used is meant to remove the existing target collection (`newDatabase.neatNamedCollection`) if it exists.

```
> db.runCommand({ renameCollection: "test.sloppyNamedCollection ", to: "
newDatabase.neatNamedCollection", dropTarget: true });
```

Also, the rename collection operation doesn't work on sharded collections.

Viewing collection stats

Perhaps one of the interesting statistics from an administrative purpose when it comes to the usage of storage, the number of documents in collection possibly to estimate the future space, and memory requirements based on the growth of the data is to get a high level statistics of the collection.

Getting ready

To find the stats of the collection we need to have a server up and running and a single node is what should be okay. Refer to the *Installing single node MongoDB* in *Chapter 1*, *Installing and Starting the Server* for information on how to start the server. The data on which we would be operating needs to be imported in the database. The steps to import the data are given in the recipe *Creating Test Data* in *Chapter 2*, *Command-line Operations and Indexes*. Once these steps are completed, we are all set to go ahead with this recipe.

How to do it...

1. We would be using `postalCodes` collection for viewing the stats.
2. Open the mongo shell and connect to the running MongoDB instance. In case you have started the mongo on default port, execute the following:

   ```
   $ mongo
   ```
3. With the data imported, create an index on the `pincode` field if one doesn't exist:

   ```
   > db.postalCodes.ensureIndex({'pincode':1})
   ```
4. On the mongo terminal, execute the following:

   ```
   > db.postalCodes.stats()
   ```
5. Observe the output and execute the following on the shell:

   ```
   > db.postalCodes.stats(1024)
   ```
6. Again, observe the output.

We will now see what these values printed out mean to us in the following section.

How it works...

If we observe the output for both these commands, we see that the second one has all the figures in KB whereas the first one is in bytes. The parameter provided is known as scale and all the figures indicating size are divided by this scale. In this case, since we gave the value as `1024`, we get all the values in KB whereas if `1024 * 1024` is passed as the value of scale (the size shown will be in MB). For our analysis, we will use the one that shows the sizes in KB.

```
> db.postalCodes.stats(1024)
{
  "ns" : "test.postalCodes",
  "count" : 39732,
  "size" : 9312,
  "avgObjSize" : 240,
  "numExtents" : 6,
  "storageSize" : 10920,
  "lastExtentSize" : 8192,
  "paddingFactor" : 1,
  "paddingFactorNote" : "paddingFactor is unused and unmaintained in
    3.0. It remains hard coded to 1.0 for compatibility only.",
  "userFlags" : 1,
  "capped" : false,
  "nindexes" : 2,
  "totalIndexSize" : 2243,
  "indexSizes" : {
    "_id_" : 1261,
    "pincode_1" : 982
  },
  "ok" : 1
}
```

The following table shows the meaning of the important fields:

Field	Description
ns	The fully qualified name of the collection with a format `<database>.<collection name>`.
count	The number of documents in the collection.

Field	Description
size	The actual storage size occupied by the documents in the collection. Addition, deletion, and updates to documents in the collection can change this figure. The scale parameter affects this field's value and in our case this value is in KB as 1024 is the scale. This number does include padding, if any.
avgObjSize	This is the average size of the document in the collection. It is simply the size field divided by the count of documents in the collection (the preceding two fields). The scale parameter affects this field's value and in our case this value is in KB as 1024 is the scale.
storageSize	Mongo preallocates the space on the disk to ensure that the documents in the collection are kept on continuous locations to provide better performance in disk access. This preallocation fills up the files with zeros and then starts allocating space to these documents inserted. This field tells the size on the storage used by this collection. This figure will generally be much more than the actual size of the collection. The scale parameter affects this field's value and in our case this value is in KB as 1024 is the scale.
numExtents	As we saw, mongo pre allocates continuous disk space to the collections for performance purpose. However as the collection grows, new space needs to be allocated. This field gives the number of such continuous chunk allocation. This continuous chunk is called an extent.
nindexes	This field gives the number of indexes present on the collection. This value would be 1 even if we do not create an index on the collection as mongo implicitly creates an index on the field _id.
lastExtentSize	The size of the last extent allocated. The scale parameter affects this field's value and in our case this value is in KB as 1024 is the scale.
paddingFactor	This parameter has been deprecated since version 3.0.0 and is hardcoded to 1 for backward compatibility reasons.
totalIndexSize	Indexes take up space to store too. This field gives the total size taken up by the indexes on the disk. The scale parameter affects this field's value and in our case this value is in KB as 1024 is the scale.
indexSizes	This field is a document with the key as the name of the index and value as the size of the index in question. In our case, we had created an index explicitly on the pincode field; thus, we see the name of the index as the key and the size of the index on disk as the value. The total of these values of all the index is same as the value given previously, totalIndexSize. The scale parameter affects this field's value and in our case this value is in KB as 1024 is the scale.

Documents are placed on the storage device in continuous locations. If a document is updated, resulting in an increase in size, Mongo will have to relocate this document. This operation turns out to be expensive affecting the performance of such update operations. Starting with Mongo 3.0.0, two data allocation strategies are used. One is *The power of 2*, where documents are allocated space in power of 2 (for example, 32, 64, 128, and so on). The other is *No Padding*, where collections do not expect document sizes to be altered.

See also

In this recipe, we discussed viewing stats of a collection. See the next recipe to view the stats at a database level.

Viewing database stats

In the previous recipe, we saw how to view some important statistics of a collection from an administrative perspective. In this recipe, we get an even higher picture, getting those (or most of those) statistics at the database level.

Getting ready

To find the stats of the database, we need to have a server up and running and a single node is what should be okay. Refer to the recipe *Installing single node MongoDB* in *Chapter 1, Installing and Starting the Server* for information on how to start the server. The data on which we would be operating needs to be imported in the database. The steps to import the data are given in the recipe *Creating Test Data* in *Chapter 2, Command-line Operations and Indexes*. Once these steps are completed, we are all set to go ahead with this recipe. Refer to the previous recipe if you need to see how to view stats at the collection level.

How to do it...

1. We will use the `test` database for the purpose of this recipe. It already has a `postalCodes` collection in it.

2. Connect to the server using the mongo shell by typing in the following command from the operating system terminal. It is assumed that the server is listening to port `27017`.

   ```
   $ mongo
   ```

3. On the shell, execute the following command and observe the output:

```
> db.stats()
```

4. On the shell, again execute the following but this time around we add the scale parameter. Observe the output:

```
> db.stats(1024)
```

How it works...

The `scale` parameter, which is a parameter to the `stats` function, divides the number of bytes with the given scale value. In this case, it is `1024` and hence all the values will be in KB. We analyze the following output:

```
> db.stats(1024)
{
        "db" : "test",
         "collections" : 3,
    "objects" : 39738,
    "avgObjSize" : 143.32699179626553,
    "dataSize" : 5562,
    "storageSize" : 16388,
    "numExtents" : 8,
    "indexes" : 2,
    "indexSize" : 2243,
    "fileSize" : 196608,
    "nsSizeMB" : 16,
"extentFreeList" : {
    "num" : 4,
    "totalSize" : 2696
  },
  "dataFileVersion" : {
        "major" : 4,
        "minor" : 5
  },
  "ok" : 1
}
```

The following table shows the meaning of the important fields:

Field	Description
db	This is the name of the database whose stats are being viewed.
collections	This is the total number of collections in the database.
objects	This is the count of documents across all collections in the database. If we find the stats of a collection using db.<collection>.stats(), we get the count of documents in the collection. This attribute is the sum of counts of all the collections in the database.
avgObjectSize	This is simply the size in bytes of all the objects in all the collections in the database divided by the count of the documents across all the collections. This value is not affected by the scale provided, although this is a size field.
dataSize	This is the total size of the data held across all the collections in the database. This value is affected by the scale provided.
storageSize	This is the total amount of storage allocated to collections in this database for storing documents. This value is affected by the scale provided.
numExtents	This is the count of all the number of extents in the database across all the collections. This is basically the number of extents (logical containers) in the collection stats for collections in this database.
indexes	This is the sum of number of indexes across all collections in the database
indexSize	This is the size in bytes for all the indexes of all the collections in the database. This value is affected by the scale provided.
fileSize	This is a sum of the size of all the database files you should find on the filesystem for this database. The files would be named test.0, test.1, and so on for test database. This value is affected by the scale provided.
nsSizeMB	This is the size of the file in MB for the .ns file of the database.
extentFreeList.num	This is the number of free extends in freelist. You can look at extent as an internal data structure of MongoDB.
extentFreeList.totalSize	Size of the extents on the freelist.

For more information on these, you can refer to books such as *Instant MongoDB* by *Packt Publishing* (`http://www.packtpub.com/big-data-and-business-inteliigence/instant-mongodb-instant`).

How it works...

Let's start by looking at the `collections` field. If you look carefully at the number and execute the show collections command on the mongo shell, you will find one extra collection in the stats as compared to those by executing the command. The difference is for one collection, which is hidden. Its name is `system.namespaces` collection. You may do a `db.system.namespaces.find()` to view its contents.

Getting back to the output of stats operation on the database, the objects field in the result has an interesting value too. If we find the count of documents in the `postalCodes` collection, we see it is `39732`. The count shown here is `39738`, which means there are six more documents. These six documents come from the `system.namespaces` and `system.indexes` collection. Executing a count query on these two collections will confirm it. Note that the `test` database doesn't contain any other collection apart from `postalCodes`. The figures would change if the database contains more collections with documents in it.

Another thing to note is the value of the `avgObjectSize` and there is something weird in this value. Unlike this very field in the collection's stats, which is affected by the value of the scale provided, in database stats this value is always in bytes. This is pretty confusing and I am not really sure why this is not scaled according to the provided scale.

Manually padding a document

Without getting too much into the internals of the storage, MongoDB uses memory mapped files, which means that the data is stored in files exactly as how it would be in memory and it would use the low level OS services to map these pages to memory. The documents are stored in continuous locations in mongo data files and problem arises when the document grows and no longer fits in the space. In such scenarios, mongo rewrites the document towards the end of the collection with the updated data and clearing up the space where it was originally placed (note that this space is not released to OS as free space).

This is not a big problem for applications that don't expect the documents to grow in size. However, this is a big performance hit for those who foresee this growth in the document size over a period of time and potentially a lot of such document movements. With the release of MongoDB 3.0, the *Power of 2* method became the default size allocation strategy. As the name suggests, this method stores documents in space allocated in powers of 2. This provides additional padding to the documents as well as better reuse of free space caused by relocation or deletion of documents.

That said, if you still wish to introduce manual padding in your strategy, read on.

Getting ready

Nothing is needed for this recipe unless you plan to try out this simple technique, in which case you would need a single instance up and running. Refer to the recipe *Installing single node MongoDB* in *Chapter 1, Installing and Starting the Server* for information on how to start the server.

How to do it...

The idea of this technique is to add some dummy data to the document to be inserted. This dummy data's size in addition to other data in the document is approximately same as the anticipated size of the document.

For example, if the average size of the document is estimated to be around 1200 bytes over a period of time and there is 300 bytes of data present in the document while inserting it, we will add a dummy field of size around 900 bytes so that the total document size sums up to 1200 bytes.

Once the document is inserted, we unset this dummy field, which leaves a hole in the file between the two consecutive documents. This empty space would then be used when the document grows over a period of time minimizing the document movements. The empty space may also be used by another document. The more foolproof way is to remove the padding only when you are using the space. However, any document growing beyond the anticipated average growth will have to be copied by the server to the end of the collection. Needless to say, documents not growing to the anticipated size will tend to waste disk space.

The applications can come up with some intelligent strategy to perhaps the adjust the size of the padding field based on say some particular field of the document to take care of these shortcomings but that is something up to the application developers.

Let's now see a sample of this approach:

1. We define a small function that will add a field called `padField` with an array of string values to the document. Its code is as follows:

```
function padDocument(doc) {
  doc.padField = []
  for(i = 0 ; i < 20 ; i++) {
    doc.padField[i] = 'Dummy'
  }
}
```

It will add an array called `padField` and add 20 times a string called `Dummy`. There is no restriction on what type you add to the document and how many times it is added as long as it consumes the space you desire. The preceding code is just a sample.

2. The next step is to insert a document. We will define another function called `insert` to do that:

```
function insert(collection, doc) {
  //1. Pad the document with the padField
  padDocument(doc);
  //2. Create or store the _id field that would be used later
  if(typeof(doc._id) == 'undefined') {
    _id = ObjectId()
    doc._id = _id
  }
  else {
    _id = doc._id
  }
  //3. Insert the document with the padded field
  collection.insert(doc)
//4. Remove the padded field, use the saved _id to find the
document to be updated.
collection.update({'_id':_id}, {$unset:{'padField':1}})
}
```

3. We will now put this into action by inserting a document in the collection `testCol` as follows:

```
insert(db.testCol, {i:1})
```

4. You may query the `testCol` using the following query and check if the document inserted exists or not:

```
> db.testCol.findOne({i:1})
```

Note that on querying you would not find the `padField` in it. However, the space once occupied by the array stays between the subsequently inserted documents even if the field was unset.

How it works...

The `insert` function is self-explanatory and has comments in it to tell what it does. An obvious question is how do we believe if this indeed what we intent to do. For this purpose, we shall do a small activity as follow. We will work on a `manualPadTest` collection for this purpose. From the mongo shell, execute the following:

```
> db.manualPadTest.drop()
```

```
> db.manualPadTest.insert({i:1})
```

```
> db.manualPadTest.insert({i:2})
```

```
> db.manualPadTest.stats()
```

Take a note of the `avgObjSize` field in the stats. Next, execute the following from the mongo shell:

```
> db.manualPadTest.drop()
> insert(db.manualPadTest , {i:1})
> insert(db.manualPadTest , {i:2})
> db.manualPadTest.stats()
```

Take a note of the `avgObjSize` field in the stats. This figure is much larger than the one we saw earlier with a regular insert without padding. The `paddingFactor` as we see in both cases still is one, but the latter case has more buffer for the document to grow.

One catch in the `insert` function we used in this recipe is that the insert into the collection and the update document operations are not atomic.

The mongostat and mongotop utilities

Most of you might find these names similar to two popular Unix commands, `iostat` and `top`. For MongoDB, `mongostat` and `mongotop` are two utilities which does pretty much the same job as these two Unix commands do and there is no prize for guessing that these are used to monitor the mongo instance.

Getting ready

In this recipe, we would be simulating some operations on a standalone mongo instance by running a script that would attempt to keep your server busy, and then in another terminal we will run these utilities to monitor the `db` instance.

You need to start a standalone server listening to any port for client connections; in this case, we will stick to the default `27017`. If you are not aware how to start a standalone server, refer to *Installing single node MongoDB* in *Chapter 1, Installing and Starting the Server*. We also need to download the script `KeepServerBusy.js` from Packt site and keep it handy for execution on local drive. Also, it is assumed that the `bin` directory of your mongo installation is present in the path variable of your operating system. If not, then these commands need to be executed with the absolute path of the executable from the shell. These two utilities `mongostat` and `mongotop` comes standard with the mongo installation.

How to do it...

1. Start the MongoDB server, and let it listen to the default port for connections.

2. In a separate terminal, execute the provided JavaScript `KeepServerBusy.js` as follows:

   ```
   $ mongo KeepServerBusy.js -quiet
   ```

3. Open a new OS terminal and execute the following command:

    ```
    $ mongostat
    ```

4. Capture the output content for some time and then hit *Ctrl + C* to stop the command from capturing more stats. Keep the terminal open or copy the stats to another file.

5. Now, execute the following command from the terminal:

    ```
    $ mongotop
    ```

6. Capture the output content for some time and then hit *Ctrl + C* to stop the command from capturing more stats. Keep the terminal open or copy the stats to another file.

7. Hit *Ctrl + C* in the shell where the provided JavaScript `KeepServerBusy.js` was executed to stop the operation that keeps the server busy.

How it works...

Let's see what we have captured from these two utilities.

We start by analyzing `mongostat`. On my laptop, the capture using `mongostat` looks like this:

```
mongostat

connected to: 127.0.0.1

insert query update delete getmore command flushes mapped vsize    res
faults idx miss % qr|qw ar|aw netIn netOut conn      time
   1000    1   950   1000      1    1|0       0 624.0M 1.4G 50.0M
0          0   0|0   0|1   431k  238k    2 08:59:21
   1000    1  1159   1000      1    1|0       0 624.0M 1.4G 50.0M
0          0   0|0   0|0   468k  252k    2 08:59:22
   1000    1   984   1000      1    1|0       0 624.0M 1.4G 50.0M
0          0   0|0   0|1   437k  240k    2 08:59:23
   1000    1  1066   1000      1    1|0       0 624.0M 1.4G 50.0M
0          0   0|0   0|1   452k  246k    2 08:59:24
   1000    1   944   1000      1    2|0       0 624.0M 1.4G 50.0M
0          0   0|0   0|1   431k  237k    2 08:59:25
   1000    1  1149   1000      1    1|0       0 624.0M 1.4G 50.0M
0          0   0|0   0|1   466k  252k    2 08:59:26
   1000    2  1015   1053      2    1|0       0 624.0M 1.4G 50.0M
0          0   0|0   0|0   450k  293k    2 08:59:27
```

You may choose to look at what the script `KeepServerBusy.js` is doing to keep the server busy. All it does is insert 1000 documents in collection `monitoringTest`, then update them one by one to set a new key in it, executes a find and iterates through all of them, and finally deletes them one by one and is basically a write intensive operation.

The output does look ugly with content wrapping, but let's analyze the fields one by one and see what the fields to keep an eye on.

Column(s)	Description
insert, query, update, delete	The first four columns are the number of insert, query, update and delete operation per second. It is per second as the time frame these figures are captured are separated by one second, which is indicated by the last column.
getmore	When the cursor runs out of data for the query, it executes a getmore operation on the server to get more results for the query executed earlier. This column shows the number of getmore operations executed in this given time frame of 1 second. In our case, there are not many getmore operations that are executed.
commands	This is the number of commands executed on the server in the given time frame of 1 second. In our case, it wasn't much and was only one. The number after a | is 0 in our case, as this was in standalone mode. Try executing mongostat connecting to a replica set primary and secondary. You should see slightly different figures there.
flushes	This is the number of times data was flushed to disk in the interval of 1 second. (fsync in case of MMAPv1 storage engine, and checkpoints triggered between polling interval in case of WiredTiger storage engine)
mapped, virtual, and resident memory	Mapped memory is the amount of memory mapped by the Mongo process to the database. This will typically be same as the size of the database. Virtual memory on other hand is the memory allocated to the entire mongod process. This will be more than twice the size of mapped memory especially when journaling is enabled. Finally, resident memory is the actual of physical memory used by mongo. All these figures are given in MB. The total amount of physical memory might be a lot more than what is being used by Mongo, but that is really not a concern unless a lot of page faults occur (which does happen in the previously mentioned output).
faults	These are the number of page faults occurring per second. These numbers should be as less as possible. It indicates the number of times mongo had to go to disk to obtain the document/index that was missing in the main memory. This problem is not as big a problem when using SSD for persistent storage as it is when using spinning disk drives.

Column(s)	Description
locked	Since version 2.2, all write operations to a collection lock the database in which the collection is and does not acquire a global level lock. This field shows the database that was locked for a majority of the time in the given time interval. In our case, the test database is locked for a majority of time.
idx miss %	This field gives the number of times a particular index was needed and was not present in memory. This causes a page fault and the disk needs to be accessed to get the index. Another disk access might be needed to get the document as well. This figure too should be low. A high percentage of index miss is something that would need attention.
qr | qw	These are the queued up reads and writes that are waiting for getting a chance to be executed. If this number goes up, it shows that the database is getting overwhelmed by the volume of read and writes than it could handle. If the values are too high, keep an eye on page faults and database lock percents in order to get more insights on increased queue counts. If the data set is too large, sharding the collection can improve the performance significantly.
ar | aw	This is the number of active readers and writers (clients). Not something to worry of even for a large number as far as other stats we saw previously are under control.
netIn and netOut	The network traffic in and out of the mongo server in the given time frame. Figure is measured in bits. For example, 271k means 271 kilobits.
conn	This indicates the number of open connections. Something to keep a watch on to see if this doesn't keep getting higher.
time	This is the time interval when this sample was captured.

There are some more fields seen if mongostat is connected to a replica set primary or secondary. As an assignment, once the stats or a standalone instance are collected, start a replica set server and execute the same script to keep the server busy. Use mongostat to connect to a primary and secondary instance and see different stats captured.

Apart from mongostat, we also used the mongotop utility to capture the stats. Let's see its output and make some sense out of it:

```
$>mongotop
connected to: 127.0.0.1
                          ns           total           read
write
2014-01-15T17:55:13
```

	ns	total	read	write
	test.monitoringTest	899ms	1ms	898ms
	test.system.users	0ms	0ms	0ms
	test.system.namespaces	0ms	0ms	0ms
	test.system.js	0ms	0ms	0ms
	test.system.indexes	0ms	0ms	0ms

	ns	total	read	write
2014-01-15T17:55:14				
	test.monitoringTest	959ms	0ms	959ms
	test.system.users	0ms	0ms	0ms
	test.system.namespaces	0ms	0ms	0ms
	test.system.js	0ms	0ms	0ms
	test.system.indexes	0ms	0ms	0ms

	ns	total	read	write
2014-01-15T17:55:15				
	test.monitoringTest	954ms	1ms	953ms
	test.system.users	0ms	0ms	0ms
	test.system.namespaces	0ms	0ms	0ms
	test.system.js	0ms	0ms	0ms
	test.system.indexes	0ms	0ms	0ms

There is not much to see in this stat. We see the total time a database was busy reading or writing in the given slice of 1 second. The value given in the total would be sum of the read and the write time. If we actually compare the mongotop and mongostat for the same time slice, the percentage of time duration for which the write was taking place would be very close to the figure given in the percentage time that the database was locked in the mongostat output.

The command `mongotop` accepts a parameter on the command line as follows:

```
$ mongotop 5
```

In this case, the interval after which the stats will be printed out will be 5 seconds as opposed to the default value of 1 second.

 Starting with MongoDB 3.0, both `mongotop` and `mongostat` utilities allow output in JSON format using `--json` option. This can be very useful if you were to use custom monitoring or metrics collection scripts, which would rely on these utilities.

See also

► In the recipe *Getting current executing operations and killing them*, we will see how to get the current executing operations from the shell and kill them if needed

► In the recipe *Using profiler to profile operations*, we will see how to use the inbuilt profiling feature of Mongo to log operation execution times.

Getting current executing operations and killing them

In this recipe, we will see how to view the current running operations and kill some operations that are running for a long time.

Getting ready

We will simulate some operations on a standalone mongo instance. We need to start a standalone server listening to any port for client connections; in this case, we will stick to the default `27017`. If you are not aware how to start a standalone server, refer to *Installing single node MongoDB* in *Chapter 1, Installing and Starting the Server*. We also need to start two shells connected to the server started. One shell would be used for background index creation and another would be used to monitor the current operation and then kill it.

How to do it...

1. We would not be able to simulate the actual long running operation in our test environment. We will try to create an index and hope it takes long to create. Depending on your target hardware configuration, the operation may take some time.

2. To start with this test, let's execute the following on the mongo shell:

```
> db.currentOpTest.drop()
> for(i = 1 ; i < 10000000 ; i++) { db.currentOpTest.
insert({'i':i}) }
```

The preceding insertion might take some time to insert 10 million documents.

3. Once the documents are inserted, we will execute an operation that would create the index in background. If you would like to know more about index creation, refer to the recipe *Creating a background and foreground index in the shell* in *Chapter 2, Command-line Operations and Indexes*, but it is not a prerequisite for this recipe.

4. Create a background index on the field i in the document. This index creation operation is what we will be viewing from the currentOp operation and is what we will attempt to kill from using the kill operation. Execute the following in one shell to initiate the background index creation operation. This takes fairly long time and on my laptop it took well over 100 seconds.

```
> db.currentOpTest.ensureIndex({i:1}, {background:1})
```

5. In the second shell, execute the following command to get the current executing operations:

```
> db.currentOp().inprog
```

6. Take a note of the progress of the operations and find the one that is necessary for index creation. In our case, it was the only in progress on test machine. It will be an operation on system.indexes and the operation will be insert. The keys to lookout for in the output document are ns and op, respectively. We need to note the first field of this operation, opid. In this case, it is 11587458. The sample output of the command is given in next section.

7. Kill the operation from the shell using the following command, using the opid (operation ID) we got earlier:

```
> db.killOp(11587458)
```

How it works...

We will split our explanation into two sections, the first about the current operation details and second about killing the operation.

In our case, index creation process is the long-running operation that we intend to kill. We create a big collection with about 10 million documents and initiate a background index creation process.

On executing the db.currentOp() operation, we get a document as the result with a field inprog whose value is an array of other documents each representing a currently running operation. It is common to get a big list of documents on a busy system. Here is a document taken for the index creation operation:

```
{
        "desc" : "conn12",
        "threadId" : "0x3be96c0",
        "connectionId" : 12,
        "opid" : 3212789,
        "active" : true,
        "secs_running" : 1,
        "microsecs_running" : NumberLong(729029),
        "op" : "query",
        "ns" : "test.$cmd",
        "query" : {
            "createIndexes" : "currentOpTest",
            "indexes" : [
                {
                    "key" : {
                        "i" : 1
                    },
                    "name" : "i_1",
                    "background" : 1
                }
            ]
        },
        "client" : "127.0.0.1:36542",
        "msg" : "Index Build (background) Index Build
          (background): 384120/1000000 38%",
        "progress" : {
            "done" : 384120,
            "total" : 1000000
        },
        "numYields" : 3003,
        "locks" : {
            "Global" : "w",
            "MMAPV1Journal" : "w",
            "Database" : "w",
            "Collection" : "W"
    "waitingForLock" : true,
        "lockStats" : {
            "Global" : {
                "acquireCount" : {
```

```
                    "w" : NumberLong(3004)
                }
            },
            "MMAPV1Journal" : {
                "acquireCount" : {
                    "w" : NumberLong(387127)
                },
                "acquireWaitCount" : {
                    "w" : NumberLong(9)
                },
                "timeAcquiringMicros" : {
                    "w" : NumberLong(60025)
                }
            },
            "Database" : {
                "acquireCount" : {
                    "w" : NumberLong(3004),
                    "W" : NumberLong(1)
                }
            },
            "Collection" : {
                "acquireCount" : {
                    "W" : NumberLong(3004)
                },
                "acquireWaitCount" : {
                    "W" : NumberLong(1)
                },
                "timeAcquiringMicros" : {
                    "W" : NumberLong(66)
                }
            },
            "Metadata" : {
                "acquireCount" : {
                    "W" : NumberLong(4)
                }
            }
        }
    }
}
```

We will see what these fields mean in the following table:

Field	Description
opid	This is a unique operation ID identifying the operation. This is the ID to be used to kill an operation.
active	The Boolean value indicating whether the operation has started or not, it is false only if it is waiting for acquiring the lock to execute the operation. The value will be true once it starts even if at a point of time where it has yielded the lock and is not executing.
secs_running	Gives the time in seconds the operation is executing for.
op	This is the type of the operation. In the case of index creation, it is inserted into a system collection of indexes. Possible values are insert, query, getmore, update, remove, and command.
ns	This is the fully qualified namespace for the target. It would be in the form <database name>.<collection name>.
insert	This is the document that would be inserted in the collection.
query	This is a field that would be present for other operations, other than insert, getmore, and command.
client	The ip address/hostname and the port of the client who initiated the operation.
desc	This is the description of the client, mostly the client connection name.
connectionId	This is the identifier of the client connection from which the request originated.
locks	This is a document containing the locks held for this operation. The document shows the type and mode of locks held for the operation being analyzed. The possible modes are as follows: **R** represents Shared (S) lock. **W** represents Exclusive (X) lock. **r** represents Intent Shared (IS) lock. **w** represents Intent Exclusive (IX) lock.
waitingForLock	This field indicates if the operation is waiting for a lock to be acquired. For instance, if the preceding index creation was not a background process, other operations on this database would queue up for the lock to be acquired. This flag for those operations would then be true.
msg	This is a human-readable message for the operation. In this case, we do see the percentage of operation complete as this is an index creation operation.
progress	The state of the operation, the total gives the total number of documents in the collection and done gives the number indexed so far. In this case, the collection already had some more documents over 10 million documents. The percentage completion is computed from these figures.

Field	Description
numYields	This is the number of times the process has yielded the lock to allow other operations to execute. Since this is the background index creation process, this number will keep on increasing as the server yields it frequently to let other operations execute. Had it been a foreground process, the lock would never be yielded till the operation completes.
lockStats	This document has more nested documents giving the stats for the total time this operation has held the read or write lock and also the time it waited to acquire the lock.

 In case you have a replica set, there would be more lot of getmore operations on the oplog on primary from secondary.

1. To see the system operations being executed too, we need to pass a true value as the parameter to the currentOp function call as follows:

```
> db.currentOp(true)
```

2. Next, we will see how to kill the user initiated operation using the killOp function. The operation is simply called as follows:

```
> db.killOp(<operation id>)
```

In our case, the index creation process had the process ID 11587458 and thus it will be killed as follows:

```
> db.killOp(11587458)
```

On killing any operation, irrespective of whether the given operation ID exists or not, we see the following message on the console:

```
{ "info" : "attempting to kill op" }
```

Thus, seeing this message doesn't mean that the operation was killed. It just means that the operation if it exists will be attempted to be killed.

3. If some operation cannot be killed immediately and if the killOp command is issued for it, the field killPending in the currentOp will start appearing for the given operation. For example, execute the following query on the shell:

```
> db.currentOpTest.find({$where:'sleep(100000)'})
```

This will not return and the thread executing the query will sleep for 100 seconds. This is an operation that cannot be killed using `killOp`. Try executing the command `currentOp` from another shell (do not press *Tab* for auto completion, your shell may just hang), get the operation ID, and then kill it using the `killOp`. You should see that the process still would be running if you execute the `currentOp` command, but the document for the process details will now contain a new key `killPending` stating that the kill for this operation is requested but pending.

Using profiler to profile operations

In this recipe, we will look at mongo's inbuilt profiler that would be used to profile the operations executed on the mongo server. It is a utility that is used to log all or slow operations that could be used for analysis of the performance of the server.

Getting ready

In this recipe, we will perform some operations on a standalone mongo instance and profile them. We need to start a standalone server listening to any port for client connections; in this case, we will stick to the default `27017`. If you are not aware how to start a standalone server, refer to *Installing single node MongoDB* in *Chapter 1, Installing and Starting the Server*. We also need to start a shell that would be used to perform querying, enabling profiling, and viewing the profiling operation.

How to do it...

1. Once the server is started and the shell is connected to it, execute the following to get the current profiling level:

   ```
   > db.getProfilingLevel()
   ```

2. The default level should be 0 (no profiling, if we have not set it earlier).

3. Let's set the profiling level to 1 (log slow operations only) and log all the operations slower than 50 ms. Execute the following on the shell:

   ```
   > db.setProfilingLevel(1, 50)
   ```

4. Now, let's execute an insert operation into a collection, and then execute a couple of queries:

   ```
   > db.profilingTest.insert({i:1})
   > db.profilingTest.find()
   > db.profilingTest.find({$where:'sleep(70)'})
   ```

5. Now, execute the query on the following collection:

   ```
   > db.system.profile.find().pretty()
   ```

How it works...

Profiling is something that would not be enabled by default. If you are happy about the performance of the database, there is no reason one would enable the profiler. It is only when one feels there is some room for improvement and wants to target some expensive operations taking place. An important question is what classifies an operation to be slow? The answer is, it depends from application to application. In mongo, slow means any operation above 100 ms. However, while setting the profiling level, you may choose the threshold value.

There are three possible values for profiling levels:

- ▶ 0: Disable profiling
- ▶ 1: Enable profiling for slow operations, where the threshold value for an operation to be classified as slow is provided with the call while setting the profiling level
- ▶ 2: Profile all operations

While profiling all operations might not be a very good idea and might not be commonly used as we shall soon see, setting the value to 1 and a threshold provided to it is a good way to monitor slow operations.

If we look at the steps that we executed, we see that we can get the current profiling level by executing the operation db.getProfilingLevel(). To get more information, for example, what value is set as a threshold for the slow operations, we can use db.getProfilingStatus(). This returns a document with the profiling level and the threshold value for slow operations.

For setting the profiling level, we call the db.setProfilingLevel() method. In our case, we set it for logging all operations taking more than 50 ms as db.setProfilingLevel(1, 50).

To disable profiling, simply execute db.setProfilingLevel(0).

Next we executed three operations, one to insert a document, one to find all documents, and finally a find that calls sleep with a value of 70 ms to slow it down.

The final step was to see these profiled operations that are logged in the system.profile collection. We execute a find to see the operations logged. For my execution, the insert and the final find operation with the sleep were logged.

Obviously, this profiling has some overhead but it is negligible. Hence, we would not enable it by default but only when we want to profile slow operations. Also, another question would be, *Will this profiling collection increase over a period of time?* The answer is *No*, as this is a capped collection. Capped collections are fixed size collections that preserve insertion orders and act as a circular queue filling in the new documents, discarding the oldest when it gets full. A query on `system.namespaces` should show the stats. The query execution would show the following for the `system.profile` collection:

```
{"name":"test.system.profile", "options":{"capped":true, "size":1048576
}}
```

As we can see, the size of the collection is 1 MB, which is incredibly small. Setting the profiling level to 2 thus would easily overwrite the data on busy systems. One may also choose to explicitly create a collection with the name `system.profile` as a capped collection and of any size they prefer should they choose to retain more operations in it. To create a capped collection explicitly, you can execute the following:

```
db.createCollection('system.profile', {capped:1, size: 1048576})
```

Obviously, the size chosen is arbitrary and you are free to allocate any size to this collection based on how frequently the data gets filled and how much of profiling data you want to keep before it gets overwritten.

As this is a capped collection and insertion order is preserved, a query with the `sort order` `{$natural:-1}` would be perfectly fine and very efficient to find the operations in the reverse order of the execution time.

We would finally take a look at the document that got inserted in the `system.profile` collection and see what all operations it has logged:

```
{
        "op" : "query",
        "ns" : "test.profilingTest",
        "query" : {
                "$where" : "sleep(70)"
        },
        "ntoreturn" : 0,
        "ntoskip" : 0,
        "nscanned" : 1,
        "keyUpdates" : 0,
        "numYield" : 0,
        "lockStats" : {
                ...<<<<snip>>>
        },
        "nreturned" : 0,
        "responseLength" : 20,
        "millis" : 188,
```

```
    "ts" : ISODate("2014-01-27T17:37:02.482Z"),
    "client" : "127.0.0.1",
    "allUsers" : [ ],
    "user" : ""
}
```

As we can see in the document, there are indeed some interesting stats. Let's look at some of them in the following table. Some of these fields are identical to the fields we see when we execute the `db.currentOp()` operation from the shell and we then discussed in the previous recipe.

Field	Description
op	This is the operation that got executed; in this case, it was a find and thus it is query in this case.
ns	This is the fully qualified name of the collection on which the operation was performed. It would be of the format `<database>.<collection name>`.
query	It shows the query that got executed on the server.
nscanned	This has a similar meaning to explain plan. It is the total number of documents and index entries scanned.
numYields	This is the number of times the lock was yielded when the operation was executed. Higher yields could indicate that the query required a lot of disk access. This could be a good indication of re-looking at the index or optimizing the query itself.
lockStats	Some interesting stats for the time taken to acquire the lock and the time for which the lock was held.
nreturned	The number of documents returned.
responseLength	The length of the response in bytes.
millis	Most important of all, the time taken in milliseconds to execute the operation. This can be a good starting point to catch slow queries.
ts	This is the time when the operation was executed.
client	This is the hostname/IP address of the client who executed the operation.

Setting up users in Mongo

Security is one of the cornerstones of any enterprise-level system. Not always would you find a system in a completely safe and secure environment to allow unauthenticated user access to it. Apart from test environments, almost every production environment requires proper access rights and perhaps audit of the system access too. Mongo security has multiple aspects:

▶ Access rights for the end users accessing the system. There would be multiple roles such as admin, read-only users, and read and write non-administrative users.

▶ Authentication of the nodes that are added to the replica set. In a replica set, one should only be allowed to add authenticated systems. The integrity of the system would be compromised if any unauthenticated node is added to the replica set.

▶ Encryption of the data that is transmitted across the wire between the nodes of the replica sets or even the client and the server (or the mongos process in case of sharded setup).

In this and the next recipe, we would be looking at how to address the first and the second point given here. The third point of encrypting the data being transmitted on the wire is not supported by default by the community edition of mongo and would need a rebuild of mongo database with the `ssl` option enabled.

Getting ready

In this recipe, we will set up users for a standalone mongo instance. We need to start a standalone server listening to any port for client connections; in this case, we will stick to the default `27017`. If you are not aware how to start a standalone server, refer to *Installing single node MongoDB* in *Chapter 1, Installing and Starting the Server*. We also need to start a shell that would be used for this admin operation. For a replica set, we will only be connected to a primary and perform these operations.

How to do it...

We will add an admin user, a read-only user for a test database, and a read-write user for test database in this recipe.

It is assumed that at this point:

▶ The server is up and running, and we are connected to it from the shell.

▶ The server is started without any special command-line argument other than those mentioned in *Chapter 1, Installing and Starting the Server* for *Starting a single node instance using command-line options* recipe. We thus have full access to the server for any user.

Perform the following steps:

1. The first step we will do is to create an admin user. All the commands assume that you are using MongoDB 3.0 and above.

2. First, we start by creating the admin user in admin database as follows:

```
> use admin
> db.createUser({
        user:'admin', pwd:'admin',
        customData:{desc:'The admin user for admin db'},
        roles:['readWrite', 'dbAdmin', 'clusterAdmin']
    })
```

3. We will add the read_user and write_user to test database. To add the users, execute the following from the mongo shell:

```
> use test
> db.createUser({
    user:'read_user', pwd:'read_user',
    customData:{desc:'The read only user for test database'},
    roles:['read']
  }
)
> db.createUser({
    user:'write_user', pwd:'write_user',
    customData:{desc:'The read write user for test database'},
    roles:['readWrite']
  }
)
```

4. Now shut down the mongo server and the close the shell too. Restart the mongo server but with the --auth option on the command line:

```
$ mongod .. <other options as provided earlier> --auth
```

If your mongod instance is using /etc/mongod.conf, then add the line auth = true in the configuration file and restart the mongod service.

5. Now connect to the server from the newly opened mongo shell and execute the following:

```
> db.testAuth.find()
```

6. The collection testAuth need not exist, but you should see an error that we are not authorized to query the collection.

7. We will now log in from the shell using a `read_user` as follows:

    ```
    > db.auth('read_user', 'read_user')
    ```

8. We will now execute the same `find` operation as follows. It should not give an error and it might not return any results depending on whether the collection exists or not:

    ```
    > db.testAuth.find()
    ```

9. Now, we will try to insert a document as follows. We should get an error that you are not authorized to insert data in this collection.

    ```
    > db.testAuth.insert({i:1})
    ```

10. We will now log out and log in again, but with a write user as follows. Note the difference in the way we login this time around as against the previous instance. We are providing a document as the parameter to the `auth` function, where as in previous case we passed two parameters for the username and password:

    ```
    > db.logout()
    > db.auth({user:'write_user', pwd:'write_user'})
    ```

    Now to execute the insert again as follows, this time around it should work

    ```
    > db.testAuth.insert({i:1})
    ```

11. Now, execute the following on the shell. You should get the unauthorized error:

    ```
    > db.serverStatus()
    ```

12. We will now switch to `admin` database. We are currently connected to the server using a `write_user` that has read-write permissions on the `test` database. From the mongo shell, try to do the following:

    ```
    > use admin
    > show collections
    ```

13. Close the mongo shell or open a new shell as follows from the operating system's console. This should take us directly to admin database:

    ```
    $ mongo -u admin -p admin admin
    ```

14. Now execute the following on the shell. It should show us the collections in the admin database:

    ```
    > show collections
    ```

15. Try and execute the following operation:

    ```
    > db.serverStatus()
    ```

How it works...

We executed a lot of steps and now we will take a closer look at them.

Initially, the server is started without `--auth` option and hence no security is enforced by default. We create an admin user with the `db.createUser` method. The signature of the method to create the user is `createUser(user, writeConcern)`. The first parameter is the user, which actually is a JSON document and second is the write concern to use for user creation. The JSON document for the user has the following format:

```
{
    'user' : <user name>,
    'pwd' : <password>,
    'customData': {<JSON document providing any user specific data>}
    'roles':[<roles of the user>]
}
```

The roles provided here can be provided as follows, assuming that the current database when the user is created is test on the shell:

```
[{'role' : 'read',   'db':'reports'}, 'readWrite']
```

This gives the user being created read access to the reports `db` and `readWrite` access to the `test` database. Let's see the complete user creation call of the `test` user:

```
> use test
> db.createUser({
      user:'test', pwd:'test',
      customData:{desc:'read access on reports and readWrite access on
test'},
      roles:[
        {role:'read', db : 'reports'},
        'readWrite'
      ]
    }
)
```

The write concern, which is an optional parameter, can be provided as the JSON document. Some examples values are `{w:1}`, `{w:'majority'}`.

Coming back to the admin user creation, we created the user in step 2 using the `createUser` method and gave three inbuilt roles to this user in the `admin` database.

In step 3, we created the `read` and `read-write` users in `test` database using the same `createUser` method.

We shut down the MongoDB server after the `admin`, `read`, and `read-write` user creation and restarted it with the `--auth` option.

On starting the server again, we will connect to it from the shell in step 8, but unauthenticated. Here, we try to execute a `find` query on a collection in test database, which fails as we are unauthenticated. This indicates that the server now requires appropriate credentials to execute operations on it. In step 8 and 9, we log in using the `read_user` and first execute a `find` operation (which succeeds), and then an insert that doesn't as the user has read privileges only. The way to authenticate a user by invoking from the shell `db.auth(<user name>, <password>)` and `db.logout()`, which will logout the current logged in user.

In steps 10 to 12, we demonstrate that we can perform `insert` operations using `write_ user` but admin operations like `db.serverStatus()` cannot be executed. This is because these operations execute an `admin command` on the server, which a non-admin user and not permitted to invoke these. Similarly, when we change the database to admin, the `write_ user`, which is from `test` database, is not permitted to perform any operations like getting a list of collections or any operation to query a collection in `admin` database.

In Step 14, we log in to the shell using the `admin` user to the `admin` database. Previously, we logged in to database using the `auth` method; in this case, we used the `-u` and `-p` options for providing the username and the password. We also provided the name of the database to connect to, which is admin in this case. Here, we are able to view the collections on the admin database and also execute admin operations like getting the server status. Executing the `db.serverStatus` call is possible as the user is given the `clusterAdmin` role.

One final thing to note, apart from writing to a collection, a user with write privileges can also create indexes on the collection in which he has write access.

There's more...

In this recipe, we saw how we can create different users and what permissions they have restricting some set of operations. In the following recipe, we will see how we can have authentication done at process level. That is, how can one mongo instance authenticate itself for being added to a replica set.

See also

- ▸ MongoDB comes with a lot of built-in user roles with various privileges associated to each of them. Refer to the following URL to get details of various in built roles: `http://docs.mongodb.org/manual/reference/built-in-roles/`.

- ▸ MongoDB also supports custom user roles. Refer to the following URL for knowing more about defining custom user roles: `http://docs.mongodb.org/manual/core/authorization/#user-defined-roles`.

Interprocess security in Mongo

In the previous recipe, we saw how authentication can be enforced for user to be logged in before allowing any operations on Mongo. In this recipe, we will look at interprocess security. By the term interprocess security, we don't mean to encrypt the communication but only to ensure that the node being added to a replica set is authenticated before being added to the replica set.

Getting ready

In this recipe, we will start multiple mongo instances as part of a replica set and thus you might have to refer to the recipe *Starting multiple instances as part of a replica set* from *Chapter 1, Installing and Starting the Server* if you are not aware of how to start a replica set. Apart from that, in this recipe, all we would be looking at how to generate key file to be used and the behavior when an unauthenticated node is added to the replica set.

How to do it...

To set the ground, we would be starting three instances, each listening to port 27000, 27001, and 27002, respectively. The first two would be started by providing it a path to the key file and the third wouldn't be. Later, we will try to add these three instances to the same replica set.

1. Let's generate key the key file first. There is nothing spectacular about generating the key file. This is as simple as having a file with 6 to 1024 characters from the base64 character set. On Linux filesystem, you may choose to generate pseudo random bytes using openssl and encode them to base64. The following command will generate 500 random bytes and those bytes will then be base64 encoded and written to the file keyfile:

    ```
    $ openssl rand -base64 500 > keyfile
    ```

2. On a Unix filesystem, the key file should not have permissions for world and group. Thus, we should do the following after it is created:

    ```
    $ chmod 400 keyfile
    ```

3. Not giving write permission to the creator ensures that we don't overwrite the contents accidently. On Windows platform, however, openssl doesn't come out of the box and thus you have to download it, the archive extracted, and the bin folder added to the OS path variable. For Windows, we can download it from the following URL: http://gnuwin32.sourceforge.net/packages/openssl.htm.

4. You may even choose not to generate the key file using the approach mentioned here (using `openssl`) and can take an easy way out by just typing in plain text in the key file from any text editor or your choice. However, note that the characters `\r`, `\n`, and spaces are stripped off by mongo and the remainder text is considered as the key. For example, we may create a file with the following content added to the key file. Again, the file will be named `keyfile` with the following content:

```
somecontentaddedtothekeyfilefromtheeditorwithoutspaces
```

5. Using any approach mentioned here, we must not have a `keyfile` in place that would be used for next steps of the recipe.

6. We will now secure the mongo processes by starting the mongo instance as follows. I will start the following on windows, and my key file ID is named `keyfile` and is placed on `c:\MongoDB`. The data path is `c:\MongoDB\data\c1`, `c:\MongoDB\data\c2`, and `c:\MongoDB\data\c3` for the three instances, respectively.

7. Start the first instance listening to port `27000` as follows:

```
C:\>mongod --dbpath c:\MongoDB\data\c1 --port 27000 --auth
--keyFile c:\MongoDB\keyfile --replSet secureSet --smallfiles
--oplogSize 100
```

8. Similarly, start the second server listening to port `27001` as follows:

```
C:\>mongod --dbpath c:\MongoDB\data\c2 --port 27001 --auth
--keyFile c:\MongoDB\keyfile --replSet secureSet --smallfiles
--oplogSize 100
```

9. The third instance would be started but without the `--auth` and the `--keyFile` option listening to port `27002` as follows:

```
C:\>mongod --dbpath c:\MongoDB\data\c3 --port 27002 --replSet
secureSet --smallfiles --oplogSize 100
```

10. We then start a mongo shell and connect it to port `27000`, which is the first instance started. From the mongo shell, we type:

```
> rs.initiate()
```

11. In few seconds, the replica set would be initiated with just one instance in it. We will now try to add two new instances to this replica set. First, add the one listening on port `27001` as follows (you will need to add the appropriate hostname, `Amol-PC` is the hostname in my case):

```
> rs.add({_id:1, host:'Amol-PC:27001'})
```

12. We will execute `rs.status()` command to see the status of our replica set. In the command's output, we should see our newly added instance.

13. We will now finally try and add an instance that was started without the `--auth` and the `--keyFile` option as follows:

```
> rs.add({_id:2, host:'Amol-PC:27002'})
```

This should add the instance to the replica set, but using `rs.status()` will show the status of the instance as UNKNOWN. The server logs for the instance running on `27002` too should show some authentication errors.

14. We would finally have to restart this instance; however, this time we provide the `--auth` and the `--keyFile` option as follows:

```
C:\>mongod --dbpath c:\MongoDB\data\c3 --port 27002 --replSet
secureSet --smallfiles --oplogSize 100 --auth --keyFile c:\
MongoDB\keyfile
```

15. Once the server is started, connect to it from the shell again and type in `rs.status()` in few moments, it should come up as a secondary instance.

There's more...

In this recipe, we saw interprocess security for preventing unauthenticated nodes from being added to the mongo replica set. We still haven't secured the transport by encrypting the data that is being sent over the wire. In the *Appendix*, we will show how to build the mongo server from the source and how to enable encryption of the contents over the wire.

Modifying collection behavior using the collMod command

This is a command that would be executed to change the behavior of a collection in mongo. It could be thought of as a *collection modify* operation (officially, it is not mentioned anywhere though).

For a part of this recipe, knowledge of TTL indexes is required.

Getting ready

In this recipe, we will execute the `collMod` operation on a collection. We need to start a standalone server listening to any port for client connections; in this case, we will stick to the default `27017`. If you are not aware how to start a standalone server, refer to *Installing single node MongoDB* in *Chapter 1, Installing and Starting the Server*. We also need to start a shell that would be used for this administration. It is highly recommended to take a look at the recipes *Expiring documents after a fixed interval using the TTL index* and *Expiring documents at a given time using the TTL index* in *Chapter 2, Command-line Operations and Indexes* if you are not aware of them.

How it works...

This operation can be used to do a couple of things:

1. Assuming we have a collection with TTL index, as we saw in *Chapter 2, Command-line Operations*, let us see the list indexes by executing the following:

   ```
   > db.ttlTest.getIndexes()
   ```

2. To change the expiry to 800 ms from 300 ms, execute the following:

   ```
   > db.runCommand({collMod: 'ttlTest', index: {keyPattern: {createDate:1}, expireAfterSeconds:800}})
   ```

How it works...

The collMod command always has the following format: {collMod : <name of the collection>, <collmod operation>}.

We use the index operation using collMod to modify the TTL index. If a TTL index is already created and the time to live needs to be changed after creation, we use the collMod command. This operation-specific field to the command is as follows:

```
{index: {keyPattern: <the field on which the index was originally created>, expireAfterSeconds:<new time to be used for TTL of the index>}}
```

The keyPattern is the field, of the collection, on which the TTL index is created and the expireAfterSeconds will contain the new time to be changed to. On successful execution, we should see the following in the shell:

```
{ "expireAfterSeconds_old" : 300, "expireAfterSeconds_new" : 800, "ok" : 1 }
```

Setting up MongoDB as a windows service

Windows services are long-running applications that run in background, similar to daemon threads. Databases are good candidates for such type of services, whereby they would start and stop when the host machines starts and stops (you may, however, choose to manually start/stop a service). Many database vendors provide a feature to start the database as a service when installed on the server. MongoDB lets you do that as well and this is what we will see in this recipe.

Refer to the recipe *Installing single node MongoDB with options from the config file* in *Chapter 1, Installing and Starting the Server* for getting information on how to start a MongoDB server using an external configuration file. Since mongo is run as a service in this case, it cannot be provided with command-like arguments and configuring it from configuration file is the only alternative. Refer to the prerequisites of the *Installing single node MongoDB* recipe in *Chapter 1, Installing and Starting the Server*, which is all we would need for this recipe.

1. We will first create a config file with three configuration values the `port`, `dbpath`, and the `logpath` file. We name the file `mongo.conf` and keep it at location `c:\conf\mongo.conf` with the following three entries in it (you may choose any path for config file location, database and logs):

   ```
   port = 27000
   dbpath = c:\data\mongo\db
   logpath = c:\logs\mongo.log
   ```

2. Execute the following from the windows terminal, which you may need to execute as an administrator. On Windows 7, the following steps were executed:

   1. Press the Windows key on your keyboard.
   2. In the Search programs and files space, type `cmd`.
   3. In the programs, the command prompt program will be seen; right-click on it and select **Run as administrator**.

3. In the shell, execute the following:

   ```
   C:\>mongod --config c:\conf\mongo.conf –install
   ```

4. The log printed out on the console should confirm that the service is installed properly.

5. The service can be started as follows from the console:

   ```
   C:\>net start MongoDB
   ```

6. The service can be stopped as follows:

   ```
   C:\>net stop MongoDB
   ```

7. Type in `services.msc` in the Run window (Windows button + R). In the management console, search for MongoDB service. We should see it as follows:

Mongo DB	Name	Description	Status	Startup Type	Log On As
	McAfee Security S...	McAfee Sec...		Manual	Local Syste..
Start the service	Media Center Exte...	Allows Med...		Disabled	Local Servic
	Microsoft .NET Fr...	Microsoft		Manual	Local Syste..
	Microsoft .NET Fr...	Microsoft		Manual	Local Syste..
Description:	Microsoft iSCSI Ini...	Manages In...		Manual	Local Syste..
Mongo DB Server	Microsoft SharePo...			Manual	Local Servic
	Microsoft Softwar...	Manages so...		Manual	Local Syste..
	Mongo DB	Mongo DB ...		Automatic	Local Syste.

8. The service is automatic, that is, it will be started when the operating system starts. It can be changed to manual by right-clicking on it and selecting **Properties**.

9. To remove a service, we need to execute the following from the command prompt:

```
C:\>mongod --remove
```

10. There are more options available that can be used to configure the name of the service, display name, description, and the user account used to run the service. These can be provided as command-line arguments. Execute the following to see the possible options and take a look at the **Windows Service Control Manager** options:

```
C:\> mongod --help
```

Replica set configurations

We have had a good discussion on what replica set is in *Chapter 1, Installing and Starting the Server* in the recipe *Starting multiple instances as part of a replica set*, and we saw how to start a simple replica set. In the recipe *Interprocess security in Mongo* in this chapter, we saw how to start a replica set with interprocess authentication. To be honest, that is pretty much what we do in setting up a standard replica set. There are a few configurations that one must know and should be aware of how it affects the replica set's behavior. Note that we still are not discussing tag aware replication in this recipe and it would be taken up later in this chapter as a separate recipe *Building tagged replica sets*.

Getting ready

Refer to the recipe *Starting multiple instances as part of a replica set* in *Chapter 1, Installing and Starting the Server* for the prerequisites and know about the replica set basics. Go ahead and set up a simple three-node replica set on your computer as mentioned in the recipe.

Before we go ahead with the configurations, we will see what elections are in a replica set and how they work from a high level. This is good to know about elections because some of the configuration options affect the voting process in the elections.

Elections in a replica set

Mongo replica set has a single primary instance and multiple secondary instances. All database writes happen only through the primary instance and are replicated to the secondary instances. Read operations can happen from secondary instances depending on the read preference. Refer to the *Understanding ReadPreference for querying* in the *Appendix* to know what read preference is. If, however, the primary goes down or is not reachable for some reason, the replica set becomes unavailable for writes. MongoDB replica set has a feature to automatically failover to a secondary, by promoting it to a primary and make the set available to clients for both read and write operations. The replica set remains unavailable for that brief moment till a new primary comes up.

It all sounds good but the question is, who decides upon who the new primary instance would be? The process of choosing a new primary happens through an election. Whenever any secondary detects that it cannot reach out to a primary, it asks all replica set nodes in the instance to elect itself as the new primary.

All other nodes in the replica set who receive this request for election of primary will perform certain checks before they vote a Yes to the secondary requesting an election:

1. They would first check if the existing primary is reachable. This is necessary because the secondary requesting the re-election is not able to reach the primary possibly because of a network partition in which case it should not be allowed to become a primary. In such case the instance receiving the request will vote a No.

2. Secondly, the instance would check the state of replication of itself with the secondary requesting the election. If it finds that the requesting secondary is behind itself in the replicated data, it would vote a No.

3. Finally, the primary is not reachable, but some instance with priority higher than the secondary requesting the re-election, is reachable from it. This is possible if the secondary requesting the re-election can't reach out to the secondary with higher priority possibly due to a network partition. In this scenario the instance receiving the request for election would vote a No.

The preceding checks are pretty much what would be happening (not necessarily in the order mentioned previously) during the re-election; if these checks pass, the instance votes a Yes.

The election is void even if a single instance votes No. However, if none of the instances have voted a No, then the secondary that requests the election would become a new primary if it receives a Yes from majority of instances. If the election becomes void, there would be a re-election with the same secondary or any other instance requesting an election with the aforementioned process till a new primary is elected.

Now that we have an idea about the elections in replica set and the terminologies, let's look at some of the replica set configurations. Few of these options are related to votes and we start by looking at these options first.

Basic configuration for a replica set

From the first chapter when we set up a replica set, we had a configuration similar to the following one. The basic replica set configuration for a three member set is as follows:

```
{
        "_id" : "replSet",
        "members" : [
                {
                        "_id" : 0,
                        "host" : "Amol-PC:27000"
                },
                {
                        "_id" : 1,
                        "host" : "Amol-PC:27001"
                },
                {
                        "_id" : 2,
                        "host" : "Amol-PC:27002"
                }
        ]
}
```

We would not be repeating the entire configuration in all the steps in the following sections. All the flags we would be mentioning would be added to the document of a particular member in the members array. In the preceding example, if node with `_id` as 2 is to be made arbiter, we would be having the following configuration for it in the configuration document shown previously:

```
{
        "_id" : 2,
        "host" : "Amol-PC:27002"
        "arbiterOnly" : true
}
```

Generally, the steps to reconfigure an existing replica set are as follows:

1. Assign the configuration document to a variable. If the replica set is already configured, it can be obtained using the `rs.conf()` call from the shell.

    ```
    > var conf = rs.conf()
    ```

2. The members field in the document is an array of documents for each individual member of a replica set. To add a new property to a particular member, we do the following. For instance, if we want to add the `votes` key and set its value to `2` for the third member of the replica set (index 2 in the array), we would do the following:

```
> conf.members[2].votes = 2
```

3. Just changing the JSON document won't change the replica set. We need to reconfigure it if the replica set is already in place, as follows:

```
> rs.reconfig(conf)
```

4. If the configuration is done for the first time, we would call the following:

```
> rs.initiate (conf)
```

For all the steps given next, you need to follow the preceding steps to reconfigure or initiate the replica set unless some other steps are mentioned explicitly.

How to do it...

In this recipe, we will look at some of the possible configurations that can be done in a replica set. The explanation will be minimal with all the explanation done in the next section, as usual.

1. The first configuration is `arbiterOnly` option. It is used to configure a replica set member as a member that holds no data but only has rights to vote. The following key need to be added to the configuration of the member who would be made an arbiter:

```
{_id: ... , 'arbiterOnly': true }
```

2. One thing to remember regarding this configuration is that once a replica set is initiated, no existing member can be changed to an arbiter from a non-arbiter node and vice versa. We can, however, add arbiter to an existing replica set using the helper function `rs.addArb(<hostname>:<port>)`. For example, add an arbiter listening to port `27004` to an existing replica set. The following was done on my machine to add an arbiter:

```
> rs.addArb('Amol-PC:27004')
```

3. When the server is started to listen to port `27004` and `rs.status()` is executed from the mongo shell, we should see that the `state` and the `strState` for this member is `7` and `ARBITER`, respectively.

4. The next option `votes` affects the number of votes a member has in the election. By default, all members have one vote each, this option can be used to change the number of votes a particular member has. It can be set as follows:

```
{_id: ... , 'votes': <0 or 1>}
```

5. Votes of existing members of a replica set can be changed and the replica set can be reconfigured using the `rs.reconfig()` helper.

6. Though the option `votes` is available, which can potentially change the number of votes to form a majority, it usually doesn't add much value and not a recommended option to use in production.

7. Next replica set configuration option is called the `priority`. It determines the eligibility of a replica set member to become a primary (or not to become a primary). The option is set as follows:

```
{_id: ... , 'priority': <priority number>}
```

8. Higher number indicates more likely hood of becoming a primary, the primary would always be the one with the highest priority amongst the members alive in a replica set. Setting this option in an already configured replica set will trigger an election.

9. Setting the priority to `0` will ensure that a member will never become primary.

10. Next option we would be looking at is `hidden`. Setting the value of this option to true ensures that the replica set member is hidden. The option is set as follows:

```
{_id: ... , 'hidden': <true/false>}
```

11. One thing to keep in mind is that when the replica set member is hidden, its priority too should be made `0` to ensure it doesn't become primary. Though this seems redundant; as of the current version, the value or priority needs to be set explicitly.

12. When a programming language client connects to a replica set, it would not be able to discover hidden members. However, after using `rs.status()` from the shell, the member's status would be visible.

13. Let's look at the `slaveDelay` option now. This option is used to set lag in time for the slave from the primary of the replica set. The option is set as follows:

```
{_id: ... , 'slaveDelay': <number of seconds to lag>}
```

14. Like the hidden member, slave delayed members too should have the priority set to `0` to ensure they don't ever become primary. This needs to be set explicitly.

15. Let's look at the final configuration option: `buildIndexes`. This value if not specified by default, is true, which indicates if an index is created on the primary, it needs to be replicated on the secondary too. The option is set as follows:

```
{_id: ... , 'buildIndexes': <true/false>}
```

16. When using this option with a value set to false, the priority is set to `0` to ensure they don't ever become primary. This needs to be set explicitly. Also, this option cannot be set after the replica set is initiated. Just like an arbiter node, this needs to be set when the replica set is being created or when a new member node is being added to the replica set.

How it works...

In this section, we will explain and understand the significance of different types of members and the configuration options we saw in the previous section.

Replica set member as an arbiter

The English meaning of the word *arbiter* is a judge who resolves a dispute. In the case of replica sets, the arbiter node is present just to vote in case of elections and not replicate any data. This is in fact, a pretty common scenario due to a fact that that a Mongo replica set needs to have at least three instances (and preferably odd number of instances, 3 or more). A lot of applications do not need to maintain three copies of data and are happy with just two instances, one primary and a secondary with the data.

Consider the scenario where only two instances are present in the replica set. When the primary goes down, the secondary instance cannot form a proper majority because it only has 50 percent votes (its own vote) and thus cannot become a primary. If a majority of secondary instances goes down, then the primary instance steps down from primary and becomes a secondary, thus making the replica set unavailable for writes. Thus, a two-node replica set is useless as it doesn't stay available even when any of the instances goes down. It defeats the purpose of setting up a replica set and thus at least three instances are needed in a replica set.

Arbiters come handy in such scenarios. We set up a replica set instance with three instances with only two having data and one acting as an arbiter. We need not maintain three copies of data at the same time we eliminate the problem we faced by setting up a two-instance replica set.

Priority of replica set members

The priority flag can be used by itself or in conjunction with other options like `hidden`, `slaveDelay`, and `buildIndexes`, where we don't want the member with one of these three options to be ever made primary. We will look at these options soon.

Some more possible use cases where we would never want a replica set to become a primary are as follows:

▶ When the hardware configuration of a member would not be able to deal with the write and read requests should it become a primary and the only reason it is being put in there is for replicating the data.

▶ We have a multi data centers setup where one replica set instance is present in another data center for the sake of geographically distributing the data for DR purposes. Ideally, the network latency between the application server hosting the application and the database should be minimal for optimum performance. This could be achieved if both the servers (application server and the database server) are in the same data center. Not changing the priority of the replica set instance in another data center makes it equally eligible for being chosen as a primary and thus compromising on the application's performance if the server in other data center gets chosen as primary. In such scenarios, we can set the priority to be 0 for the server in the second data center and a manual cutover would be needed by the administrator to fail over to another data center should an emergency arise.

In both scenarios mentioned here, we could also have the respective members hidden so that the application client doesn't have a view of these members in the first place.

Similar to setting a priority to 0 for not allowing one to be primary, we can also be biased to one member to be primary whenever it is available by setting its priority to a value greater than 1, because the default value of priority is 1.

Suppose we have a scenario for budget reasons we have one of the members storing data on SSDs and remaining on spinning disks. We would ideally want the member with SSDs to be the primary whenever it is up and running. It is only when it is not available we would want another member to become a primary, In such scenarios we can set the priority of the member running on SSD to a value greater than 1. The value doesn't really matter as long as it is greater than the rest, that is, setting it to 1.5 or 2 makes no difference as long as priority of other members is less.

Hidden, slave delayed, and build index configuration

The term hidden for a replica set node is from an application client that is connected to the replica set and not for an administrator. For an administrator, the hidden members are equally important to be monitored and thus their state is seen in the rs.status() response. Hidden members participate in elections too like all other members.

For the slaveDelay option, most common use case is to ensure that the data in a member as a particular point of time lags behind the primary by the provided number of seconds and can be restored in case some unforeseen error has happened, say a human error for erroneously updating some data. Remember, longer the time delay, more is the time we get recover but at the cost of possibly stale data.

The `buildIndexes` option is useful in cases where we have a replica set member with non-production standard hardware and the cost of maintaining the indexes are not worth it. You may choose to set this option for members where no queries are executed on it. Obviously, if you set this option it can never become a primary member, and thus the priority option is forced to be set to `0`.

There's more...

You can achieve some interesting things using tags in replica sets. This would be discussed in a later recipe, after we learn about tags in the recipe *Building tagged replica sets*.

Stepping down as primary from the replica set

There are times when for some maintenance activity during business hours we would like to take a server out from the replica set, perform the maintenance and put it back in the replica set. If the server to be worked upon is the primary, we somehow need to step down from the primary member position, perform re-election and ensure that it doesn't get re-elected for a minimum given time frame. After the server becomes secondary once the step down operation is successful, we can take it out of the replica set, perform the maintenance activity and put it back in the replica set.

Getting ready

Refer to the recipe *Starting multiple instances as part of a replica set* from *Chapter 1, Installing and Starting the Server* for the prerequisites and know about the replica set basics. Set up a simple three-node replica set on your computer, as mentioned in the recipe.

How to do it...

Assuming at this point of time we have a replica set up and running, do the following:

1. Execute the following from the shell connected to one of the replica set members and see which instance currently is the primary:

   ```
   > rs.status()
   ```

2. Connect to that primary instance from the mongo shell and execute the following on the shell:

   ```
   > rs.stepDown()
   ```

3. The shell should reconnect again and you should see that the instance connected to and initially a primary instance now becomes secondary. Execute the following from the shell so that a new primary is now re-elected:

```
> rs.status()
```

4. You can now connect to the primary, modify the replica set configuration and go ahead with the administration on the servers.

How it works...

The preceding steps mentioned are pretty simple, but there are a couple of interesting things that we will see.

The method we saw previously, `rs.stepDown()` did not have any parameters. The function can in fact take a numeric value, which is the number of seconds for which the instance stepped down won't participate in the elections and won't become a primary and the default value for this is `60` seconds.

Another interesting thing to try out is what if the instance that was asked to step down has a higher priority than other instances. Well, it turns out that the priority doesn't matter when you step down. The instance stepped down will not become primary no matter what for the provided number of seconds. However, if priority is set for the instance stepped down and it is higher than others, then after the time given to `stepDown` elapses an election will happen and the instance with higher priority will become primary again.

Exploring the local database of a replica set

In this recipe, we will explore the local database from a replica set's perspective. The local database may contain collections that are not specific to replica sets, but we will focus only on the replica set specific collections and try to take a look at what's in them and what they mean.

Getting ready

Refer to the recipe *Starting multiple instances as part of a replica set* from *Chapter 1, Installing and Starting the Server* for the prerequisites and know about the replica set basics. Go ahead and set up a simple three-node replica set on your computer, as mentioned in the recipe.

How to do it...

1. With the replica set up and running, we need to open a shell connected to the primary. You may connect randomly to any one member; use `rs.status()` and then determine the primary.

2. With shell open, first switch to `local` database and the view the collections in the `local` database as follows:

```
> use local
switched to db local
> show collections
```

3. You should find a collection called `me`. Querying this collection should show us one document and it contains the hostname of the server to which we are currently connected to:

```
>db.me.findOne()
```

4. There would be two fields, the hostname and the `_id` field. Take a note of the `_id` field—it is important.

5. Take a look at the `replset.minvalid` collection. You will have to connect to a secondary member from the shell to execute the following query. Switch to the `local` database first:

```
> use local
switched to db local
> db.replset.minvalid.find()
```

6. This collection just contains the single document with a key `ts` and a value that is the timestamp till the time the secondary we are connected to is synchronized. Note down this time.

7. From the shell in primary, insert a document in any collection. We will use the database as test. Execute the following from the shell of the primary member:

```
> use test
switched to db test
> db.replTest.insert({i:1})
```

8. Query the secondary again, as follows:

```
> db.replset.minvalid.find()
```

9. We should see that the time against the field `ts` has now incremented corresponding to the time this replication happened from primary to secondary. With a slave delayed node, you will see this time getting updated only after the delay period has elapsed.

10. Finally, we will see the collection `system.replset`. This collection is the place where the replica set configuration is stored. Execute the following:

```
> db.system.replset.find().pretty()
```

11. Actually, when we execute `rs.conf()`, the following query gets executed:

```
db.getSisterDB("local").system.replset.findOne()
```

How it works...

The database local is a special (non-replicated) database that is used to hold the replication and instance specific details in it. Try creating a collection of your own in the local database and insert some data in it; it would not be replicated to the secondary nodes.

This database gives us some view of the data stored by mongo for internal use. However, as an administrator, it is good to know about these collections and the type of data in it.

Most the collections are pretty straightforward. From the shell of the secondary execute the query `db.me.findOne()` in the local database and we should see that `_id` there should match the `_id` field of the document present in the slaves collection.

The config document we see gives the hostname of the secondary instance that we are referring to. Note that the port and other configuration options of the replica set member are not present in this document. Finally, the `syncedTo` time tells us till what time the secondary instances are synced up with the primary. We saw the collection `replset.minvalid` on the secondary, which tells us the time till which it is synced with primary. This value in the `syncedTo` time on primary would be same as in `replset.minvalid` on respective secondary.

There's more...

We have not seen the oplog, which is interesting to look at. We would take a look at this special collection in a separate recipe, *Understanding and analyzing oplogs*.

Understanding and analyzing oplogs

Oplog is a special collection and forms the backbone of the MongoDB replication. When any write operation or configuration changes are done on the replica set's primary, they are written to the oplog on the primary. All the secondary members then tail this collection to get the changes to be replicated. Tailing is synonymous to tail command in Unix and can only be done on a special type of collection called capped collection. Capped collections are fixed size collections which maintain the insertion order just like a queue. When the collection's allocated space becomes full, the oldest data is overwritten. If you are not aware of capped collections and what tailable cursors are, please refer to *Creating and tailing a capped collection cursors in MongoDB* in *Chapter 5, Advanced Operations* for more details.

Oplog is a capped collection present in the non-replicated database called **local**. In our previous recipe, we saw what a `local` database is and what collections are present in it. Oplog is something we didn't discuss in last recipe, as it demands a lot more explanation and a dedicated recipe is needed to do justice.

Getting ready

Refer to the recipe *Starting multiple instances as part of a replica set* from *Chapter 1, Installing and Starting the Server* for the prerequisites and know about the replica set basics. Go ahead and set up a simple three-node replica set on your computer as mentioned in the recipe. Open a shell and connect to the primary member of the replica set. You will need to start the mongo shell and connect to the primary instance.

How to do it...

1. Execute the following steps after connecting to a primary from the shell to get the timestamp of the last operation present in the oplog. We would be interested in looking at the operations after this time.

   ```
   > use test
   > local = db.getSisterDB('local')
   > var cutoff = local.oplog.rs.find().sort({ts:-1}).limit(1).next().ts
   ```

2. Execute the following from the shell. Keep the output in the shell or copy it to some place. We will analyze it later:

   ```
   > local.system.namespaces.findOne({name:'local.oplog.rs'})
   ```

3. Insert 10 documents as follows:

   ```
   > for(i = 0; i < 10; i++) db.oplogTest.insert({'i':i})
   ```

4. Execute the following update to set a string value for all documents with value of i greater than 5, which is 6, 7, 8 and 9 in our case. It would be a multiupdate operation:

   ```
   > db.oplogTest.update({i:{$gt:5}}, {$set:{val:'str'}}, false, true)
   ```

5. Now, create the index as follows:

   ```
   > db.oplogTest.ensureIndex({i:1}, {background:1})
   ```

6. Execute the following query on oplog:

   ```
   > local.oplog.rs.find({ts:{$gt:cutoff}}).pretty()
   ```

How it works...

For those aware of messaging and its terminologies, Oplog can be looked at as a topic in messaging world with one producer, the primary instance, and multiple consumers, the secondary instances. Primary instance writes to an oplog all the contents that need to be replicated. Thus, any create, update, and delete operations as well as any reconfigurations on the replica sets would be written to the oplog and the secondary instances would tail (continuously read the contents of the oplog being added to it, similar to a tail with `-f` option command in Unix) the collection to get documents written by the primary. If the secondary has a `slaveDelay` configured, it will not read documents more than the maximum time minus the `slaveDelay` time from the oplog.

We started by saving an instance of the local database in the variable called `local` and identified a cutoff time that we would use for querying all the operations we will perform in this recipe from the oplog.

Executing a query on the `system.namespaces` collection in the local database shows us that the collection is a capped collection with a fixed size. For performance reasons capped collections are allocated continuous space on the filesystem and are preallocated. The size allocated by the server is dependent on the OS and CPU architecture. While starting the server the option `oplogSize` can be provided to mention the size of the oplog. The defaults are generally good enough for most cases. However, for development purpose, you can choose to override this value for a smaller value. Oplogs are capped collections that need to be preallocated a space on disk. This preallocation not only takes time when the replica set is first initialized but takes up a fixed amount of disk space. For development purpose, we generally start multiple MongoDB processes as part of the same replica set on same machine and would want them to be up and running as quickly as possible with minimum resource usage. Also, having the entire oplog in memory becomes possible if the oplog size is small. For all these reasons, it is advisable to start the local instances for development purpose with a small oplog size.

We performed some operations such as insert 10 documents and update four documents using a multi update and create an index. If we query the oplog for entries after the cutoff, we computed earlier we see 10 documents for each insert in it. The document looks something like this:

```
{
        "ts" : Timestamp(1392402144, 1),
        "h" : NumberLong("-4661965417977826137"),
        "v" : 2,          "op" : "i",
        "ns" : "test.oplogTest",
        "o" : {
                "_id" : ObjectId("52fe5edfd473d2f623718f51"),
                "i" : 0
        }
}
```

As we can see, we first look at the three fields: op, ns, and o. These stand for the operation, the fully qualified name of the collection into which the data is being inserted, and the actual object to be inserted. The operation i stand for insert operation. Note that the value of o, which is the document to be inserted, contains the _id field that got generated on the primary. We should see 10 such documents, one for each insert. What is interesting to see is what happens on a multi update operation. The primary puts four documents, one for each of them affected for the updates. In this case, the value op is u, which is for update and the query used to match the document is not the same as what we gave in the update function, but it is a query that uniquely finds a document based on the _id field. Since there is an index already in place for the _id field (created automatically for each collection), this operation to find the document to be updated is not expensive. The value of the field o is the same document we passed to the update function from the shell. The sample document in the oplog for the update is as follows:

```
{
    "ts" : Timestamp(1392402620, 1),
    "h" : NumberLong("-7543933489976433166"),
    "v" : 2,
    "op" : "u",
    "ns" : "test.oplogTest",
    "o2" : {
            "_id" : ObjectId("52fe5edfd473d2f623718f57")
    },
    "o" : {
            "$set" : {
                    "val" : "str"
            }
    }
}
```

The update in the oplog is the same as the one we provided. This is because the $set operation is idempotent, which means you may apply an operation safely any number of times.

However, update using $inc operator is not idempotent. Let's execute the following update:

```
> db.oplogTest.update({i:9}, {$inc:{i:1}})
```

In this case, the oplog would have the following as the value of o.

```
"o" : {
    "$set" : {
            "i" : 10
    }
}
```

This non-idempotent operation is put into oplog by Mongo smartly as an idempotent operation with the value of i set to a value that is expected to be after the increment operation once. Thus it is safe to replay an oplog any number of times without corrupting the data.

Finally, we can see that the index creation process is put in the oplog as an insert operation in the `system.indexes` collection. For large collections, index creation can take hours and thus the size of the oplog is very important to let the secondary catch up from where it hasn't replicated since the index creation started. However, since version 2.6, index creation initiated in background on primary will also be built in background on secondary instances.

For more details on the index creation on replica sets, visit the following URL: `http://docs.mongodb.org/master/tutorial/build-indexes-on-replica-sets/`.

Building tagged replica sets

In *Chapter 1, Installing and Starting the Server*, we saw how to set up a simple replica in *Starting multiple instances as part of a replica set* and saw what is the purpose of a replica set. We also have a good deal of explanation on what `WriteConcern` is in the *Appendix* of the book and why it is used. What we saw about write concerns is that it offers a minimum level guarantee for a certain write operation. However, with the concept of tags and write concerns, we can define a variety of rules and conditions which must be satisfied before a write operation is deemed successful and a response is sent to the user.

Consider some common use cases such as the following:

1. Application wants the write operation to be propagated to at least one server in each of its data center. This ensures that in event of a data center shutdown, other data centers will have the data that was written by the application.

2. If there are no multiple data centers, at least one member of a replica set is kept on different rack. For instance, if the rack's power supply goes down, the replica set will still be available (not necessarily for writes) as at least one member is running on a different rack. In such scenarios, we would want the write to be propagated to at least two racks before responding back to the client with a successful write.

3. It is possible that a reporting application queries a group of secondary of a replica set for generating some reports regularly. (Such secondary might be configured to never become a primary). After each write, we want to ensure that the write operation is replicated to at least one reporting replica member before acknowledging the write as successful.

The preceding use cases are a few of the common use cases that arise and are not addressed using simple write concerns that we have seen earlier. We need a different mechanism to cater to these requirements and replica sets with tags is what we need.

Obviously, the next question is what exactly are tags? Let's take an example of a blog. Various posts in the blog have different tags attached to them. These tags allow us to easily search, group, and relate posts together. Tags are some user defined text with some meaning attached to it. If we draw an analogy between the blog post and the replica set members, similar to how we attach tags to a post, we can attach tags to each replica set member. For example, in a multiple data center scenario with two replica set members in data center 1 (dc1) and one member in data center 2 (dc2), we can have the following tags assigned to the members. The name of the key and the value assigned to the tag is arbitrary and is chosen during design of the application; you may choose to even assign any tags like the administrator who set up the server if you really find it useful to address your use case:

Replica Set Member	Tag
Replica set member 1	`{'datacentre': 'dc1', 'rack': 'rack-dc1-1'}`
Replica set member 2	`{'datacentre': 'dc1', 'rack': 'rack-dc1-2'}`
Replica set member 3	`{'datacentre': 'dc2', 'rack': 'rack-dc2-2'}`

That is good enough to lay the foundation of what a replica set tags are. In this recipe, we will see how to assign tags to replica set members and more importantly, how to make use of them to address some of the sample use cases we saw earlier.

Getting ready

Refer to the recipe *Starting multiple instances as part of a replica set from Chapter 1, Installing and Starting the Server* for the prerequisites and know about the replica set basics. Go ahead and set up a simple three-node replica set on your computer, as mentioned in the recipe. Open a shell and connect to the primary member of the replica set.

If you need to know about write concerns, refer to the overview of write concerns in the *Appendix* of the book.

For inserting documents in the database, we will use Python as it gives us an interactive interface like the mongo shell. Refer to the recipe *Connecting to a single node using a Python client* in *Chapter 1, Installing and Starting the Server* for steps on how to install pymongo. Mongo shell would have been the most ideal candidate for the demonstration of the insert operations, but there are certain limitations around the usage of the shell with our custom write concern. Technically, any programming language with the write concerns mentioned in the recipe for insert operations would work fine.

How to do it...

1. With the replica set started, we will add tags to it and reconfigure it as follows. The following commands are executed from the mongo shell:

```
> var conf = rs.conf()
> conf.members[0].tags = {'datacentre': 'dc1', 'rack': 'rack-dc1-1'}
> conf.members[1].tags = {'datacentre': 'dc1', 'rack': 'rack-dc1-2'}
> conf.members[2].priority = 0
> conf.members[2].tags = {'datacentre': 'dc2', 'rack': 'rack-dc2-1'}
```

2. With the replica set tags set (not that we have not yet reconfigured the replica set), we need to define some custom write concerns. First, we define one that will ensure that the data gets replicated to at least to one server in each data center. Execute the following in the mongo shell again:

```
> conf.settings = {'getLastErrorModes' : {'MultiDC':{datacentre : 2}}}
> rs.reconfig(conf)
```

3. Start the python shell and execute the following:

```
>>> import pymongo
>>> client = pymongo.MongoClient('localhost:27000,localhost:27001', replicaSet='replSetTest')
>>> db = client.test
```

4. We will now execute the following insert:

```
>>>db.multiDCTest.insert({'i':1}, w='MultiDC', wtimeout=5000)
```

5. The preceding insert goes through successfully and the ObjectId would be printed out; you may query the collection to confirm from either the mongo shell or Python shell.

6. Since our primary is one of the servers in data centre 1, we will now stop the server listening to port 27002, which is the one with priority 0 and tagged to be in a different data center.

7. Once the server is stopped (you may confirm using the rs.status() helper function from the mongo shell), execute the following insert again, this insert should error out:

```
>>>db.multiDCTest.insert({'i':2}, w='MultiDC', wtimeout=5000)
```

8. Restart the stopped mongo server.

9. Similarly, we can achieve rack awareness by ensuring that the write propagates to at least two racks (in any data centre) by defining a new configuration as follows from the mongo shell:

```
{'MultiRack':{rack : 2}}
```

10. The settings value of the conf object would then be as follows. Once set, reconfigure the replica set again using `rs.reconfig(conf)` from the mongo shell:

```
{
    'getLastErrorModes' : {
            'MultiDC':{datacentre : 2},
            'MultiRack':{rack : 2}
    }
}
```

11. We saw `WriteConcern` used with replica set tags to achieve some functionality like data center and rack awareness. Let's see how we can use replica set tags with read operations.

12. We will see how to make use of replica set tags with read preference. Let's reconfigure the set by adding one more tag to mark a secondary member that will be used to execute some hourly stats reporting.

13. Execute the following steps to reconfigure the set from the mongo shell:

```
> var conf = rs.conf()
> conf.members[2].tags.type = 'reports'
> rs.reconfig(conf)
```

14. This will configure the same member with priority 0 and the one in a different data center with an additional tag called type with a value reports.

15. We now go back to the python shell and perform the following steps:

```
>>> curs = db.multiDCTest.find(read_preference=pymongo.
ReadPreference.SECONDARY,
 tag_sets=[{'type':'reports'}])
>>> curs.next()
```

16. The preceding execution should show us one document from the collection (as we has inserted data in this test collection in previous steps).

17. Stop the instance which we have tagged for reporting, that is, the server listening to connections on port `27002` and execute the following on the python shell again:

```
>>> curs = db.multiDCTest.find(read_preference=pymongo.
ReadPreference.SECONDARY,
  tag_sets=[{'type':'reports'}])
>>> curs.next()
```

18. This time around, the execution should fail and state that no secondary found with the required tag sets.

How it works...

In this recipe, we did a lot of operations on tagged replica sets and saw how it can affect the write operations using `WriteConcern` and read operations using `ReadPreference`. Let's look at them in some details now.

WriteConcern in tagged replica sets

We set up a replica set that was up and running, which we reconfigured to add tags. We tagged the first two servers in datacenter 1 and in different racks (servers running listening to port `27000` and `27001` for client connections) and the third one in datacenter 2 (server listening to port `27002` for client connections). We also ensured that the member in datacenter 2 doesn't become a primary by setting its priority to `0`.

Our first objective is to ensure that the write operations to the replica set gets replicated to at least one member in the two datacenters. To ensure this, we define a write concern as follows `{'MultiDC':{datacentre : 2}}`. Here, we first define the name of the write concern as MultiDC. The value which is a JSON object has one key with name datacenter, which is same as the key used for the tag we attached to the replica set and the value is a number 2, which will be looked as the number of distinct values of the given tag that should acknowledge the write before it is deemed successful.

For instance, in our case, when the write comes to server 1 in datacenter 1, the number of distinct values of the tag datacenter is 1. If the write operation gets replicated to the second server, the number still stays one as the value of the tag datacenter is same as the first member. It is only when the third server acknowledges the write operation, the write satisfies the defined condition of replicating the write to distinct two values of the tag *datacenter* in the replica set. Note that the value can only be a number and not have something like `{datacentre : 'dc1'}` this definition is invalid and an error will be thrown while re-configuring the replica set.

But we need to register this write concern somewhere with the server. This is done in the final step of the configuration by setting the settings value in configuration JSON. The value to set is `getLastErrorModes`. The value of `getLastErrorModes` is a JSON document with all possible write concerns defined in it. We later defined one more write concern for write propagated to at least two racks. This is conceptually in line with MultiDC write concern and thus we will not be discussing it in details here. After setting all the required tags and the settings, we reconfigure the replica set for the changes to take effect.

Once reconfigured, we perform some write operations using the MultiDC write concern. When two members in two distinct datacenters are available, the write goes through successfully. However, when the server in second datacenter goes down, the write operation times out and throws an exception to the client initiating the write. This demonstrates that the write operation will succeed or fail as per how we intended.

We just saw how these custom tags can be used to address some interesting use cases, which are not supported by the product implicitly as far as write operations are concerned. Similar to write operations, read operations can take full advantages of these tags to address some use cases such as reading from a fixed set of secondary members that are tagged with a particular value.

ReadPreference in tagged replica sets

We added another custom tag annotating a member to be used for reporting purposes, we then fire a query operation with the read preference to query a secondary and provide the tag sets that should be looked for before considering the member as a candidate for read operation. Remember that when using primary as the read preference, we cannot use tags and that is reason we explicitly specified the value of the `read_preference` to `SECONDARY`.

Configuring the default shard for non-sharded collections

In the recipe *Starting a simple sharded environment of two shards* in *Chapter 1, Installing and Starting the Server* we set up a simple two-shard server. In the recipe *Connecting to a shard in the shell and performing operations* in *Chapter 1, Installing and Starting the Server* we added data to a person collection that was sharded. However, for any collection that is not sharded, all the documents end up on one shard called the primary shard. This situation is acceptable for small databases with relatively small number of collections. However, if the database size increases and at the same time the number of un-sharded collections increase, we end up overloading a particular shard (which is the primary shard for a database) with a lot of data from these un-sharded collections. All query operations for such un-sharded collections as well as those on the collections whose particular range in the shard reside on this server instance will be directed to this it. In such scenario, we can have the primary shard of a database changed to some other instance so that these un-sharded collections get balanced out across different instances.

In this recipe, we will see how to view this primary shard and change it to some other server whenever needed.

Getting ready

Following the recipe *Starting a simple sharded environment of two shards* in *Chapter 1, Installing and Starting the Server* set up and start a sharded environment. From the shell, connect to the started mongos process. Also, assuming that the two shards servers are listening to port `27000` and `27001`, connect from the shell to these two processes. So, we have a total of three shells opened, one connected to the mongos process and two to these individual shards.

We need are using the `test` database for this recipe and sharding has to be enabled on it. If it not, then you need to execute the following on the shell connected to the mongos process:

```
mongos> use test
mongos> sh.enableSharding('test')
```

How to do it...

1. From the shell connected to the mongos process, execute the following two commands:

    ```
    mongos> db.testCol.insert({i : 1})
    mongos> sh.status()
    ```

2. In the databases, look out for `test` database and take a note of the `primary`. Suppose the following is a part (showing the part under databases only) of the output of `sh.status()`:

    ```
    databases:
        {  "_id" : "admin",  "partitioned" : false,  "primary" : "config"
    }
        {  "_id" : "test",  "partitioned" : true,  "primary" :
    "shard0000" }
    ```

    The second document under the databases shows us that the database `test` is enabled for sharding (because partitioned is true) and the primary shard is `shard0000`.

3. The primary shard, which is `shard0000` in our case, is the mongod process listening to port `27000`. Open the shell connected to this process and execute the following in it:

    ```
    > db.testCol.find()
    ```

4. Now, connect to another mongod process listening to port `27001` and again execute the following query:

    ```
    > db.testCol.find()
    ```

    Note that the data would be found only on the primary shard and not on other shard.

5. Execute the following command from the mongos shell:

    ```
    mongos> use admin

    mongos> db.runCommand({movePrimary:'test', to:'shard0001'})
    ```

6. Execute the following command from mongo shell connected to the mongos process:

    ```
    mongos> sh.status()
    ```

7. From the shell connected to the mongos processes running on port `27000` and `27001`, execute the following query:

    ```
    > db.testCol.find()
    ```

How it works...

We started a sharded setup and connected to it from the mongos process. We started by inserting a document in the `testCol` collection that is not enabled for sharding in the test database, which is not enabled for sharding as well. In such cases, the data lies on shard called the **primary shard**. Do not misunderstand this for the primary of a replica set. This is a shard (that itself can be a replica set) and it is the shard chosen by default for all database and collection for which sharding is not enabled.

When we add the data to a non-sharded collection, it was seen only on the shard that is primary. Executing `sh.status()` tells us the primary shard. To change the primary, we need to execute a command from the admin database from the shell connected to the mongos process. The command is as follows:

```
db.runCommand({movePrimary:'<database whose primary shard is to be
changed>', to:'<target shard>'})
```

Once the primary shard was changed, all existing data of non-sharded database and collection was migrated to the new primary and all subsequent writes to non-sharded collections will go to this shard.

Use this command with caution as it will migrate all the unsharded collections to the new primary, which may take time for big collections.

Manual split and migration of chunks

Though MongoDB does a good job of splitting and migrating chunks across shards to maintain the balance, under some circumstances such as a small number of documents or relatively large number of small documents where the automatic balancer doesn't split the collection, an administrator might want to split and migrate the chunks manually. In this recipe, we will see how to split and migrate the collection manually across shards. For this recipe, we will set up a simple shard as we saw in *Chapter 1, Installing and Starting the Server*.

Getting ready

Refer to the recipe *Starting a simple sharded environment of two shards* in *Chapter 1, Installing and Starting the Server* to set up and start a sharded environment. It is preferred to start a clean environment without any data in it. From the shell, connect to the started mongos process.

How to do it...

1. Connect to the mongos process from the mongo shell and enable sharding on the test database and the splitAndMoveTest collection as follows:

```
> sh.enableSharding('test')
> sh.shardCollection('test.splitAndMoveTest', {_id:1}, false)
```

2. Let's load the data in the collection as follows:

```
> for(i = 1; i <= 10000 ; i++) db.splitAndMoveTest.insert({_id : i})
```

3. Once the data is loaded, execute the following:

```
> db. splitAndMoveTest.find().explain()
```

Note the number of documents in two shards in the plan. The value to lookout for is in the two documents under the shards key in the result of explain plan. Within these two documents the field to lookout for is n.

4. Execute the following to see the splits of the collection:

```
> config = db.getSisterDB('config')
> config.chunks.find({ns:'test.splitAndMoveTest'}).pretty()
```

5. Split the chunk into two at 5000 as follows:

```
> sh.splitAt('test.splitAndMoveTest', {_id:5000})
```

6. Splitting it doesn't migrate it to the second server. See what exactly happened with the chunks by executing the following query again:

```
> config.chunks.find({ns:'test.splitAndMoveTest'}).pretty()
```

7. We will now move the second chunk to the second shard:

```
> sh.moveChunk('test.splitAndMoveTest', {_id:5001}, 'shard0001')
```

8. Execute the following query again and confirm the migration:

```
> config.chunks.find({ns:'test.splitAndMoveTest'}).pretty()
```

9. Alternatively, the following explain plan will show a split of about 50-50:

```
> db. splitAndMoveTest.find().explain()
```

How it works...

We simulate a small data load by adding monotonically increasing numbers and discover that the numbers are not split across two shards evenly by viewing the query plan. It is not a problem as the chunk size needs to reach a particular threshold, 64 MB by default, before the balancer decides to migrate the chunks across the shards to maintain balance. This is pretty perfect as in real world, when the data size gets huge we will see that eventually over a period of time the shards are well balanced.

However, if the administration does decide to split and migrate the chunks, it is possible to do it manually. The two helper functions `sh.splitAt` and `sh.moveChunk` are there to do this work. Let's look at their signatures and see what they do.

The function `sh.splitAt` takes two arguments, first is the namespace, which has the format `<database>.<collection name>` and the second parameter is the query that acts as the split point to split the chunk into two, possibly two uneven portions depending on where the given document is in the chunk. There is another method, `sh.splitFind`, which will try and split the chunk in two equal portions.

Splitting doesn't mean the chunk moves to another shard, it just breaks one big chunk into two, but the data stays on the same shard. It is an inexpensive operation which involves updating the config DB.

Next, we executed was to migrate the chunk to a different shard after we split it into two. The operation `sh.MoveChunk` is used just to do that. This function takes three parameters, first one is again the namespace of the collection that has the format `<database>.<collection name>`, second parameter is a query a document whose chunk would be migrated, and the third parameter is the destination chunk.

Once the migration is done, the query's plan shows us that the data is split in two chunks.

Domain-driven sharding using tags

The recipes *Starting a simple sharded environment of two shards* and *Connecting to a shard in the shell and performing operations* in *Chapter 1, Installing and Starting the Server* explained how to start a simple two server shard and then insert data in a collection after choosing a shard key. The data that gets sharded is more technical where the data chunk is kept to a manageable size by Mongo by splitting it into multiple chunks and migrating the chunks across shards to keep the chunk distribution even across shards. But what if we want the sharding to be more domain oriented? Suppose we have a database for storing postal addresses and we shard based on postal codes where we know the postal code range of a city. What we can do is tag the shard servers according to the city name as the tag, add shard range (postal codes), and associate this range with the tag. This way, we can state which servers can contain the postal addresses of which cities. For instance, we know that Mumbai being most populous city, the number of addresses would be huge and thus we add two shards for Mumbai. On the other hand, one shard should be enough to cope up with the volumes of the Pune city. For now we tag just one shard. In this recipe, we will see how to achieve this use case using tag aware sharding. If the description is confusing, don't worry, we will see how to implement what we just discussed.

Getting ready

Refer to the recipe *Starting a simple sharded environment of two shard* in *Chapter 1, Installing and Starting the Server* for information on how to start a simple shard. However, for this recipe, we will add an additional shard. So, we will now start three mongo servers listening to port `27000`, `27001`, and `27002`. Again, it is recommended to start off with a clean database. For the purpose of this recipe, we will be using the collection `userAddress` to store the data.

How to do it...

1. Assuming that we have three shard up and running, let's execute the following:

   ```
   mongos> sh.addShardTag('shard0000', 'Mumbai')

   mongos> sh.addShardTag('shard0001', 'Mumbai')

   mongos> sh.addShardTag('shard0002', 'Pune')
   ```

2. With tags defined, let's define range of pin codes that will map to a tag:

   ```
   mongos> sh.addTagRange('test.userAddress', {pincode:400001},
   {pincode:400999}, 'Mumbai')

   mongos> sh.addTagRange('test.userAddress', {pincode:411001},
   {pincode:411999}, 'Pune')
   ```

3. Enable sharding for the test database and the `userAddress` collection as follows:

```
mongos> sh.enableSharding('test')
mongos> sh.shardCollection('test.userAddress', {pincode:1})
```

4. Insert the following documents in the `userAddress` collection:

```
mongos> db.userAddress.insert({_id:1, name: 'Varad', city: 'Pune',
pincode: 411001})

mongos> db.userAddress.insert({_id:2, name: 'Rajesh', city:
'Mumbai', pincode: 400067})

mongos> db.userAddress.insert({_id:3, name: 'Ashish', city:
'Mumbai', pincode: 400101})
```

5. Execute the following plans:

```
mongos> db.userAddress.find({city:'Pune'}).explain()
mongos> db.userAddress.find({city:'Mumbai'}).explain()
```

How it works...

Suppose we want to partition data driven by domain in a shard, we can use tag aware sharding. It is an excellent mechanism that lets us tag the shards and then split the data range across shards identified by the tags. We don't really have to bother about the actual machines and their address hosting the shard. Tags act as a good abstraction in the way, we can tag a shard with multiple tags and one tag can be applied to multiple shards.

In our case, we have three shards and we apply tags to each of them using the `sh.addShardTag` method. The method takes the shard ID, which we can see in the `sh.status` call with the *shards* key. This `sh.addShardTag` method can be used to keep adding tags to a shard. Similarly, there is a helper method `sh.removeShardTag` to remove an assignment of the tag from the shard. Both these methods take two parameters, the first one is the shard ID and second one of the tag to remove.

Once the tagging is done, we assign range of the values of the shard key to the tag. The method `sh.addTagRange` is used to do that. It accepts four parameters, first one is the namespace, which is the fully qualified name of the collection, second and third parameters are the start and end value of the range for this shard key and the fourth parameter is the tag name of the shards hosting the range being added. For example, the call `sh.addTagRange('test.userAddress', {pincode:400001}, {pincode:400999}, 'Mumbai')` says we are adding the shard range `400001` to `400999` for the collection `test.userAddress`, and this range will be stored in the shards tagged as `Mumbai`.

Once the tagging and adding tag range is done, we enabled sharding on database and collection and add data to it from Mumbai and Pune city with respective pin codes. We then query and explain the plan to see that the data did indeed reside on the shards we have tagged for Pune and Mumbai city. We can also add new shards to this sharded setup and accordingly tag the new shard. The balancer will then accordingly balance the data based on the value it is tagged. For instance, if the addresses in Pune increase overloading a shard, we can add a new shard with tag as Pune. The postal address for Pune will then be sharded across these two server instances for tagged for Pune city.

Exploring the config database in a sharded setup

Config database is the backbone of a sharded setup in Mongo. It stores all the metadata of the shard setup and has a dedicated mongod process running for it. When a mongos process is started we provide it with the config servers' URL. In this recipe, we will take a look at some collections in the config database and dive deep into their content and significance.

Getting ready

We need a sharded setup for this recipe. Refer to the recipe *Starting a simple sharded environment of two shard* in *Chapter 1, Installing and Starting the Server* for information on how to start a simple shard. Additionally, connect to the mongos process from a shell.

How to do it...

1. From the console connected to the mongos process, switch to the config database and execute the following:

   ```
   mongos> use config
   mongos>show collections
   ```

2. From the list of all collections, we will visit a few. We start with the databases collection. This keeps a track of all the databases on this shard. Execute the following from the shell:

   ```
   mongos> db.databases.find()
   ```

3. The content of the result is pretty straightforward, the value of the field _id is for the database. The value of field partitioned tells us whether sharding is enabled for the database or not; true indicates it is enabled and the field primary gives the primary shard where the data of non-sharded collections reside upon.

4. Next, we will visit the collections collection. Execute the following from the shell:

   ```
   mongos> db.collections.find().pretty()
   ```

This collection, unlike the databases collection we saw earlier, contains only those collections for which we have enabled sharding. The field _id gives the namespace of the collection in the <database>.<collection name> format, the field key gives the shard key and the field unique, indicates whether the shard key is unique or not. These three fields come as the three parameters of the sh.shardCollection function in that very order.

5. Next, we look at the chunks collection. Execute the following on the shell. If the database was clean when we started this recipe, we won't have a lot of data in this:

```
mongos> db.chunks.find().pretty()
```

6. We then look at the tags collection and execute the following query:

```
mongos> db.tags.find().pretty()
```

7. Let's query the mongos collection as follows.

```
mongos> db.mongos.find().pretty()
```

This is a simple collection that gives the list of all mongos instances connected to the shard with the details like the host and port on which the mongos instance is running, which forms the _id field. The version and figures like for how much time the process is up and running in seconds.

8. Finally, we look at the version collection. Execute the following query. Note that is not similar to other queries we execute:

```
mongos>db.getCollection('version').findOne()
```

How it works...

We saw the collections and databases collection while we queried them and they are pretty simple. Let's look at the collection called chunks. Here is a sample document from this collection:

```
{
        "_id" : "test.userAddress-pincode_400001.0",
        "lastmod" : Timestamp(1, 3),
        "lastmodEpoch" : ObjectId("53026514c902396300fd4812"),
        "ns" : "test.userAddress",
        "min" : {
                "pincode" : 400001
        },
        "max" : {
                "pincode" : 411001
        },
        "shard" : "shard0000"
}
```

The fields of interest are ns, min, max, and shard, which are the namespace of the collection, the minimum value present in the chunk, the maximum value present in the chunk, and the shard on which this chunk lies, respectively. The value of the chunk size is 64 MB by default. This can be seen in the settings collection. Execute db.settings.find() from the shell and look at the value of the field value, which is the size of the chunk in MB. Chunks are restricted to this small size to ease the migration process across shards, if needed. When the size of the chunk exceeds this threshold, mongo server finds a suitable point in the existing chunk to break it into two and adds a new entry in this chunks collection. This operation is called splitting, which is inexpensive as the data stays where it is; it is just logically split into multiple chunks. The balancer on mongo tries to keep the chunks across shards balanced and the moment it sees some imbalance, it migrates these chunks to a different shard. This is expensive and also depends largely on the network bandwidth. If we use sh.status(), the implementation actually queries the collections we saw and prints the pretty formatted result.

5

Advanced Operations

In this chapter, we will cover the following recipes:

- ▶ Atomic find and modify operations
- ▶ Implementing atomic counters in Mongo
- ▶ Implementing server-side scripts
- ▶ Creating and tailing a capped collection cursors in MongoDB
- ▶ Converting a normal collection to capped collection
- ▶ Storing binary data in Mongo
- ▶ Storing large data in Mongo using GridFS
- ▶ Storing data to GridFS from Java client
- ▶ Storing data to GridFS from Python client
- ▶ Implementing triggers in Mongo using oplog
- ▶ Flat plane (2D) geospatial queries in Mongo using geospatial indexes
- ▶ Spherical indexes and GeoJSON compliant data in Mongo
- ▶ Implementing full text search in Mongo
- ▶ Integrating MongoDB for full text search with Elasticsearch

Introduction

In *Chapter 2, Command-line Operations and Indexes*, we saw how to perform basic operations from the shell to query, update, and insert documents, and also saw different types of indexes and index creation. In this chapter, we will see some of the advanced features of Mongo, such as GridFS, Geospatial Indexes, and Full text search. Other recipes we will see include an introduction and use of capped collections and implementing server-side scripts in MongoDB.

Atomic find and modify operations

In *Chapter 2, Command-line Operations and Indexes*, we had some recipes that explained various CRUD operations we perform in MongoDB. There was one concept that we didn't cover and it is atomically find and modify documents. Modification consists of both update and delete operations. In this recipe, we will go through the basics of MongoDB's `findAndModify` operation. In the next recipe, we will use this method to implement a counter.

Getting ready

Look at the recipe *Installing single node MongoDB* in *Chapter 1, Installing and Starting the Server* and start a single instance of MongoDB. That is the only prerequisite for this recipe. Start a mongo shell and connect to the started server.

How to do it...

1. We will test a document in `atomicOperationsTest` collection. Execute the following from the shell:

    ```
    > db.atomicOperationsTest.drop()
    > db.atomicOperationsTest.insert({i:1})
    ```

2. Execute the following from the mongo shell and observe the output:

    ```
    > db.atomicOperationsTest.findAndModify({
        query: {i: 1},
        update: {$set : {text : 'Test String'}},
        new: false
      }
    )
    ```

3. We will execute another one this time but with slightly different parameters; observe the output for this operation:

    ```
    > db.atomicOperationsTest.findAndModify({
        query: {i: 1},
        update: {$set : {text : 'Updated String'}}, fields: {i:
          1, text :1, _id:0},
        new: true
      }
    )
    ```

4. We will execute another update this time that would upsert the document as follows:

```
>db.atomicOperationsTest.findAndModify({
    query: {i: 2},
    update: {$set : {text : 'Test String'}},
    fields: {i: 1, text :1, _id:0},
    upsert: true,
    new: true
    }
)
```

5. Now, query the collection once as follows and see the documents present:

```
> db.atomicOperationsTest.find().pretty()
```

6. We will finally execute the delete as follows:

```
>db.atomicOperationsTest.findAndModify({
    query: {i: 2},
    remove: true,
    fields: {i: 1, text :1, _id:0},
    new: false
    }
)
```

How it works...

If we perform find and update operations independently by first finding the document and then updating it in MongoDB, the results might not be as expected. There might be an interleaving update between the find and the update operations, which may have changed the document state. In some of the specific use cases, like implementing atomic counters, this is not acceptable and thus we need a way to atomically find, update, and return a document. The returned value is either the one before the update is applied or after the update is applied and is decided by the invoking client.

Now that we have executed the steps in the preceding section, let's see what we actually did and what all these fields in the JSON document passed as the parameter to the findAndModify operation mean. Starting with step 3, we gave a document as a parameter to the findAndModify function that contains the fields query, update, and new.

The query field specifies the search parameters that would be used to find the document and the update field contains the modifications that need to be applied. The third field, new, if set to true, tells MongoDB to return the updated document.

In step 4, we actually added a new field to the document passed as a parameter called **fields** that is used to select a limited set of fields from the result document returned. Also, the value of the field new is `true`, which tells that we want the updated document that is, the one after the update operation is executed and not the one before.

In step 5 contains a new field called `upsert`, which upserts (update + insert) the document. That is, if the document with the given query is found, it is updated else a new one is created and updated. If the document didn't exist and an upsert happened, having the value of the parameter `new` as `false` will return `null`. This is because there was nothing present before the update operation was executed.

Finally, in step 7, instead of the `update` field, we used the `remove` field with the value `true` indicating that the document is to be removed. Also, the value of the new field is `false`, which means that we expect the document that got deleted.

See also

An interesting use case of atomic `FindandModify` operations is developing an atomic counter in Mongo. In our next recipe, we will see how to implement this use case.

Implementing atomic counters in Mongo

Atomic counters are a necessity for a large number of use cases. Mongo doesn't have a built in feature for atomic counters; nevertheless, it can be easily implemented using some of its cool offerings. In fact, with the help of previously described `findAndModify()` command, implementing is quite simple. Refer to the previous recipe *Atomic find and modify operations* to know what atomic find and modify operations are in Mongo.

Getting ready

Look at the recipe *Installing single node MongoDB* in *Chapter 1, Installing and Starting the Server* and start a single instance of Mongo. That is the only prerequisite for this recipe. Start a mongo shell and connect to the started server.

How to do it...

1. Execute the following piece of code from the mongo shell:

```
> function getNextSequence(counterId) {
  return db.counters.findAndModify(
    {
      query: {_id : counterId},
      update: {$inc : {count : 1}},
```

```
        upsert: true,
        fields:{count:1, _id:0},
        new: true
    }
  ).count
}
```

2. Now from the shell invoke the following:

```
> getNextSequence('Posts Counter')
> getNextSequence('Posts Counter')
> getNextSequence('Profile Counter')
```

How it works...

The function is as simple as a `findAndModify` operation on a collection used to store all the counters. The counter identifier is the `_id` field of the document stored and the value of the counter is stored in the field `count`. The document passed to the `findAndModify` operations accepts the query, which uniquely identifies the document storing the current count—a query using the `_id` field. The update operation is an `$inc` operation that will increment the value of the `count` field by 1. But what if the document doesn't exist? This will happen on the first invocation of the counter. To take care of this scenario, we will set the `upsert` flag to `true`. The value of `count` will always start with 1 and there is no way it would accept any user-defined start number for the sequence or a custom increment step. To address such requirements, we will have to specifically add a document with the initialized values to the counters collection. Finally, we are interested in the state of the counter after the value is incremented; hence, we set the value of the field `new` as `true`.

On invoking this method thrice (as we did), we should see the following in the collection counters. Simply execute the following query:

```
>db.counters.find()
{ "_id" : "Posts Counter", "count" : 2 }
{ "_id" : "Profile Counter", "count" : 1 }
```

Using this small function, we now have implemented atomic counters in Mongo.

See also

We can store such common code on a Mongo server that would be available for execution in other functions. Look at the recipe *Implementing server-side scripts* to see how we can store JavaScript functions on the Mongo server. This allows us even to invoke this function from other programming language clients.

Implementing server-side scripts

In this recipe, we will see how to write server stored JavaScript similar to stored procedures in relational databases. This is a common use case where other pieces of code require access to these common functions and we have them in one central place. To demonstrate server-side scripts, the function will simply add two numbers.

There are two parts to this recipe. First, we see how to load the scripts from the collections on the client-side JavaScript shell and secondly, we will see how to execute these functions on the server.

 The documentation specifically mentions that it is not recommended to use server-side scripts. Security is one concern though if the data is not properly audited and hence we need to be careful with what functions are defined. Since Mongo 2.4, the server-side JavaScript engine is V8, which can execute multiple threads in parallel as opposed to the engine prior to version 2.4 of Mongo, which executes only one thread at a time.

Getting ready

Look at the recipe *Installing single node MongoDB* in *Chapter 1, Installing and Starting the Server* and start a single instance of Mongo. That is the only prerequisite for this recipe. Start a mongo shell and connect to the started server.

How to do it...

1. Create a new function called `add` and save it to the collection `db.system.js` as follows. The current database should be test:

   ```
   > use test
   > db.system.js.save({ _id : 'add', value : function(num1, num2)
   {return num1 + num2}})
   ```

2. Now that this function is defined, load all the functions as follows:

   ```
   > db.loadServerScripts()
   ```

3. Now, invoke `add` and see if it works:

   ```
   > add(1, 2)
   ```

4. We will now use this function and execute this on the server-side instead: Execute the following from the shell:

   ```
   > use test
   > db.eval('return add(1, 2)')
   ```

5. Execute the following steps (you can execute the preceding command):

```
> use test1
> db.eval('return add(1, 2)')
```

How it works...

The collection `system.js` is a special MongoDB collection used to store JavaScript code. We add a new server-side JavaScript using the `save` function in this collection. The `save` function is just a convenience function that inserts the document if it is not present or updates an existing one. The objective is to add a new document to this collection which you may add even using `insert` or `upsert`.

The secret lies in the method `loadServerScripts`. Let's look at the code of this method: `this.system.js.find().forEach(function(u){eval(u._id + " = " + u.value);});`

It evaluates a JavaScript using the `eval` function and assigns the function defined in the `value` attribute of the document to a variable named with the name given in the `_id` field of the document for each document present in the collection `system.js`.

For example, if the following document is present in the collection `system.js`, `{ _id : 'add', value : function(num1, num2) {return num1 + num2}}`, then the function given in the `value` field of the document will be assigned to the variable named as `add` in the current shell. The value `add` is given in the `_id` field of the document.

These scripts do not really execute on the server but their definition is stored on the server in a collection. The JavaScript method `loadServerScripts`, just instantiates some variables in the current shell and make those functions available for invocation. It is the JavaScript interpreter of the shell that executes these functions and not the server. The collection `system.js` is defined in the scope of the database. Once loaded, these act as JavaScript functions defined in the shell and hence the functions are available throughout the scope of the shell irrespective of the database currently active.

As far as security is concerned, if the shell is connected to the server with security enabled, then the user invoking `loadServerScripts` must have privileges to read the collections in the database. For more details on enabling security and various roles a user can have, refer to the recipe *Setting up users in Mongo* in *Chapter 4, Administration*. As we saw earlier, the function `loadServerScripts` reads data from the collection `system.js` and if the user doesn't have privileges to read from the collection, the function invocation will fail. Apart from that, the functions executed from the shell after being loaded should have appropriate privileges. For instance, if a function inserts/updates in any collection, the user should have read and write privileges on that particular collection accessed from the function.

Executing scripts on the server is perhaps what one would expect to be server-side script as opposed to executing in the shell connected. In this case, the functions are evaluated on the server's JavaScript engine and the security checks are more stringent as long running functions can hold locks, having detrimental effects on the performance. The wrapper to invoke the execution of a JavaScript code on the server-side is the db.eval function accepting the code to evaluate on the server-side along with the parameters if any.

Before evaluating the function, the write operation takes a global lock; this can be skipped if the parameter nolock is used. For instance, the preceding add function can be invoked as follows instead of calling db.eval and achieving the same results. We additionally provided the nolock field to instruct the server not to acquire the global lock before evaluating the function. If this function were to perform write operations on a collection, then the nolock field is ignored.

```
> db.runCommand({eval: function (num1, num2) {return num1 + num2},
args:[1, 2],nolock:true})
```

If security is enabled on the server, the invoking user needs to have the following four roles: userAdminAnyDatabase, dbAdminAnyDatabase, readWriteAnyDatabase, and clusterAdmin (on the admin database) to successfully invoke the db.eval function.

Programming languages do provide a way for invocation of such server-side scripts using the eval function. For instance, in Java API, the class com.mongodb.DB has the method eval to invoke server-side JavaScript code. Such server-side executions are highly useful when we want to avoid unnecessary network traffic for the data and get the result to the clients. However, too much logic on the database server can quickly make things difficult to maintain and affect the performance of the server badly.

 As of MongoDB 3.0.3, the db.eval() method is being deprecated and it is advised that users do not rely on this method but instead use client-side scripts. See https://jira.mongodb.org/browse/ SERVER-17453 for more details.

Creating and tailing a capped collection cursors in MongoDB

Capped collections are fixed size collections where documents are added towards the end of the collection, similar to a queue. As capped collection have a fixed size, older documents are removed if the limit is reached.

They are naturally sorted by the order of the insertion and any retrieval needed on them required ordered by time can be retrieved using the $natural sort order. This makes document retrieval very fast.

The following figure gives a pictorial representation of a capped collection of a size which is good enough to hold up to three documents of equal size (which is too small for any practical use, but good for understanding). As we can see in the image, the collection is similar to a circular queue where the oldest document is replaced by the newly added document should the collection become full. The tailable cursors are special types of cursors that tail the collection similar to a tail command in Unix. These cursors iterate through the collection similar to a normal cursors do, but additionally wait for data to be available in the collection if it is not available. We will see capped collections and tailable cursors in detail in this recipe.

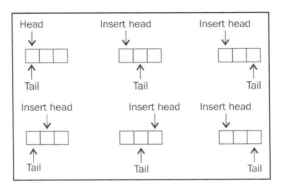

Getting ready

Look at the recipe *Installing single node MongoDB* recipe in *Chapter 1, Installing and Starting the Server* and start a single instance of Mongo. That is the only prerequisite for this recipe. Start a MongoDB shell and connect to the started server.

How to do it...

There are two parts to this recipe: in the first part, we will create a capped collection called `testCapped` and try performing some basic operations on it. Next, we will be creating a tailable cursor on this capped collection.

1. Drop the collection if one already exists with this name.

    ```
    > db.testCapped.drop()
    ```

2. Now create a capped collection as follows. Note the size given here is the size in bytes allocated for the collection and not the number of documents it contains:

    ```
    > db.createCollection('testCapped', {capped : true, size:100})
    ```

3. We will now insert 100 documents in the capped collection as follows:

    ```
    > for(i = 1; i < 100; i++) {
    db.testCapped.insert({'i':i, val:'Test capped'})
      }
    ```

4. Now query the collection as follows:

```
> db.testCapped.find()
```

5. Try to remove the data from the collection as follows:

```
> db.testCapped.remove()
```

6. We will now create and demonstrate a tailable cursor. It is recommended that you type/copy the following pieces of code into a text editor and keep it handy for execution.

7. To insert data in a collection, we will be using the following fragment of code. Execute this piece of code in the shell:

```
> for(i = 101 ; i < 500 ; i++) {
  sleep(1000)
  db.testCapped.insert({'i': i, val :'Test Capped'})
}
```

8. To tail a capped collection, we use the following piece of code:

```
> var cursor = db.testCapped.find().addOption(DBQuery.Option.
tailable).addOption(DBQuery.Option.awaitData)
while(cursor.hasNext()) {
  var next = cursor.next()
  print('i: ' + next.i + ', value: ' + next.val)
}
```

9. Open a shell and connect to the running mongod process. This will be the second shell opened and connected to the server. Copy and paste the code mentioned in step 8 in this shell and execute it.

10. Observe how the records inserted are shown as they are inserted into the capped collection.

How it works...

We will create a capped collection explicitly using the `createCollection` function. This is the only way a capped collection is created. There are two parameters to the `createCollection` function. The first one is the name of the collection and the second is a JSON document that contains the two fields, `capped` and `size`, which are used to inform the user that the collection is capped or not and the size of the collection in bytes respectively. An additional field `max` can be provided to specify the maximum number of documents in the collection. The field size is required even if the `max` field is specified. We then insert and query the documents. When we try to remove the documents from the collection, we would see an error that removal is not permitted from the capped collection. It allows the documents to be deleted only when new documents are added and there isn't space available to accommodate them.

What we see next is a tailable cursor we created. We start two shells and one of them is a normal insertion of documents with an interval of 1 second between subsequent insertions. In the second shell, we create a cursor and iterate through it and print the documents that we get from the cursor onto the shell. The additional options we added to the cursor make the difference though. There are two options added, DBQuery.Option.tailable and DBQuery.Option.awaitData. These options are for instructing that the cursor is tailable, rather than normal, where the last position is marked and we can resume where we left off, and secondly to wait for more data for some time rather than returning immediately when no data is available and when we reach towards the end of the cursor, respectively. The awaitData option can be used with tailable cursors only. The combination of these two options gives us a feel similar to the tail command in Unix filesystem.

For a list of available options, visit the following page: http://docs.mongodb.org/manual/reference/method/cursor.addOption/.

There's more...

In the next recipe, we will see how to convert a normal collection to a capped collection.

Converting a normal collection to a capped collection

This recipe will demonstrate the process of converting a normal collection to a capped collection.

Getting ready

Look at the recipe *Installing single node MongoDB* in *Chapter 1, Installing and Starting the Server* and start a single instance of Mongo. That is the only prerequisite for this recipe. Start a mongo shell and connect to the started server.

How to do it...

1. Execute the following to ensure you are in the test database:

   ```
   > use test
   ```

2. Create a normal collection as follows. We will be adding 100 documents to it, type/copy the following code snippet on to the mongo shell and execute it. The command is as follows:

   ```
   for(i = 1 ; i <= 100 ; i++) {
       db.normalCollection.insert({'i': i, val :'Some Text Content'})
   }
   ```

3. Query the collection as follows to confirm it contains the data:

   ```
   > db.normalCollection.find()
   ```

4. Now, query the collection `system.namespaces` as follows and note the result document:

   ```
   > db.system.namespaces.find({name : 'test.normalCollection'})
   ```

5. Execute the following command to convert the collection to capped collection:

   ```
   > db.runCommand({convertToCapped : 'normalCollection', size : 100})
   ```

6. Query the collection to take a look at the data:

   ```
   > db.normalCollection.find()
   ```

7. Query the collection `system.namespaces` as follows and note the result document:

   ```
   > db.system.namespaces.find({name : 'test.normalCollection'})
   ```

How it works...

We created a normal collection with 100 documents and then tried to convert it to a capped collection with 100 bytes size. The command has the following JSON document passed to the `runCommand` function, `{convertToCapped : <name of normal collection>, size: <size in bytes of the capped collection>}`. This command creates a capped collection with the mentioned size and loads the documents in natural ordering from the normal collection to the target capped collection. If the size of the capped collection reaches the limit mentioned, the old documents are removed in the FIFO order making space for new documents. Once this is done, the created capped collection is renamed. Executing a find on the capped collection confirms that not all 100 documents originally present in the normal collection are present in the capped collection. A query on the `system.namespaces` collection before and after the execution of the `convertToCapped` command shows the change in the `collection` attributes. Note that, this operation acquires a global write lock blocking all read and write operations in this database. Also, any indexes present on the original collection are not created for the capped collection, upon conversion.

There's more...

Oplog is an important collection used for replication in MongoDB and is a capped collection. For more information on replication and oplogs, refer to the recipe *Understanding and analyzing oplogs* in *Chapter 4, Administration*. In a recipe later in this chapter, we will use this oplog to implement a feature similar to after insert/update/delete trigger of a relational database.

Storing binary data in Mongo

So far, we saw how to store text values, dates, and numbers fields in a document. Binary content also needs to be stored at times in the database. Consider cases where users would need to store files in a database. In relational databases, the BLOB data type is most commonly used to address this requirement. MongoDB also supports binary contents to be stored in a document in the collection. The catch is that the total size of the document shouldn't exceed 16 MB, which is the upper limit of the document size as of the writing this book. In this recipe, we will store a small image file into Mongo's document and also retrieve it later. If the content you wish to store in MongoDB collections is greater than 16 MB, then MongoDB offers an out of the box solution called **GridFS**. We will see how to use GridFS in another recipe later in this chapter.

Getting ready

Look at the recipe *Installing single node MongoDB* in *Chapter 1, Installing and Starting the Server* and start a single instance of MongoDB. Also, the program to write binary content to the document is written in Java. Refer to the recipes *Executing query and insert operations using a Java client, Implementing aggregation in Mongo using a Java client* and *Executing MapReduce in Mongo using a Java client* in *Chapter 3, Programming Language Drivers*, for more details on Java drivers. Open a mongo shell and connect to the local MongoDB instance listening to port 27017. For this recipe, we will be using the project mongo-cookbook-bindata. This project is available in the source code bundle downloadable from Packt site. The folder needs to be extracted on the local filesystem. Open a command line shell and go to the root of the project extracted. It should be the directory where the file pom.xml is found.

How to do it...

1. On the operating system shell with the pom.xml present in the current directory of the mongo-cookbook-bindata project, execute the following command:

   ```
   $ mvn exec:java -Dexec.mainClass=com.packtpub.mongo.cookbook.
   BinaryDataTest
   ```

2. Observe the output; the execution should be successful.

3. Switch to mongo shell that is connected to the local instance and execute the following query:

   ```
   > db.binaryDataTest.findOne()
   ```

4. Scroll through the document and take a note of the fields in the document.

How it works...

If we scroll through the large document printed out, we see that the fields are `fileName`, `size`, and `data`. The first two fields are of type string and number respectively, which we populated on document creation and hold the name of the file we provide and the size in bytes. The data field is a field of BSON type BinData, where we see the data encoded in Base64 format.

The following lines of code show how we populated the DBObject that we added to the collection:

```
DBObject doc = new BasicDBObject("_id", 1);
doc.put("fileName", resourceName);
doc.put("size", imageBytes.length);
doc.put("data", imageBytes);
```

As we see above, two fields `fileName` and `size` are used to store the name of the file and the size of the file and are of type string and number respectively. The field data is added to the `DBObject` as a byte array, it gets stored automatically as the BSON type BinData in the document.

See also

What we saw in this recipe is straightforward as long as the document size is less than 16 MB. If the size of the files stored exceeds this value, we have to resort to solutions like GridFS, which is explained in next recipe *Storing large data in Mongo using GridFS*.

Storing large data in Mongo using GridFS

A document size in MongoDB can be up to 16 MB. But does that mean we cannot store data more than 16 MB in size? There are cases where you prefer to store videos and audio files in database rather than in a filesystem for a number of advantages such as a few of them are storing metadata along with them, when accessing the file from an intermediate location, and replicating the contents for high availability if replication is enabled on the MongoDB server instances. GridFS can be used to address such use cases in MongoDB. We will also see how GridFS manages large content that exceeds 16 MB and analyzes the collections it uses for storing the content behind the scene. For test purpose, we will not use data exceeding 16 MB but something smaller to see GridFS in action.

Getting ready

Look at the recipe *Installing single node MongoDB* in *Chapter 1, Installing and Starting the Server* and start a single instance of Mongo. That is the only prerequisite for this recipe. Start a Mongo shell and connect to the started server. Additionally, we will use the mongofiles utility to store data in GridFS from command line.

How to do it...

1. Download the code bundle of the book and save the image file `glimpse_of_universe-wide.jpg` to your local drive (you may choose any other large file as the matter of fact and provide appropriate names of the file with the commands we execute). For the sake of the example, the image is saved in the home directory. We will split our steps into three parts.

2. With the server up and running, execute the following command from the operating system's shell with the current directory being the home directory. There are two arguments here. The first one is the name of the file on the local filesystem and the second one is the name that would be attached to the uploaded content in MongoDB.

   ```
   $ mongofiles put -l glimpse_of_universe-wide.jpg universe.jpg
   ```

3. Let's now query the collections to see how this content is actually stored in the collections behind the scenes. With the shell open, execute the following two queries. Make sure that in the second query, you ensure to mention not selecting the data field.

   ```
   > db.fs.files.findOne({filename:'universe.jpg'})
   > db.fs.chunks.find({}, {data:0})
   ```

4. Now that we have put a file to GridFS from the operating system's local filesystem, we will see how we can get the file to the local filesystem. Execute the following from the operating system shell:

   ```
   $ mongofiles get -l UploadedImage.jpg universe.jpg
   ```

5. Finally, we will delete the file we uploaded as follows. From the operating system shell, execute the following:

   ```
   $ mongofiles delete universe.jpg
   ```

6. Confirm the deletion using the following queries again:

   ```
   > db.fs.files.findOne({filename:'universe.jpg'})
   > db.fs.chunks.find({}, {data:0})
   ```

How it works...

Mongo distribution comes with a tool called mongofiles, which lets us upload the large content to Mongo server that gets stored using the GridFS specification. GridFS is not a different product but a specification that is standard and followed by different drivers for MongoDB for storing data greater than 16 MB, which is the maximum document size. It can even be used for files less than 16 MB, as we did in our recipe, but there isn't really a good reason to do that. There is nothing stopping us from implementing our own way of storing these large files, but it is preferred to follow the standard. This is because all drivers support it and does the heavy lifting of splitting of big file into small chunks and assembling them back when needed.

We kept the image downloaded from the Packt Publishing site and uploaded using mongofiles to MongoDB. The command to do that is `put` and the `-l` option gives the name of the file on the local drive that we want to upload. Finally, the name `universe.jpg` is the name of the file we want it to be stored as on GridFS.

On successful execution, we should see something like the following on the console:

```
connected to: 127.0.0.1
added file: { _id: ObjectId('5310d531d1e91f93635588fe'), filename:
"universe.jpg
", chunkSize: 262144, uploadDate: new Date(1393612082137), md5:
d894ec31b8c5add
d0c02060971ea05ca", length: 2711259 }
done!
```

This gives us some details of the upload, the unique `_id` for the uploaded file, the name of the file, the chunk size, which is the size of the chunk this big file is broken into (by default 256 KB), the date of upload, the checksum of the uploaded content, and the total length of upload. This checksum can be computed beforehand and then compared after the upload to check if the uploaded content was not corrupt.

Execute the following query from the mongo shell in test database:

```
> db.fs.files.findOne({filename:'universe.jpg'})
```

We see that the output we saw for the `put` command of mongofiles same as the document queried above in the collection `fs.files`. This is the collection where all the uploaded file details are put when some data is added to GridFS. There will be one document per upload. Applications can later also modify this document to add their own custom meta data along with the standard details added to my Mongo when adding the data. Applications can very well use this collection to add details like, the photographer, the location where the image was taken, where was it taken, and details like tags for individuals in the image in this collection if the document is for an image upload.

The file content is something that contains this data. Let's execute the following query:

```
> db.fs.chunks.find({}, {data:0})
```

We have deliberately left out the data field from the result selected. Let's look at the structure of the result document:

```
{
_id: <Unique identifier of type ObjectId representing this chunk>,
file_id: <ObjectId of the document in fs.files for the file whose
  chunk this document represent>,
n:<The chunk identifier starts with 0, this is useful for knowing
  the order of the chunks>,
data: <BSON binary content  for the data uploaded for the file>
}
```

For the file we uploaded, we have 11 chunks of a maximum 256 KB each. When a file is being requested, the fs.chunks collection is searched by the file_id that comes from the _id field of fs.files collection and the field n, which is the chunk's sequence. A unique index is created on these two fields when this collection is created for the first time when a file is uploaded using GridFS for the fast retrieval of chunks using the file ID sorted by chunk sequence number.

Similar to put, the get option is used to retrieve the files from the GridFS and put them on local filesystem. The difference in the command is to use the get instead of put, the -l still is used to provide the name of the file that this file would be saved as on the local filesystem and the final command line parameter is the name of the file as stored in GridFS. This is the value of the filename field in fs.files collection. Finally, the delete command of mongofiles simply removes the entry of the file from fs.files and fs.chunks collections. The name of the file given for delete is again the value present in the filename field of the fs.files collection.

Some important use cases of using GridFS are when there is some user generated contents like large reports on some static data that doesn't change too often and are expensive to generate frequently. Instead of running them all the times, it can be run once and stored until a change in the static data is detected; in which case, the stored report is deleted and re-executed on next request of the data. The filesystem may not always be available to the application to write the files to, in which case this is a good alternative. There are cases where one might be interested in some intermediate chunk of the data stored, in which case the chunk containing the required data be accessed. You get some nice features like the MD5 content of the data, which is stored automatically and is available for use by the application.

Now that we have seen what GridFS is, let's see some scenarios where using GridFS might not be a very good idea. The performance of accessing the content from MongoDB using GridFS and directly from the filesystem will not be same. Direct filesystem access will be faster than GridFS and **Proof of Concept** (**POC**) for the system to be developed is recommended to measure the performance hit and see if it is within the acceptable limits; if so, the trade off in performance might be worth for the benefits we get. Also, if your application server is fronted with CDN, you might not actually need a lot of IO for static data stored in GridFS. Since GridFS stores the data in multiple documents in collections, atomically updating them is not possible. If we know the content is less than 16 MB, which is the case in lot of user-generated content, or some small files uploaded, we may skip GridFS altogether and store the content in one document as BSON supports storing binary content in the document. Refer to the previous recipe *Storing binary data in Mongo* for more details.

We would rarely use mongofiles utility to store, retrieve, and delete data from GridFS. Though it may occasionally be used, we will mostly perform these operations from an application. In the next couple of recipes, we will see how to connect to GridFS to store, retrieve, and delete files using Java and Python clients.

There's more...

Though this is not much to do with Mongo, Openstack is an **Infrastructure as a Service** (**IaaS**) platform and offers a variety of services for Compute, Storage, Networking, and so on. One of the image storage service called **Glance** supports a lot of persistent stores to store the images. One of the supported stores by Glace is MongoDB's GridFS. You can find more information on how to configure Glance to use GridFS at the following URL: `http://docs.openstack.org/trunk/config-reference/content/ch_configuring-openstack-image-service.html`.

See also

You can refer to the following recipes:

 ▶ *Storing data to GridFS from Java client*
 ▶ *Storing data to GridFS from Python client*

Storing data to GridFS from Java client

In the previous recipe, we saw how to store data to GridFS using a command-line utility that comes with MongoDB to manage large data files: mongofiles. To get an idea of what GridFS is and what collections are used behind the scenes to store the data, refer to the previous recipe *Storing large data in Mongo using GridFS*.

In this recipe, we will look at storing data to GridFS using a Java client. The program will be a highly scaled down version of mongofiles utility and focus only on how to store, retrieve, and delete data rather than trying to provide a lot of options like mongofiles do.

Getting ready

Refer to the recipe *Installing single node MongoDB* from *Chapter 1*, *Installing and Starting the Server*, for all the necessary setup for this recipe. If you are interested in more details on Java drivers, refer to the recipes *Implementing aggregation in Mongo using a Java client* and *Executing MapReduce in Mongo using a Java client* in *Chapter 3*, *Programming Language Drivers*. Open a mongo shell and connect to the local mongod instance listening to port `27017`. For this recipe, we will be using the project `mongo-cookbook-gridfs`. This project is available in the source code bundle downloadable from Packt site. The folder needs to be extracted on the local filesystem. Open a terminal of your operating system and go to the root of the project extracted. It should be the directory where the file `pom.xml` is found. Also, save the file `glimpse_of_universe-wide.jpg` on the local filesystem, similar to the previous recipe, found in the downloadable bundle for the book from the Packt site.

How to do it...

1. We are assuming that the collections of GridFS are clean and no prior data is uploaded. If there is nothing crucial in the database, you can execute the following to clear the collection. Do exercise caution before dropping the collections.

```
> use test
> db.fs.chunks.drop()
> db.fs.files.drop()
```

2. Open an operating system shell and execute the following:

```
$ mvn exec:java -Dexec.mainClass=com.packtpub.mongo.cookbook.
GridFSTests -Dexec.args="put ~/glimpse_of_universe-wide.jpg
universe.jpg"
```

3. The file I need to upload was placed in the home directory. You can choose to give the file path of the image file after the `put` command. Bear in mind if the path contains spaces, the whole path need to be given within single quotes.

4. If the preceding command runs successfully, we should expect the following output to the command line:

```
Successfully written to universe.jpg, details are:
Upload Identifier: 5314c05e1c52e2f520201698
Length: 2711259
MD5 hash: d894ec31b8c5addd0c02060971ea05ca
Chunk Side in bytes: 262144
Total Number Of Chunks: 11
```

5. Once the preceding execution is successful, which we can confirm from the console output, execute the following from the mongo shell:

```
> db.fs.files.findOne({filename:'universe.jpg'})
> db.fs.chunks.find({}, {data:0})
```

6. Now, we will get the file from GridFS to local filesystem, execute the following to perform this operation:

```
$ mvn exec:java -Dexec.mainClass=com.packtpub.mongo.cookbook.
GridFSTests -Dexec.args="get '~/universe.jpg' universe.jpg"
```

Confirm the file is present on the local filesystem at the mentioned location. We should see the following printed to the console output to indicate a successful write operation:

```
Connected successfully..
Successfully written 2711259 bytes to ~/universe.jpg
```

7. Finally, we will delete the file from GridFS:

```
$ mvn exec:java -Dexec.mainClass=com.packtpub.mongo.cookbook.
GridFSTests -Dexec.args="delete universe.jpg"
```

8. On successful deletion, we should see the following output in the console:

```
Connected successfully..
Removed file with name 'universe.jpg' from GridFS
```

How it works...

The class `com.packtpub.mongo.cookbook.GridFSTests` accepts three types of operations: `put` to upload file to GridFS, `get` to get contents from GridFS to local filesystem, and `delete` to delete files from GridFS.

The class accepts up to three parameters, the first one is the operation with valid values as `get`, `put`, and `delete`. The second parameter is relevant for `get` and `put` operations and is the name of the file on local filesystem to write the downloaded content to be written or source the content from for upload respectively. The third parameter is the name of the file in GridFS, which is not necessarily same as the name on local filesystem. For `delete`, however, only the filename on GridFS is needed which would be deleted.

Let's see some important snippets of code from the class which is specific to GridFS.

Open the class `com.packtpub.mongo.cookbook.GridFSTests` in your favorite IDE and look for the methods `handlePut`, `handleGet`, and `handleDelete`. These are the methods where all the logic is. We will start with the `handlePut` method first, which is for uploading the contents of the file from local filesystem to GridFS.

Irrespective of the operation we perform, we will create an instance of the class `com.mongodb.gridfs.GridFS`. In our case, we instantiated it as follows:

```
GridFS gfs = new GridFS(client.getDB("test"));
```

The constructor of this class takes the database instance of class `com.mongodb.DB`. Once the instance of GridFS is created, we will invoke the method `createFile` on it. This method accepts two parameters, the first one is the `InputStream` sourcing the bytes of the content to be uploaded and the second parameter is the name of the file on GridFS for the file that would be saved on GridFS. However, this method doesn't create the file on GridFS but returns and instance of `com.mongodb.gridfs.GridFSInputFile`. The upload will happen only when we call `save` method in this returned object. There are few overloaded variants of this `createFile` method. Please refer to Javadocs of the class `com.mongodb.gridfs.GridFS` for more details.

Our next method is `handleGet`, which gets the contents of the file saved on GridFS to the local filesystem. Similar to the `com.mongodb.DBCollection` class, the class `com.mongodb.gridfs.GridFS` has the `find` and `findOne` methods for searching. However, instead of accepting any DBObject query, `find` and `findOne` in GridFS accept filename or the ObjectID value of the document to search in `fs.files` collection. Similarly, the return value is not a DBCursor but an instance of `com.mongodb.gridfs.GridFSDBFile`. This class has various methods that get the `InputStream` of the bytes of content present in the file on GridFS, `writeTo` file or `OutputStream` and a method, `getLength` that gives the number of bytes in the file. Refer to the Javadocs of the class `com.mongodb.gridfs.GridFSDBFile` for details.

Finally, we look at the method `handleDelete`, which is used to delete the files on GridFS and is the simplest of the lot. The method on the object of GridFS is `remove`, which accepts a string argument: the name of the file to delete on the server. The `return` type of this method is `void`. So irrespective of whether the content is present on GridFS or not, the method will not return a value nor throw an exception if a name is provided to this method for a file that doesn't exist.

See also

You can refer to the following recipes:

- ▶ *Storing binary data in Mongo*
- ▶ *Storing data to GridFS from Python client*

Storing data to GridFS from Python client

In the recipe *Storing large data in Mongo using GridFS*, we saw what GridFS is and how it could be used to store the large files in MongoDB. In the previous recipe, we saw to use GridFS API from a Java client. In this recipe, we will see how to store image data into MongoDB using GridFS from a Python program.

Getting ready

Refer to the recipe *Connecting to the single node using a Java client* from *Chapter 1, Installing and Starting the Server*, for all the necessary setup for this recipe. If you are interested in more detail on Python drivers refer to the following recipes: *Executing query and insert operations with PyMongo* and *Executing update and delete operations using PyMongo* in *Chapter 3, Programming Language Drivers*. Download and save the image `glimpse_of_universe-wide.jpg` from the downloadable bundle available with the book from the Packt site to local filesystem as we did in the previous recipe.

How to do it...

1. Open a Python interpreter by typing in the following in the operating system shell. Note that the current directory is same as the directory where the image file `glimpse_of_universe-wide.jpg` is placed:

   ```
   $ python
   ```

2. Import the required packages as follows:

   ```
   >>>import pymongo
   >>>import gridfs
   ```

3. Once the Python shell is opened, create a `MongoClient` and a database object to the test database as follows:

   ```
   >>>client = pymongo.MongoClient('mongodb://localhost:27017')
   >>>db = client.test
   ```

4. To clear the GridFS-related collections execute the following:

```
>>> db.fs.files.drop()
>>> db.fs.chunks.drop()
```

5. Create the instance of GridFS as follows:

```
>>>fs = gridfs.GridFS(db)
```

6. Now, we will read the file and upload its contents to GridFS. First, create the file object as follows:

```
>>>file = open('glimpse_of_universe-wide.jpg', 'rb')
```

7. Now put the file into GridFS as follows

```
>>>fs.put(file, filename='universe.jpg')
```

8. On successfully executing `put`, we should see the ObjectID for the file uploaded. This would be same as the `_id` field of the `fs.files` collection for this file.

9. Execute the following query from the Python shell. It should print out the `dict` object with the details of the upload. Verify the contents

```
>>> db.fs.files.find_one()
```

10. Now, we will get the uploaded content and write it to a file on the local filesystem. Let's get the `GridOut` instance representing the object to read the data out of GridFS as follows:

```
>>> gout = fs.get_last_version('universe.jpg')
```

11. With this instance available, let's write the data to the file to a file on local filesystem as follows. First, open a handle to the file on local filesystem to write to as follows:

```
>>> fout = open('universe.jpg', 'wb')
```

12. We will then write content to it as follows:

```
>>>fout.write(gout.read())
>>>fout.close()
>>>gout.close()
```

13. Now verify the file on the current directory on the local filesystem. A new file called `universe.jpg` will be created with same number of bytes as the source present in it. Verify it by opening it in an image viewer.

How it works...

Let's look at the steps we executed. In the Python shell, we import two packages, `pymongo` and `gridfs`, and instantiate the `pymongo.MongoClient` and `gridfs.GridFS` instances. The constructor of the class `gridfs.GridFS` takes on an argument, which is the instance of `pymongo.Database`.

We open a file in binary mode using the `open` function and pass the file object to the GridFS `put` method. There is an additional argument called `filename` passed, which would be the name of the file put into GridFS. The first parameter need not be a file object but any object with a `read` method defined.

Once the `put` operation succeeds, the `return` value is an ObjectID for the uploaded document in `fs.files` collection. A query on `fs.files` can confirm that the file is uploaded. Verify that the size of the data uploaded matches the size of the file.

Our next objective is to get the file from GridFS on to the local filesystem. Intuitively, one would imagine if the method to put a file in GridFS is `put`, then the method to get a file would be `get`. True, the method is indeed `get`, however, it will get only based on the `ObjectId` that was returned by the `put` method. So, if you are okay to fetch by `ObjectId`, `get` is the method for you. However, if you want to get by the filename, the method to use is `get_last_version`. It accepts the name of the filename that we uploaded and the return type of this method is of type `gridfs.gridfs_file.GridOut`. This class contains the method `read`, which will read out all the bytes from the uploaded file to GridFS. We open a file called `universe.jpg` for writing in binary mode and write all the bytes read from the `GridOut` object.

See also

You can refer to the following recipes:

- *Storing binary data in Mongo*
- *Storing data to GridFS from Java client*

Implementing triggers in Mongo using oplog

In a relational database, a trigger is a code that gets invoked when an `insert`, `update`, or a `delete` operation is executed on a table in the database. A trigger can be invoked either before or after the operation. Triggers are not implemented in MongoDB out of the box and in case you need some sort of notification for your application whenever any `insert/update/delete` operations are executed, you are left to manage that by yourself in the application. One approach is to have some sort of data access layer in the application, which is the only place to query, insert, update, or delete documents from the collections. However, there are few challenges to it. First, you need to explicitly code the logic to accommodate this requirement in the application, which may or may not be feasible. If the database is shared and multiple applications access it, things become even more difficult. Secondly, the access needs to be strictly regulated and no other source of insert/update/delete be permitted.

Alternatively, we need to look at running some sort of logic in a layer close to the database. One way to track all write operations is by using an oplog. Note that read operations cannot be tracked using oplogs. In this recipe, we will write a small Java application that would tail an oplog and get all the `insert`, `update` and `delete` operations happening on a Mongo instance. Note that this program is implemented in Java and works equally well in any other programming language. The crux lies in the logic for the implementation, the platform for implementation can be any. Also, this works only if the mongod instance is started as a part of replica set and not a standalone instance. Also, this trigger like functionality can only be invoked only after the operation is performed and not before the data gets inserted/updated or deleted from the collection.

Getting ready

Refer to the recipe *Starting multiple instances as part of a replica set* from *Chapter 1, Installing and Starting the Server*, for all the necessary setup for this recipe. If you are interested in more details on Java drivers, refer to the following recipes *Executing query and insert operations using a Java client* and *Executing update and delete operations using a Java client* in *Chapter 3, Programming Language Drivers*. Prerequisites of these two recipes are all we need for this recipe.

Refer to the recipe *Creating and tailing a capped collection cursors in MongoDB* in this chapter to know more about capped collections and tailable cursors if you are not aware or need a refresher. Finally, though not mandatory, *Chapter 4, Administration*, explains oplog in depth in the recipe *Understanding and analyzing oplogs*. This recipe will not explain oplog in depth as we did in *Chapter 4, Administration*. Open a shell and connect it to the primary of the replica set.

For this recipe, we will be using the project `mongo-cookbook-oplogtrigger`. This project is available in the source code bundle downloadable from Packt site. The folder needs to be extracted on the local filesystem. Open a command line shell and go to the root of the project extracted. It should be the directory where the file `pom.xml` is found. Also, the `TriggerOperations.js` file would be needed to trigger operations in the database that we intend to capture.

How to do it...

1. Open an operating system shell and execute the following:

```
$ mvn exec:java -Dexec.mainClass=com.packtpub.mongo.cookbook.
OplogTrigger -Dexec.args="test.oplogTriggerTest"
```

2. With the Java program started, we will open the shell as follows with the file `TriggerOperations.js` present in the current directory and the mongod instance listening to port `27000` as the primary:

```
$ mongo --port 27000 TriggerOperations.js --shell
```

3. Once the shell is connected, execute the following function we loaded from the JavaScript:

```
test:PRIMARY> triggerOperations()
```

4. Observe the output printed out on the console where the Java program `com.packtpub.mongo.cookbook.OplogTrigger` is being executed using Maven.

How it works...

The functionality we implemented is pretty handy for a lot of use cases but let's see what we did at a higher level first. The Java program `com.packtpub.mongo.cookbook.OplogTrigger` is something that acts as a trigger when new data is inserted, updated, or deleted from a collection in MongoDB. It uses oplog collection that is the backbone of the replication in Mongo to implement this functionality.

The JavaScript we have just acts as a source of producing, updating, and deleting data from the collection. You may choose to open the `TriggerOperations.js` file and take a look at how it is implemented. The collection on which it performs is present in the test database and is called `oplogTriggerTest`.

When we execute the JavaScript function, we should see something like the following printed to the output console:

```
[INFO] <<< exec-maven-plugin:1.2.1:java (default-cli) @ mongo-cookbook-
oplogtriger <<<

[INFO]

[INFO] --- exec-maven-plugin:1.2.1:java (default-cli) @ mongo-cookbook-
oplogtriger ---

Connected successfully..

Starting tailing oplog...

Operation is Insert ObjectId is 5321c4c2357845b165d42a5f

Operation is Insert ObjectId is 5321c4c2357845b165d42a60

Operation is Insert ObjectId is 5321c4c2357845b165d42a61

Operation is Insert ObjectId is 5321c4c2357845b165d42a62

Operation is Insert ObjectId is 5321c4c2357845b165d42a63

Operation is Insert ObjectId is 5321c4c2357845b165d42a64

Operation is Update ObjectId is 5321c4c2357845b165d42a60

Operation is Delete ObjectId is 5321c4c2357845b165d42a61

Operation is Insert ObjectId is 5321c4c2357845b165d42a65

Operation is Insert ObjectId is 5321c4c2357845b165d42a66

Operation is Insert ObjectId is 5321c4c2357845b165d42a67

Operation is Insert ObjectId is 5321c4c2357845b165d42a68

Operation is Delete ObjectId is 5321c4c2357845b165d42a5f

Operation is Delete ObjectId is 5321c4c2357845b165d42a62

Operation is Delete ObjectId is 5321c4c2357845b165d42a63

Operation is Delete ObjectId is 5321c4c2357845b165d42a64

Operation is Delete ObjectId is 5321c4c2357845b165d42a60

Operation is Delete ObjectId is 5321c4c2357845b165d42a65

Operation is Delete ObjectId is 5321c4c2357845b165d42a66

Operation is Delete ObjectId is 5321c4c2357845b165d42a67

Operation is Delete ObjectId is 5321c4c2357845b165d42a68
```

The Maven program will be continuously running and never terminate as the Java program doesn't. You may hit *Ctrl + C* to stop the execution.

Let's analyze the Java program, which is where the meat of the content is. The first assumption is that for this program to work, a replica set must be set up as we will use Mongo's oplog collection. The Java programs created a connection to the primary of the replica set members, connects to the local database, and gets the `oplog.rs` collection. Then, all it does is find the last or nearly the last timestamp in the oplog. This is done to prevent the whole oplog to be replayed on startup but to mark a point towards the end in the oplog. Here is the code to find this timestamp value:

```
DBCursor cursor = collection.find().sort(new BasicDBObject("$natural",
-1)).limit(1);
int current = (int) (System.currentTimeMillis() / 1000);
return cursor.hasNext() ? (BSONTimestamp)cursor.next().get("ts") : new
BSONTimestamp(current, 1);
```

The oplog is sorted in the reverse natural order to find the time in the last document in it. Since oplogs follow the first in first out pattern, sorting the oplog in the descending natural order is equivalent to sorting by the timestamp in descending order.

Once this is done, finding the timestamp as before, we query the oplog collection as usual but with two additional options:

```
DBCursor cursor = collection.find(QueryBuilder.start("ts")
            .greaterThan(lastreadTimestamp).get())
            .addOption(Bytes.QUERYOPTION_TAILABLE)
            .addOption(Bytes.QUERYOPTION_AWAITDATA);
```

The query finds all documents greater than a particular timestamp and adds two options, `Bytes.QUERYOPTION_TAILABLE` and `Bytes.QUERYOPTION_AWAITDATA`. The latter option can only be added when the former option is added. This not only queries and returns the data, but also waits for some time when the execution reaches the end of the cursor for some more data. Eventually, when no data arrives, it terminates.

During every iteration, store the last seen timestamp as well. This is used when the cursor closes when no more data is available and we query again to get a new tailable cursor instance. The query this time will use the timestamp we have stored on previous iteration, when the last document was seen. This process continues indefinitely and we basically tail the collection in a similar way to how we tail a file in Unix using the `tail` command.

The oplog document contains a field called `op` for the operation whose value is `i`, `u`, and `d` for insert, update, and delete, respectively. The field `o` contains the inserted or deleted object's ID (`_id`) in case of insert and delete. In case of update, the file `o2` contains the `_id`. All we do is simply check for these conditions and print out the operation and the ID of the document inserted/deleted or updated.

Something to be careful about is as follows. Obviously, the deleted documents would not be available in the collection so, the `_id` would not really be useful if you intend to query. Also, be careful when selecting a document after update using the ID we get as some other operation later in the oplog might already have performed more updates on the same document and our application's tailable cursor has yet to reach that point. This is common in case of high-volume systems. Similarly, for inserts we have a similar problem. The document we might query using the provided ID might be updated/deleted already. Applications using this logic to track these operations must be aware of them.

Alternatively, take a look at the oplog that contains more details. Like the document inserted, the `update` statement executed, and so on. Updates in the oplog collection are idempotent, which means they can be applied any number of times without unintended side effects. For instance, if the actual update was to increment the value by 1, the update in the oplog collection will have the `set` operator with the final value to be expected. This way, the same update can be applied multiple times. The logic you would use would then have to be more sophisticated to implement such scenarios.

Also, failovers are not handled here. This is needed for production based systems. The infinite loop on the other hand opens a new cursor as soon as the first one terminates. There could be a sleep duration introduced before the oplog is queried again to avoid overwhelming the server with queries. Note that the program given here is not a production quality code but just a simple demo of the technique that is being used by a lot of other systems to get notified for new data insert, delete, and updates to collections in MongoDB.

MongoDB didn't have the text search feature until version 2.4 and prior to that all full text search was handled using external search engines like Solr or Elasticsearch. Even now, though the text search feature in MongoDB is production ready, many would still use an external dedicated search indexer. It won't be a surprise if the decision is taken to use an external full text index search tool instead of leveraging the MongoDB's inbuilt one. In case of Elasticsearch, the abstraction to flow the data in to the indexes is known as a river. The MongoDB river in Elasticsearch, which adds data to the indexes as and when the data gets added to the collections in Mongo is built on the same logic as we saw in the simple program implemented in Java.

Flat plane 2D geospatial queries in Mongo using geospatial indexes

In this recipe, we will see what geospatial queries are and then see how to apply these queries on flat planes. We will put it to use in a test map application.

Geospatial queries can be executed on data in which geospatial indexes are created. There are two types of geospatial indexes. The first one is called the 2D indexes and is the simpler of the two, it assumes that the data is given as *x,y* coordinates. The second one is called 3D or spherical indexes and is relatively more complicated. In this recipe, we will explore the 2D indexes and execute some queries on 2D data. The data on which we are going to work upon is a 25 x 25 grid with some coordinates representing bus stops, restaurants, hospitals, and gardens.

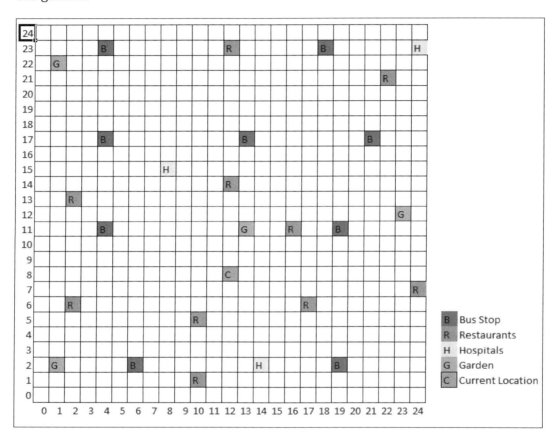

Getting ready

Refer to the recipe *Connecting to the single node using a Java client* from *Chapter 1, Installing and Starting the Server*, for all the necessary setup for this recipe. Download the data file `2dMapLegacyData.json` and keep it on the local filesystem ready to import. Open a mongo shell connecting to the local MongoDB instance.

How to do it...

1. Execute the following command from the operating system shell to import the data into the collection. The file `2dMapLegacyData.json` is present in the current directory.

   ```
   $ mongoimport -c areaMap -d test --drop 2dMapLegacyData.json
   ```

2. If we see something like the following on the screen, we can confirm that the import has gone through successfully:

   ```
   connected to: 127.0.0.1
   Mon Mar 17 23:58:27.880 dropping: test.areaMap
   Mon Mar 17 23:58:27.932 check 9 26
   Mon Mar 17 23:58:27.934 imported 26 objects
   ```

3. After the successful import, from the opened mongo shell, verify the collection and its content by executing the following query:

   ```
   > db.areaMap.find()
   ```

   This should give you the feel of the data in the collection.

4. The next step is to create 2D geospatial index on this data. Execute the following to create a 2D index:

   ```
   $ db.areaMap.ensureIndex({co:'2d'})
   ```

5. With the index created, we will now try to find the nearest restaurant from the place an individual is standing. Assuming the person is not fussy about the type of cuisine, let's execute the following query assuming that the person is standing at location (12, 8), as shown in the image. Also, we are interested in just three nearest places.

   ```
   $ db.areaMap.find({co:{$near:[12, 8]}, type:'R'}).limit(3)
   ```

6. This should give us three results, starting with the nearest restaurant with the subsequent ones given in increasing distance. If we look at the image given earlier, we kind of agree with the results given here.

7. Let's add more options to the query. The individual has to walk and thus wants the distance to be restricted to a particular value in the results. Let's rewrite the query with the following modification:

   ```
   $ db.areaMap.find({co:{$near:[12, 8], $maxDistance:4}, type:'R'})
   ```

8. Observe the number of results retrieved this time around.

How it works...

Let's now go through what we did. Before we continue, let's define what exactly we mean by the distance between two points. Suppose on a cartesian plane that we have two points (x_1, y_1) and (x_2, y_2), the distance between them would be computed using the formula:

$$\sqrt{(x_1 - x_2)^2 + (y_1 - y_2)^2}$$

Suppose the two points are (2, 10) and (12, 3), the distance would be: $\sqrt{(2 - 12)^2 + (10 - 3)^2}$ $= \sqrt{(-10)^2 + (7)^2} = \sqrt{149} = 12.207$.

After knowing how calculations for distance calculation are done behind the scenes by MongoDB, let's see what we did right from step 1.

We started by importing the data normally into a collection, `areaMap` in the `test` database and created an index as `db.areaMap.ensureIndex({co:'2d'})`. The index is created on the field `co` in the document and the value is a special value, `2d`, which denotes that this is a special type of index called 2D geospatial index. Usually, we give this value as `1` or `-1` in other cases denoting the order of the index.

There are two types of indexes. The first is a 2D index that is commonly used for planes whose span is less and do not involve spherical surfaces. It could be something like a map of the building, a locality, or even a small city where the curvature of the earth covering the portion of the land is not really significant. However, once the span of the map increases and covers the globe, 2D indexes will be inaccurate for predicting the values as the curvature of the earth needs to be considered in the calculations. In such cases, we go for spherical indexes, which we will discuss soon.

Once the 2D index is created, we can use it to query the collection and find some points near the point queried. Execute the following query:

```
> db.areaMap.find({co:{$near:[12, 8]}, type:'R'}).limit(3)
```

It will query for documents that are of the type R, which are of type `restaurants` and closes to the co-ordinates (12,8). The results returned by this query will be in the increasing order of the distance from the point in question, (12, 8) in this case. The limit just limits the result to top three documents. We may also provide the `$maxDistance` in the query, which will restrict the results with a distance less than or equal to the provided value. We queried for locations not more than four units away, as follows:

```
> db.areaMap.find({co:{$near:[12, 8], $maxDistance:4}, type:'R'})
```

Spherical indexes and GeoJSON compliant data in Mongo

Before we continue with this recipe, we need to look at the previous recipe *Flat plane 2D geospatial queries in Mongo using geospatial indexes* to get an understanding of what geospatial indexes are in MongoDB and how to use the 2D indexes. So far, we have imported the JSON documents in a non-standard format in MongoDB collection, created geospatial indexes, and queried them it. This approach works perfectly fine and in fact, it was the only option available until MongoDB 2.4. version 2.4 of MongoDB supports an additional way to store, index, and query the documents in the collections. There is a standard way to represent geospatial data particularly meant for geodata exchange in JSON and the specification of GeoJSON mentions it in detail in the following link: `http://geojson.org/geojson-spec.html`. We can now store the data in this format.

There are various geographic figure types supported by this specification. However, for our use case, we will be using the type `Point`. First let's see how the document we imported before using a non-standard format looked and how the one using GeoJSON format looks.

- ▶ Document in non-standard format:

  `{"_id":1, "name":"White Street", "type":"B", co:[4, 23]}`

- ▶ Document in GeoJSON format:

  `{"_id":1, "name":"White Street", "type":"B", co:{type: 'Point', coordinates : [4, 23]}}`

It looks more complicated than the non-standard format and for our particular case I do agree. However, when representing polygons and other lines, the non-standard format might have to store multiple documents. In this case, it can be stored in a single document just by changing the value of the `type` field. Refer to the specification for more details.

Getting ready

The prerequisites for this recipe are same as the prerequisites for the previous recipe except that the file to be imported would be `2dMapGeoJSONData.json` and `countries.geo.json`. Download these files from the Packt site and keep them on the local filesystem for importing them later.

 Special thanks to Johan Sundström for sharing the world data. The GeoJSON for the world is taken from `https://github.com/johan/world.geo.json`. The file is massaged to enable importing and index creation in Mongo. Version 2.4 doesn't support MultiPolygon and thus all MultiPolygon type of shapes are omitted. The shortcoming seems to be fixed in Version 2.6 though.

How to do it...

1. Import the GeoJSON compatible data in a new collection as follows. This contains 26 documents similar to what we imported last time around, except that they are formatted using the GeoJSON format.

```
$ mongoimport -c areaMapGeoJSON -d test --drop 2dMapGeoJSONData.json
$ mongoimport -c worldMap -d test --drop countries.geo.json
```

2. Create a Geospatial index on this collections as follows:

```
> db.areaMapGeoJSON.ensureIndex({"co" : "2dsphere"})
> db.worldMap.ensureIndex({geometry:'2dsphere'})
```

3. We will now first query the collection areaMapGeoJSON collection as follows:

```
> db.areaMapGeoJSON.find(
{   co:{
     $near:{
       $geometry:{
         type:'Point',
         coordinates:[12, 8]
       }
     }
   },
   type:'R'
}).limit(3)
```

4. Next, we will try to find all the restaurants that fall within the square drawn between the points (0, 0), (0, 11), (11, 11), and (11, 0). Refer to the figure given in the introduction of the previous recipe for getting a clear visual of the points and the results to expect.

5. Write the following query and observe the results:

```
> db.areaMapGeoJSON.find(
{   co:{
     $geoIntersects:{
       $geometry:{
         type:'Polygon',
         coordinates:[[[0, 0], [0, 11], [11, 11], [11, 0], [0, 0]]]
       }
     }
```

```
  },
  type:'R'
})
```

Check if it contains the three restaurants at coordinates (2, 6), (10, 5), and (10, 1) as expected.

6. We will next try and perform some operations that would find all the matching objects that lie completely within another enclosing polygon. Suppose that we want to find some bus stops that lie within a given square block. Such use cases can be addressed using the $geoWithin operator, and the query to achieve it is as follows:

```
> db.areaMapGeoJSON.find(
  {co:{
    $geoWithin:{
    $geometry:{
      type: 'Polygon',
      coordinates : [[ [3, 9], [3, 24], [6, 24], [6, 9], [3, 9]] ]}
      }
    },
    type:'B'
  }
)
```

7. Verify the results; we should have three bus stops in the result. Refer to the image of the map in the previous recipe's introduction to get the expected results of the query.

8. When we execute the above commands, they just print the documents in ascending order of the distance. However, we don't see the actual distance in the result. Let's execute the same query as in point number 3 and additionally, get the calculated distances as following:

```
> db.runCommand({
            geoNear: "areaMapGeoJSON",
    near: [ 12, 8 ],
    spherical: true,
            limit:3,
            query:{type:'R'}
  }
)
```

9. The query returns one document with an array within the field called results containing the matching documents and the calculated distances. The result also contains some additional stats giving the maximum distance, the average of the distances in the result, the total documents scanned, and the time taken in milliseconds.

10. We will finally query on the world map collection to find which country the provided coordinate lies in. Execute the following query as follows from the mongo shell:

```
> db.worldMap.find(
  {geometry:{
    $geoWithin:{
      $geometry:{
          type:'Point',
          coordinates:[7, 52]
        }
      }
    }
  }
  ,{properties:1, _id:0}
)
```

11. All the possible operations we can perform with the `worldMap` collection are numerous and not all are practically possible to cover in this recipe. I would encourage you to play around with this collection and try out different use cases.

How it works...

Starting from version MongoDB 2.4, the standard way for storing geospatial data in JSON is also supported. Note that the legacy approach that we saw is also supported. However, if you are starting afresh, it is recommended to go ahead with this approach for the following reasons.

▶ It is a standard and anybody aware of the specification would easily be able to understand the structure of the document

▶ It makes storing complex shapes, polygons, and multiple lines easy

▶ It also lets us query easily for the intersection of the shapes using the `$geoIntersect` and other new set of operators

For using GeoJSON-compatible documents, we import JSON documents in the file `2dMapGeoJSONData.json` into the collection `areaMapGeoJSON` and create the index as follows:

```
> db.areaMapGeoJSON.ensureIndex({"co" : "2dsphere"})
```

The collection has data similar to what we had imported into the `areaMap` collection in the previous recipe but with a different structure that is compatible to JSON format. The type here used is 2Dsphere and not 2D. The 2Dsphere type of index also considers the spherical surfaces in calculations. Note that the field `co`, on which we are creating the geospatial index, is not an array of coordinates but a document itself that is GeoJSON compatible.

We query where the value of the `$near` operator is not an array of the coordinates, as we did in our previous recipe, but a document with the key `$geometry` and the value is a GeoJSON-compatible document for a point with the coordinates. The results, irrespective of the query we use are identical. Refer to point 3 in this recipe and point 5 in the previous recipe to see the difference in the query. The approach using GeoJSON looks more complicated but it has some advantages which we will soon see.

It is important to note that we cannot mix two approaches. Try executing the query in the GeoJSON format that we just executed on the collection `areaMap` and see that although we do not get any errors, the results are not correct.

We used the `$geoIntersects` operator in point 5 of this recipe. This is only possible when the documents are stored in GeoJSON format in the database. The query simply finds all the points in our case that intersect any shape we create. We create a polygon using the GeoJSON format as follows:

```
{
  type:'Polygon',
  coordinates:[[[0, 0], [0, 11], [11, 11], [11, 0], [0, 0]]]
}
```

The coordinates are for the square, giving the four corners in a clockwise direction with the last coordinate the same as the first denoting it to be complete. The query executed is the same as `$near`, apart from the fact that the `$near` operator is replaced by the `$geoIntersects` and the value of the `$geometry` field is the GeoJSON document of the polygon with which we wish to find the intersecting points in the `areaMapGeoJSON` collection. If we look at the results obtained and look at the figure in the introduction section or previous recipe, they indeed are what we expected.

We also saw what the `$geoWithin` operator is in point number 12, which is pretty handy to use when we want to find the points or even within another polygon. Note that only shapes completely inside the given polygon will be returned. Suppose that, similar to our `worldMap` collection, we have a `cities` collection with their coordinates specified in a similar manner. We can then use the polygon of a country to query all the polygons that lie within it in the `cities` collection, thus giving us the cities. Obviously, an easier and faster way would be to store the country code in the city document. Alternatively, if we have some data missing in the city's collection and the country is not present, one point anywhere within the city's polygon (since a city entirely lies in one country) can be used and a query can be executed on the `worldMap` collection to get its country, which we have demonstrated in point number 12.

A combination of what we saw previously can be put to good use to compute the distances between two points or even execute some geometric operation.

Some of the functionalities like getting the centroid of a polygon figure stored as GeoJSON in the collection or even the area of a polygon are not supported out of the box and there should have been some utility functions to help compute these given the coordinates. These features are good and are commonly required, and perhaps we might have some support in future release; such operations are to be implemented by developers themselves. Also, there is no straightforward way to find if there is an overlap between two polygons, what the coordinates are, where they overlap, the area of overlap, and so on. The `$geoIntersects` operator we saw does tell us what polygons do intersect with the given polygon, point, or line.

Though nothing related to Mongo, the GeoJSON format doesn't have support for circles, and hence storing circles in Mongo using GeoJSON format is not possible. Refer to the following link `http://docs.mongodb.org/manual/reference/operator/query-geospatial/` for more details on geospatial operators.

Implementing full text search in Mongo

Many of us (I won't be wrong to say all of us) use Google every day to search content on the web. To explain in short: the text that we provide in the text box on Google's page is used to search the pages on the web it has indexed. The search results are then returned to us in some order determined by Google's page rank algorithm. We might want to have a similar functionality in our database that lets us search for some text content and give the corresponding search results. Note that this text search is not same as finding the text as part of the sentence, which can easily be done using regex. It goes way beyond that and can be used to get results that contain the same word, a similar sounding word, have a similar base word, or even a synonym in the actual sentence.

Since MongoDB Version 2.4, text indexes have been introduced, which let us create text indexes on a particular field in the document and enable text search on those words. In this recipe, we will be importing some documents and creating text indexes on them, which we will later query to retrieve the results.

Getting ready

A simple, single node is what we would need for the test. Refer to the recipe *Installing single node MongoDB* from *Chapter 1*, *Installing and Starting the Server*, for how to start the server. However, do not start the server yet. There would be an additional flag provided during the startup to enable text search. Download the file `BlogEntries.json` from the Packt site and keep it on your local drive ready to be imported.

How to do it...

1. Start the MongoDB server listening to port `27017` as follows. Once the server is started, we will be creating the test data in a collection as follows. With the file `BlogEntries.json` placed in the current directory, we will be creating the collection `userBlog` as follows using `mongoimport`:

   ```
   $ mongoimport -d test -c userBlog --drop BlogEntries.json
   ```

2. Now, connect to the `mongo` process from a mongo shell by typing the following command from the operating system shell:

   ```
   $ mongo
   ```

3. Once connected, get a feel of the documents in the `userBlog` collection as follows:

   ```
   > db.userBlog.findOne()
   ```

4. The field `blog_text` is of our interest and this is the one on which we will be creating a text search index.

5. Create a text index on the field `blog_text` of the document as follows:

   ```
   > db.userBlog.ensureIndex({'blog_text':'text'})
   ```

6. Now, execute the following search on the collection from the mongo shell:

   ```
   $ db.userBlog.find({$text: {$search : 'plot zoo'}})
   ```

   Look at the results obtained.

7. Execute another search as follows:

   ```
   $ db.userBlog.find({$text: {$search : 'Zoo -plot'}})
   ```

How it works...

Let's now see how it all works. A text search is done by a process called reverse indexes. In simple terms, this is a mechanism where the sentences are broken up into words and then those individual words point back to the document which they belong to. The process is not straightforward though, so let's see what happens in this process step by step at a high level:

1. Consider the following input sentence, `I played cricket yesterday`. The first step is to break this sentence into tokens and they become [`I`, `played`, `cricket`, `yesterday`].

2. Next, the stop words from the broken down sentence are removed and we are left with a subset of these. Stop words are a list of very common words that are eliminated as it makes no sense to index them as they can potentially affect the accuracy of the search when used in the search query. In this case, we will be left with the following words [`played`, `cricket`, `yesterday`]. Stop words are language specific and will be different for different languages.

3. Finally, these words are stemmed to their base words, in this case it will be [`play`, `cricket`, `yesterday`]. Stemming is process of reduction of a word to its root. For instance, all the words `play`, `playing`, `played`, and `plays` have the same root word, `play`. There are a lot of algorithms and frameworks present for stemming a word to its root form. Refer to the Wikipedia `http://en.wikipedia.org/wiki/Stemming` page for more information on stemming and the algorithms used for this purpose. Similar to eliminating stop words, the stemming algorithm is language dependent. The examples given here were for the English language.

If we look at the index creation process, it is created as follows `db.userBlog.ensureIndex({'blog_text':'text'})`. The key given in the JSON argument is the name of the field on which the text index is to be created and the value will always be the text denoting that the index to be created is a text index. Once the index is created, at a high level, the preceding three steps get executed on the content of the field on which the index is created in each document and a reverse index is created. You can also choose to create a text index on more than one field. Suppose that we had two fields, `blog_text1` and `blog_text2`; we can create the index as `{'blog_text1': 'text', 'blog_text2':'text'}`. The value `{'$**':'text'}` creates an index on all fields of the document.

Finally, we executed the search operation by invoking the following: `db.userBlog.find({$text: {$search : 'plot zoo'}})`.

This command runs the text search on the collection `userBlog` and the search string used is `plot zoo`. This searches for the value `plot` or `zoo` in the text in any order. If we look at the results, we see that we have two documents matched and the documents are ordered by the score. This score tells us how relevant the document searched is, and the higher the score, the more relevant it is. In our case, one of the documents had both the words plot and zoo in it, and thus got a higher score than a document, as we see here:

To get the scores in the result, we need to modify the query a bit, as follows:

```
db.userBlog.find({$text:{$search:'plot zoo'}}, {score: { $meta:
"textScore"}})
```

We now have an additional document provided in the `find` method that asks for the score calculated for the text match. The results still are not ordered in descending order of score. Let's see how to sort the results by score:

```
db.userBlog.find({$text:{$search:'plot zoo'}}, { score: { $meta:
"textScore" }}).sort({score: { $meta: "textScore"}})
```

As we can see, the query is same as before, it's just the additional `sort` function that we have added, which will sort the results by descending order of score.

When the search is executed as `{$text:{$search:'Zoo -plot'}`, it searches for all the documents that contain the word `zoo` and do not contain the word `plot`, thus we get only one result. The - sign is for negation and leaves out the document from the search result containing that word. However, do not expect to find all documents without the word plot by just giving `-plot` in the search.

If we look at the contents returned as the result of the search, it contains the entire matched document in the result. If we are not interested in the entire document, but only a few documents, we can use projection to get the desired fields of the document. The following query, for instance, `db.userBlog.find({$text: {$search : 'plot zoo'}},{_ id:1})` will be same as finding all the documents in the `userBlog` collection containing the words zoo or plot, but the results will contain the `_id` field from the resulting documents.

If multiple fields are used for creation of index, then we may have different weights for different fields in the document. For instance, suppose blog_text1 and blog_text2 are two fields of a collection. We can create an index where `blog_text1` has higher weight than `blog_text2` as follows:

```
    db.collection.ensureIndex(
      {
        blog_text1: "text",
        blog_text2: "text"
      },
      {
        weights: {
          blog_text1: 2,
          blog_text2: 1,
        },
        name: "MyCustomIndexName"
      }
    )
```

This gives the content in `blog_text1` twice as much weight as that in `blog_text2`. Thus, if a word is found in two documents but is present in the `blog_text1` field of the first document and `blog_text2` of second document, then the score of first document will be more than the second. Note that we also have provided the name of the index using the name field as `MyCustomIndexName`.

We also see from the language key that the language in this case is English. MongoDB supports various languages for implementing text search. Languages are important when indexing the content as they decide the stop words, and stemming of words is language specific too.

Visit the link `http://docs.mongodb.org/manual/reference/command/text/#text-search-languages` for more details on the languages supported by Mongo for text search.

So, how do we choose the language while creating the index? By default, if nothing is provided, the index is created assuming the language is English. However, if we know the language is French, we create the index as follows:

```
db.userBlog.ensureIndex({'text':'text'}, {'default_language':'french'})
```

Suppose that we had originally created the index using the French language, the `getIndexes` method would return the following document:

```
[
  {
    "v" : 1,
    "key" : {
      "_id" : 1
    },
    "ns" : "test.userBlog",
    "name" : "_id_"
  },
  {
    "v" : 1,
    "key" : {
      "_fts" : "text",
      "_ftsx" : 1
    },
    "ns" : "test.userBlog",
    "name" : "text_text",
    "default_language" : "french",
    "weights" : {
      "text" : 1
    },
```

```
      "language_override" : "language",
      "textIndexVersion" : 1
   }
]
```

However, if the language was different per document basis, which is pretty common in scenarios like blogs, we have a way out. If we look at the document above, the value of the `language_override` field is language. This means that we can store the language of the content using this field on a per document basis. In its absence, the value will be assumed as the default value, `french` in the preceding case. Thus, we can have the following:

```
{_id:1, language:'english', text: ….}  //Language is English
{_id:2, language:'german', text: ….}  //Language is German
{_id:3, text: ….}       //Language is the default one, French in this
case
```

There's more...

To use MongoDB text search in production, you would need version 2.6 or higher. Integrating MongoDB with other systems like Solr and Elasticsearch is also an option. In the next recipe, we will see how to integrate Mongo with Elasticsearch using the mongo-connector.

See also

▶ For more information on the `$text` operator, visit `http://docs.mongodb.org/manual/reference/operator/query/text/`

Integrating MongoDB for full text search with Elasticsearch

MongoDB has integrated text search features, as we saw in the previous recipe. However, there are multiple reasons why one would not use the Mongo text search feature and fall back to a conventional search engine like Solr or Elasticsearch, and the following are few of them:

▶ The text search feature is production ready in version 2.6. In version 2.4, it was introduced in beta and not suitable for production use cases.

▶ Products like Solr and Elasticsearch are built on top of Lucene, which has proven itself in the search engine arena. Solr and Elasticsearch are pretty stable products too.

▶ You might already have expertise on products like Solr and Elasticsearch and would like to use it as a full text search engine rather than MongoDB.

▶ Some particular feature that you might find missing in MongoDB search which your application might require, for example, facets.

Setting up a dedicated search engine does need additional efforts to integrate it with a MongoDB instance. In this recipe, we will see how to integrate a MongoDB instance with a search engine, Elasticsearch.

We will be using the mongo-connector for integration purpose. It is an open source project that is available at `https://github.com/10gen-labs/mongo-connector`.

Getting ready
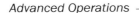

Refer to the recipe *Connecting to a single node using a Python client*, in *Chapter 1, Installing and Starting the Server* for installing and setting up Python client. The tool pip is used for getting the mongo-connector. However, if you are working on a Windows platform, the steps to install pip was not mentioned earlier. Visit the URL `https://sites.google.com/site/pydatalog/python/pip-for-windows` to get pip for windows.

The prerequisites for starting the single instance are all we need for this recipe. We would, however, start the server as a one node replica set for demonstration purpose in this recipe.

Download the file `BlogEntries.json` from the Packt site and keep it on your local drive ready to be imported.

Download elastic search from the following URL for your target platform: `http://www.elasticsearch.org/overview/elkdownloads/`. Extract the downloaded archive and from the shell, go to the `bin` directory of the extraction.

We will get the mongo-connector source from GitHub.com and run it. A Git client is needed for this purpose. Download and install the Git client on your machine. Visit the URL `http://git-scm.com/downloads` and follow the instructions for installing Git on your target operating system. If you are not comfortable installing Git on your operating system, then there is an alternative available that lets you download the source as an archive.

Visit the following URL `https://github.com/10gen-labs/mongo-connector`. Here, we will get an option that lets us download the current source as an archive, which we can then extract on our local drive. The following image shows that the download option available on the bottom-right corner:

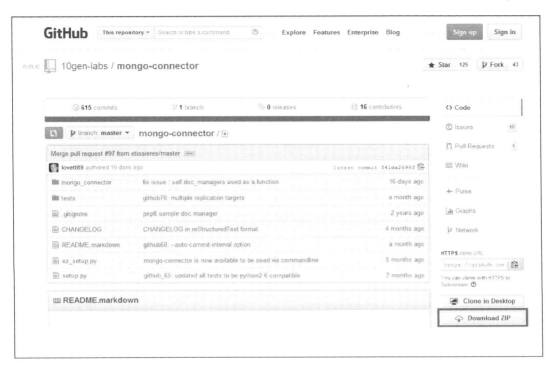

Note that we can also install mongo-connector in a very easy way using pip as follows:

```
pip install mongo-connector
```

However, the version in PyPi is a very old with not many features supported and thus using the latest from the repository is recommended.

Similar to the previous recipe, where we saw text search in Mongo, we will use the same five documents to test our simple search. Download and keep the `BlogEntries.json` file.

How to do it...

1. At this point, it is assumed that Python and PyMongo are installed and pip for your operating system platform is installed. We will now get mongo-connector from source. If you have already installed the Git client, we will be executing the following on the operating system shell. If you have decided to download the repository as an archive, you may skip this step. Go to the directory where you would like to clone the connector repository and execute the following:

```
$ git clone https://github.com/10gen-labs/mongo-connector.git
$ cd mongo-connector
$ python setup.py install
```

2. The preceding setup will also install the Elasticsearch client that will be used by this application.

3. We will now start a single mongo instance but as a replica set. From the operating system console, execute the following:

```
$  mongod --dbpath /data/mongo/db --replSet textSearch
--smallfiles --oplogSize 50
```

4. Start a mongo shell and connect to the started instance:

```
$ mongo
```

5. From the mongo shell initiate the replica set as follows:

```
> rs.initiate()
```

6. The replica set will be initiated in a few moments. Meanwhile, we can proceed to starting the elasticsearch server instance.

7. Execute the following from the command after going to the bin directory of the extracted elasticsearch archive:

```
$ elasticsearch
```

8. We won't be getting into the Elasticsearch settings, and we will start it in the default mode.

9. Once started, enter the following URL in the browser http://localhost:9200/_nodes/process?pretty.

10. If we see a JSON document as the following, giving the process details, we have successfully started `elasticsearch`.

```
{
    "cluster_name" : "elasticsearch",
    "nodes" : {
        "p0gMLKzsT7CjwoPdrl-unA" : {
            "name" : "Zaladane",
            "transport_address" : "inet[/192.168.2.3:9300]",
            "host" : "Amol-PC",
            "ip" : "192.168.2.3",
            "version" : "1.0.1",
            "build" : "5c03844",
            "http_address" : "inet[/192.168.2.3:9200]",
            "process" : {
                "refresh_interval" : 1000,
                "id" : 5628,
                "max_file_descriptors" : -1,
                "mlockall" : false
            }
        }
    }
}
```

11. Once the `elasticsearch` server and mongo instance are up and running, and the necessary Python libraries are installed, we will start the connector that will sync the data between the started mongo instance and the `elasticsearch` server. For the sake of this test, we will be using the collection `user_blog` in the `test` database. The field on which we would like to have text search implemented is the field `blog_text` in the document.

12. Start the mongo-connector from the operating system shell as follows. The following command was executed with the mongo-connector's directory as the current directory.

```
$ python mongo_connector/connector.py -m localhost:27017 -t
http://localhost:9200 -n test.user_blog --fields blog_text -d
mongo_connector/doc_managers/elastic_doc_manager.py
```

13. Import the `BlogEntries.json` file into the collection using `mongoimport` utility as follows. The command is executed with the `.json` file present in the current directory.

```
$ mongoimport -d test -c user_blog BlogEntries.json --drop
```

14. Open a browser of your choice and enter the following URL in it: `http://localhost:9200/_search?q=blog_text:facebook`.

15. You should see something like the following in the browser:

How it works...

Mongo-connector basically tails the oplog to find new updates that it publishes to another endpoint. We used elasticsearch in our case, but it could be even be Solr. You may choose to write a custom DocManager that would plugin with the connector. Refer to the wiki `https://github.com/10gen-labs/mongo-connector/wiki` for more details, and the readme for `https://github.com/10gen-labs/mongo-connector` gives some detailed information too.

We gave the connector the options `-m`, `-t`, `-n`, `--fields`, and `-d` and what they mean is explained in the table as follows:

Option	Description
`-m`	URL of the MongoDB host to which the connector connects to get the data to be synchronized.
`-t`	The target URL of the system with which the data is to be synchronized with. Elasticsearch in this case. The URL format will depend on the target system. Should you choose to implement your own DocManager, the format will be one that your DocManager understands.
`-n`	This is the namespace that we would like keep synchronized with the external system. The connector will just be looking for changes in these namespaces while tailing the oplog for data. The value will be comma separated if more than one namespaces are to be synchronized.
`--fields`	These are the fields from the document that will be sent to the external system. In our case, it doesn't make sense to index the entire document and waste resources. It is recommended to add to the index just the fields that you would like to add text search support. The identifier `_id` and the namespace of the source is also present in the result, as we can see in the preceding screenshot. The `_id` field can then be used to query the target collection.

Option	Description
-d	This is the document manager to be used, in our case we have used the elasticsearch's document manager.

For more supported options, refer to the readme of the connector's page on GitHub.

Once the insert is executed on the MongoDB server, the connector detects the newly added documents to the collection of its interest, `user_blog`, and starts sending the data to be indexed from the newly documents to the elasticsearch. To confirm the addition, we execute a query in the browser to view the results.

Elasticsearch will complain that the index names have upper case characters in them. The mongo-connector doesn't take care of this, and thus the name of the collection has to be in lower case. For example, the name `userBlog` will fail.

There's more...

We have not done any additional configuration on elasticsearch as that was not the objective of the recipe. We were more interested in integrating MongoDB and elasticsearch. You will have to refer to elasticsearch documentation for more advanced config options. If integrating with elasticsearch is required, there is a concept called rivers in elasticsearch that can be used as well. Rivers are elasticsearch's way to get data from another data source. For MongoDB, the code for the river can be found at `https://github.com/richardwilly98/elasticsearch-river-mongodb/`. The readme in this repository has steps on how to set it up.

In this chapter, we saw a recipe, *Implementing triggers in Mongo using oplog*, on how to implement trigger-like functionalities using Mongo. This connector and MongoDB river for elasticsearch rely on the same logic for getting the data out of Mongo as and when it is needed.

See also

- ▶ You may find additional elasticsearch documentation at `http://www.elasticsearch.org/guide/en/elasticsearch/reference/`

6
Monitoring and Backups

In this chapter, we will take a look at the following recipes:

- ▶ Signing up for MMS and setting up an MMS monitoring agent
- ▶ Managing users and groups in MMS Console
- ▶ Monitoring instances and setting up alerts in MMS
- ▶ Setting up monitoring alerts in MMS
- ▶ Back up and restore data in Mongo using out-of-the-box tools
- ▶ Configuring MMS Backup service
- ▶ Managing backups in MMS Backup service

Introduction

Monitoring and backup is an important aspect of any mission-critical software in production. Monitoring proactively lets us take action whenever an abnormal event occurs in the system that can compromise data consistency, availability, or the performance of the system. Issues may come to light after having a significant impact in the absence of monitoring the systems proactively. We covered administration-related recipes in *Chapter 4*, *Administration*, and both these activities are part of it; however, they demand a separate chapter as the content to be covered is extensive. In this chapter, we will see how to monitor various parameters and set up alerts for various parameters of your MongoDB cluster using the **Mongo Monitoring Service** (**MMS**). We will look at some mechanisms to backup data using the out-of-the-box tools and also using the MMS backup service.

Signing up for MMS and setting up an MMS monitoring agent

MMS is a cloud-based or on-premise service that enables you to monitor your MongoDB cluster. The on-premise version is available with an enterprise subscription only. It gives you one central place that lets the administrators monitor the health of the server instances and the boxes on which the instances are running. In this recipe, we will see what the software requirements are and how to set up MMS for Mongo.

Getting ready

We will be starting a single instance of `mongod`, which we will use for monitoring purposes. Refer to the recipe *Installing single node MongoDB* from *Chapter 1, Installing and Starting the Server* to start a MongoDB instance and connect to it from a Mongo shell. The monitoring agent used for sending the statistics of the mongo instance to the monitoring service uses Python and pymongo. Refer to the recipe *Connecting to a single node using a Python client* in *Chapter 1, Installing and Starting the Server* to learn more about how to install Python and pymongo, the Python client of MongoDB.

How to do it...

If you don't already have a MMS account, then log in to `https://mms.mongodb.com/` and sign up for an account. On signing up and logging in, you should see the following page:

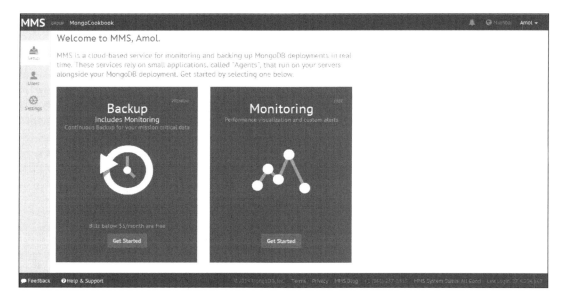

Click on the **Get Started** button under **Monitoring**.

1. Once we reach the **Download Agent** option in the menu, click on the appropriate OS platform to download the agent. Follow the instructions given after selecting the appropriate OS platform. Note down the **apiKey** too. For example, if the Windows platform is selected, we would see the following:

Install or Update the Monitoring Agent on Windows

         Install   Update

1. Download and run the 32-bit or 64-bit MSI file. During the installation process, you will be prompted for a folder in which to store configuration and log files. It is strongly advised that you encrypt or restrict access to this folder.

2. In the configuration/log folder that you selected, the setup program will create a file called `monitoring-agent.config`. Open this file in a text editor. Insert your API key into the file as indicated by the comments.

    `apiKey=`▉▉▉▉▉▉▉▉▉▉▉▉▉▉▉▉▉▉

3. In the Administrative Tools section of Control Panel, select Services. Find MMS Monitoring Agent in the list of services. Right-click on it and select Start.

If you are using MongoDB authentication, please consult the docs

If you are using Kerberos authentication, or your Monitoring Agent must connect to the internet via proxy, you will need to continue to use our legacy Python Monitoring Agent. You may download a zip or tar.gz file. See the docs for installation instructions.

---

2. Once the installation is complete, open the file `monitoring-agent.config`. It will be present in the configuration folder selected while installing the agent.

3. Look out for the key `mmsApiKey` in the file and set its value to the API key that was noted down in step 1.

4. Once the service is started (we have to go to `services.msc` on Windows, which can be done by typing `services.msc` in the run dialog (Windows + *R*) and start the service manually). The service would be named **MMS Monitoring Agent**. On the web page, click on the **Verify Agent** button. If all goes well, the started agent will be verified and a success message will be shown.

5. The next step is to configure the host. This host is the one that is seen from the agent's perspective running on the organization or individual's infrastructure. The following screen shows the screen used for the addition of a host. The hostname is the internal hostname (the hostname on the client's network), and the MMS on the cloud doesn't need to reach out to the MongoDB processes. It is the agent that collects the data from these mongodb processes and sends the data to the MMS service.

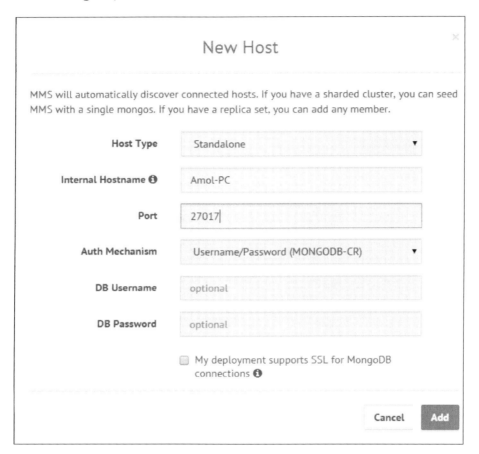

Once the host's details are added, click on the **Verify Host** button. Once verification is done, click the **Start Monitoring** button.

We have successfully set up MMS and added one host to it that will be monitored.

How it works...

In this recipe, we set up an MMS agent and monitoring for a standalone MongoDB instance. The installation and setup process is pretty simple. We also added a standalone instance and all was okay.

Suppose we have a replica set up and running (refer to the recipe *Starting multiple instances as part of a replica set* in *Chapter 1, Installing and Starting the Server*, for more details on how to start a replica set) and the three members are listening to ports `27000`, `27001`, and `27002`. Refer to point number 6 in the *How to do it...* section where we set up one standalone host. In the drop-down menu for **Host Type** select **Replica Set** and in the **Internal hostname**, give a valid hostname of any member of the replica set (in my case **Amol-PC** and port **27001** were given, which is a secondary instance); all other instances will be automatically discovered and will be visible under the hosts, as shown here:

We didn't see what is to be done when security is enabled on the cluster, which is pretty common in production environments and we have replica sets or shard setup. If authentication is enabled, we need proper credentials for the MMS agent to gather the statistics. The **DB Username** and **DB Password** that we give while adding a new host (point number 6 in the *How to do it...* section) should have a minimum of `clusterAdmin` and `readAnyDatabase` role.

There's more...

What we saw in this recipe was how to set up MMS agent and create an account from the MMS console. However, we can add groups and users for the MMS console as an administrator granting various users privileges for performing various operations on different groups. In the next recipe, we will throw some light on user and group management in the MMS console.

Managing users and groups in MMS console

In the previous recipe, we saw how to set up an MMS account and set up an MMS agent. In this recipe, we will throw some light on how to set up the groups and user access to the MMS console.

Getting ready

Refer to the previous recipe for setting up the agent and MMS account. This is the only prerequisite for this recipe.

How to do it...

1. Start by going to **Administration | Users** on the left-hand side of the screen, as shown here:

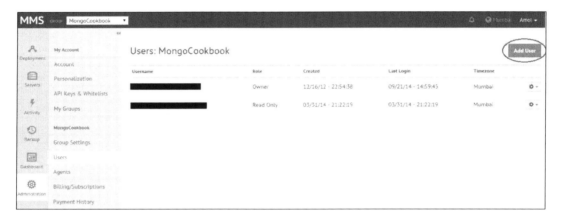

Here, you can view the existing users and also add new users. On clicking the **Add User** (encircled in the top right corner of the preceding image) button, you should see the following popup window that allows you to add a new user:

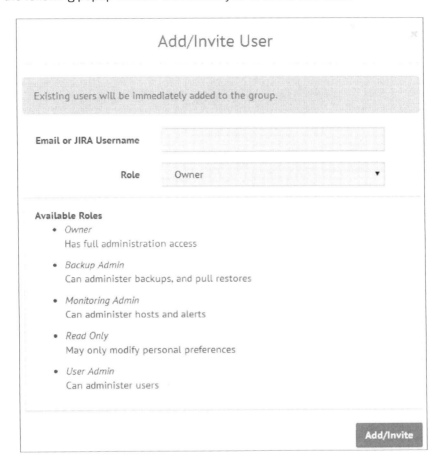

The preceding screen will be used to add users. Take a note of the various available roles.

2. Similarly, go to **Administration | My Groups** to view and add new groups by clicking on the **Add Group** button. In the text box, type the name of the group. Remember that the name of the group you enter should be available globally. The given name of the group should be unique across all users of MMS and not just your account.

3. When a new group is created, it will be visible in the top left corner in a drop-down menu for all the groups, as shown here:

4. You can switch between the groups using this drop-down menu, which should show all the details and stats relevant to the selected group.

Remember that a group once created cannot be deleted. So be careful while creating one.

How it works...

The tasks we did in the recipe are pretty straightforward and don't need a lot of explanation except for one question. When and why do we add a group? It is when we want to segregate our MongoDB instances by different environments or applications. There will be a different MMS agent running for each group. Creating a new group is necessary when we want to have separate monitoring groups for different environments of an application (Development, QA, Production, and so on), and each group has different privileges for the users. That is, the same agent cannot be used for two different groups. While configuring the MMS agent, we give it an API key unique to the group. To view the API key for the group, select the appropriate group from the drop-down menu at the top of the screen (if your user has access to only group, the drop-down menu won't be seen) and go to **Administration | Group Settings** as shown in the next screenshot. The **Group ID** and the **API Key** will both be shown on the top of the page.

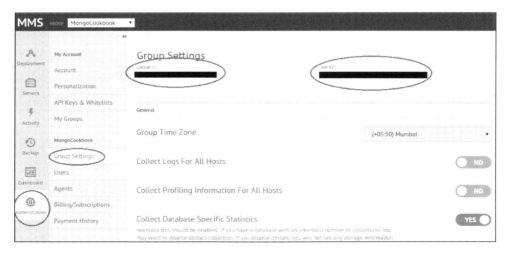

Note that not all user roles will see this option. For example, read-only users can only personalize their profile and most of the other options will not be visible.

Monitoring instances and setting up alerts on MMS

The previous couple of recipes showed us how to set up an MMS account, set up an agent, add hosts, and manage user access to MMS console. The core objective of MMS is monitoring the host instances, which has not been discussed yet. In this recipe, we will perform some operations on the host that we added to MMS in the first recipe and monitor it from the MMS console.

Getting ready

Follow the recipe *Signing up for MMS and setting up an MMS monitoring agent*, and that is pretty much all that is needed for this recipe. You may choose to have a standalone instance or a replica set, either way is fine. Also, open a mongo shell and connect to the primary instance from it (it is a replica set).

How to do it...

1. Start by logging into MMS console and clicking on **Deployment** on the left. Then, click on the **Deployment** link in the submenu again, as shown in the following screenshot:

Click on one of the hostnames to see a large variety of graphs showing various statistics. In this recipe, we will analyze the majority of these.

2. Open the bundle downloaded for the book. In *Chapter 4, Administration*, we used a JavaScript to keep the server busy with some operations named `KeepServerBusy.js`. We will be using the same script this time around.

3. In the operating system shell, execute the following with the `.js` file in current directory. The shell connects to port `27000` in my case for the primary:

```
$ mongo KeepServerBusy.js --port 27000 --quiet
```

4. Once it's started, keep it running and give it some 5 to 10 minutes before you start monitoring the graphs on MMS console.

How it works...

In *Chapter 4, Administration*, we saw a recipe, *The mongostat and mongotop utilities* that demonstrated how these utilities can be used to get the current operations and resource utilization. That is a fairly basic and helpful way to monitor a particular instance. MMS, however, gives us one place to monitor the MongoDB instance with pretty easy-to-understand graphs. MMS also gives us historical stats, which `mongostat` and `mongotop` cannot give.

Before we go ahead with the analysis of the metrics, I would like to mention that in the case of MMS monitoring, the data is not queried nor sent out over the public network. It is just the statistics that are sent over a secure channel by the agent. The source code for the agent is open source and is available for examination if needed. The mongod servers need not be accessible from the public network as the cloud-based MMS service never communicates with the server instances directly. It is the MMS agent that communicates with the MMS service. Typically, one agent is enough to monitor several servers unless you plan to segregate them into different groups. Also, it is recommended to run the agent on a dedicated machine/virtual machine and not share it with any of the mongod or mongos instances unless it is a less crucial test instance group you are monitoring.

Let's see some of these statistics on the console; we start with the memory-related ones. The following graph shows the resident, mapped, and virtual memory.

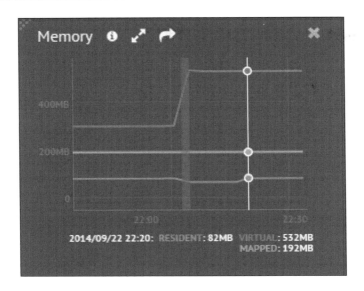

As we can see, the resident memory for the data set is 82 MB, which is very low and it is the actual physical memory used up by the mongod process. This current value is significantly below the free memory available and generally this will increase over a period of time till it reaches a point where it has used up a large chunk of the total physical available memory. This is automatically taken care of by the mongod server process, and we can't force it to use up more memory even though it is available on the machine it is running on.

The mapped memory, on other hand, is about the total size of the database and is mapped by MongoDB. This size can be (and usually is) much higher than the physical memory available, which enables the mongod process to address the entire dataset as it is present in memory even if it isn't. MongoDB offloads the responsibility of mapping and loading data to and from disk to the underlying operating system. Whenever a memory location is accessed and it is not available in the RAM (that is, the resident memory), the operating system fetches the page into memory, evicting some pages to make space for the new page if necessary. What exactly is a memory mapped file? Let's try to see with a super scaled down version. Suppose we have a file of 1 KB (1024 bytes) and the RAM is only 512 bytes, then obviously we cannot have the whole file in memory. However, you can ask the operating system to map this file to available RAM in pages. Suppose each page is 128 bytes, then the total file is 8 pages (128 * 8 = 1024). But the OS can only load four pages, and we assume it loaded the first 4 pages (up to 512 bytes) in the memory. When we access byte number 200, it is okay and found in the memory as it is in present on page 2. But what if we access byte 800, which is logically on page 7 that is not loaded in memory? What OS does is takes one page out from the memory and loads this page 7 containing byte number 800. MongoDB as an application gives the impression that everything was loaded in the memory and was accessed by the byte index, but actually it wasn't and the OS transparently did the work for us. Since the page accessed was not present in the memory and we had to go to the disk to load it in the memory it is called a **page fault**.

Getting back to the stats shown in the graph, the virtual memory contains all the memory usage including the mapped memory plus any additional memory used, such as the memory associated with the thread stack associated with each connection. If journaling is enabled, this size will definitely be more than twice than that of the mapped memory as journaling too will have a separate memory mapping for the data. Thus, we have two addresses mapping the same memory location. This doesn't mean that the page will be loaded twice. It just means that two different memory locations can be used to address the same physical memory. Very high virtual memory might need some investigation. There is no predetermined definition of a too high or low value; generally these values are monitored for your system under normal circumstances when you are happy with the performance of your system. These benchmark values should then be compared with the figures seen when system performance goes down and then appropriate action can be taken.

As we saw earlier, page faults are caused when an accessed memory location is not present in the resident memory, causing the OS to load the page from memory. This IO activity will definitely cause performance to go down and too many page faults can bring down database performance dramatically. The following screenshot shows quite a few page faults happening per minute. However, if the disk used is an SSD instead of spinning disks, the hit in terms of seek time from the drive might not be significantly high.

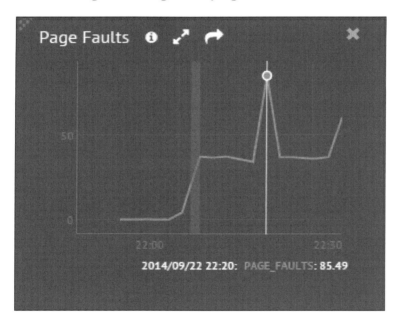

A large number of page faults usually occur when there isn't enough physical memory to accommodate the data set and the OS needs to get the data from the disk into memory. Note that this stat shown in the preceding screenshot is taken on a Windows platform and might seem high for a very trivial operation. This value is the sum of hard and soft page faults and doesn't really give a true figure of how good (or bad) the system is. These figures would be different on a Unix-based OS. There is a JIRA (`https://jira.mongodb.org/browse/ SERVER-5799`) open as of the writing of this book which reports this problem.

One thing you might need to remember is that in production systems, MongoDB doesn't work well with a NUMA architecture and you might see a lot of page faults happening even if the available memory seems to be high enough. Refer to the URL `http://docs.mongodb.org/ manual/administration/production-notes/` for more details.

There is an additional graph which gives some details about non-mapped memory. As we saw earlier in this section, there are three types of memory: mapped, resident, and virtual. Mapped memory is always less than virtual memory. Virtual memory will be more than twice that of mapped memory if journaling is enabled. If we look at the image given in this section earlier, we see that the mapped memory is 192 MB whereas the virtual memory is 532MB. Since journaling is enabled, the memory is more than twice that of the mapped memory. When journaling is enabled, the same page of data is mapped twice in memory. Note that the page is physically loaded only once, it is just that the same location can be accessed using two different addresses. Let's find the difference between the virtual memory, which is 532MB, and twice the mapped memory that is 384 MB (2 * 192 = 384). The difference between these figures is 148 MB (532 - 384).

What we see here is the portion of virtual memory that is not mapped memory. This value is the same as what we just calculated.

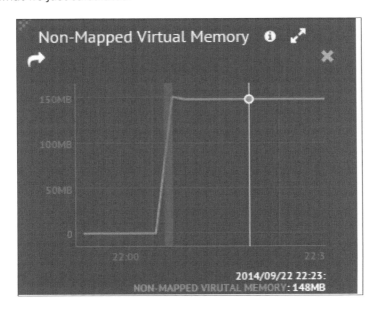

As mentioned earlier, a high or low value for non-mapped memory is not defined, however when the value reaches GBs we might have to investigate; possibly the number of open connections is high and we need to check if there is a leak with client applications not closing them after using it. There is a graph that gives us the number of connections open and it looks as follows:

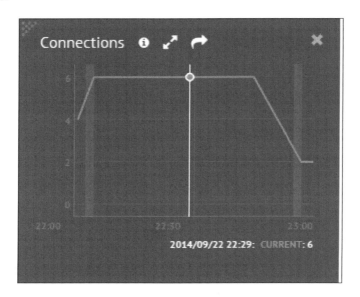

Once we know the number of connections and find it too high as compared to the expected count, we will need to find the clients who have opened the connections to that instance. We can execute the following JavaScript code from the shell to get those details. Unfortunately, at the time of writing this book, MMS doesn't have this feature to list out the client connection details.

```
testMon:PRIMARY> var currentOps = db.currentOp(true).inprog;
 currentOps.forEach(function(c) {
  if(c.hasOwnProperty('client')) {
    print('Client: ' + c.client + ", connection id is: " + c.desc);
  }
  //Get other details as needed
});
```

The `db.currentOp` method returns all the idle and system operations in the result. We then iterate through all the results and print out the client host and the connection details. A typical document in the result of the `currentOp` looks like this. You can choose to tweak the preceding code to include more details as per your need:

```
{
  "opid" : 62052485,
  "active" : false,
  "op" : "query",
  "ns" : "",
  "query" : {
    "replSetGetStatus" : 1,
    "forShell" : 1
  },
  "client" : "127.0.0.1:64460",
  "desc" : "conn3651",
  "connectionId" : 3651,
  "waitingForLock" : false,
  "numYields" : 0,
  "lockStats" : {
  "timeLockedMicros" : {

  },
  "timeAcquiringMicros" : {

  }
  }
}
```

In *Chapter 4, Administration*, we saw a recipe, *The mongostat and mongotop utilities* that was used to get some details on the percent of time a database was locked and the number of update, insert, delete, and getmore operations executed per second. You may refer to these recipes and try them out. We had used the same JavaScript that we have used currently to keep the server busy.

In MMS console, we have graphs giving these details as follows:

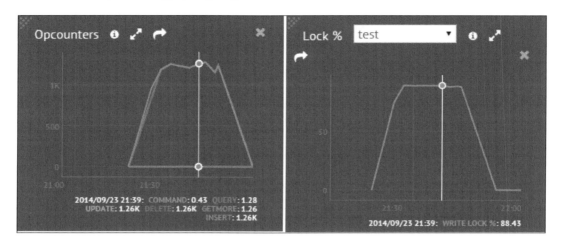

The first one, `opcounters`, shows the number of operations executed at a particular point in time. This should be similar to what we saw using the `mongostat` utility. The one on the right shows us the percentage of time a database was locked. The drop-down menu lists the database names. We can select an appropriate database that we want to see the stats for. Again, this statistic can be seen using the `mongostat` utility. The only difference is that with the command-line utility, we see the stats as of the current time, whereas here we see the historical stats too.

In MongoDB, indexes are stored in BTrees and the next graph shows the number of times the BTree index was accessed, hit, and missed. At the minimum, the RAM should be enough to accommodate the indexes for optimum performance. So in this metric, the misses should be 0 or very low. A high number of misses results in a page fault for the index and possibly additional page faults for the corresponding data if the query is not covered, that is, all its data cannot be sourced from the index, which is a double blow for performance. One good practice while querying is to use projections and fetch only the necessary fields from the document. This is helpful whenever we have our selected fields present in an index, in which case the query becomes covered and all the necessary data is sourced from the index only. To learn more about on covered indexes, refer to the recipe *Creating index and viewing plans of queries* in *Chapter 2, Command-line Operations and Indexes*.

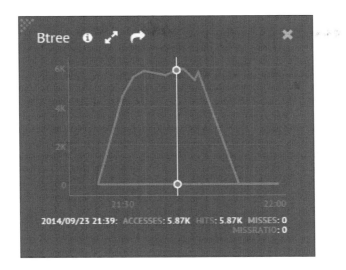

For busy applications if the volumes are very high, with multiple write and read operations contending for lock, the operations queue up. Untill Version 2.4 of MongoDB, the locks are at the database level. Thus, even if the writes are happening on another collection, read operations on any collection in that database will block. This queuing operation affects the performance of the system and is a good indicator that the data might need to be sharded across to scale the system.

Remember, no value is defined as high or low; it is the acceptable value on an application-to-application basis.

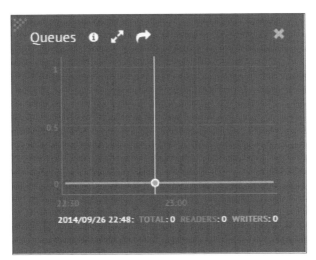

MongoDB flushes the data from the journal immediately and the data file periodically to disk. The following metrics give us the flush time per minute at a given point of time. If the flush takes up a significant percentage of the time per minute, we can safely say that the write operations are forming a bottleneck for performance.

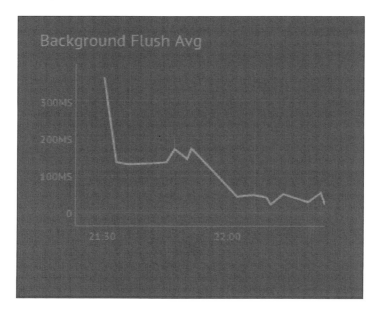

There's more...

We have seen monitoring of the MongoDB instances/cluster in this recipe. However, setting up alerts to get notifications when certain threshold values are crossed is what we still haven't seen. In the next recipe, we will see how to achieve this with a sample alert that is sent out over an e-mail when the page faults exceed a predetermined value.

See also

▶ Monitoring the hardware, such as CPU usage, is pretty useful and MMS console does support that. However, it needs munin-node to be installed to enable CPU monitoring. Refer to the page http://mms.mongodb.com/help/monitoring/configuring/ for setting up munin-node and hardware monitoring.

▶ For updating the monitoring agent, refer to the page http://mms.mongodb.com/help/monitoring/tutorial/update-mms/.

Setting up monitoring alerts in MMS

In the previous recipe, we saw how to monitor various metrics from MMS console. This is a great way to see all the stats in one place and get an overview of the health of the MongoDB instances and cluster. However, it is not possible to monitor the system continuously, 24/7, for the support personnel and there has to be some mechanism to automatically send out alerts in case some threshold is exceeded. In this recipe we will set up an alert whenever the page faults exceeds 1000.

Getting ready

Refer to the previous recipe to set up Monitoring Mongo Instances using MMS. That is the only prerequisite for this recipe.

How to do it...

1. Click on the **Activity** option on the left side menu, and then **Alert Settings**. On the **Alert Settings** page, click on **Add Alert**.

2. Add a new alert for the **Host** that is a primary instance and if the page faults exceed a given number, which is 1000 page faults per minute. The notification is chosen to be an e-mail in this case and the interval after which the alert will be sent is 10 minutes.

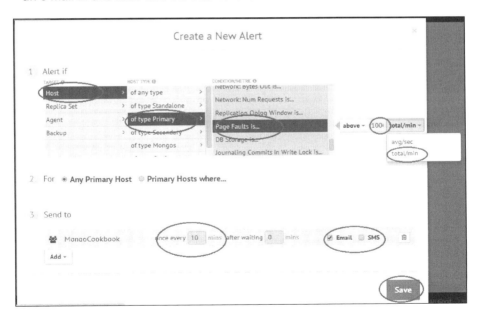

3. Click on **Save** to save the alert.

How it works...

The steps were pretty simple and we were successful in setting up MMS alerts when the page faults exceeded 1000 per minute. As we saw in the previous recipe, no fixed value is classified as high or low. It is something that is acceptable for your system, which comes with benchmarking the system during the testing phases in your environment. Similar to page faults, there is a vast array of alerts that can be set up. Once an alert is raised, it will be sent every 10 minutes, as we have set, until the condition for sending the alerts is not met. In this case, if the number of page faults falls below 1000 or somebody manually acknowledges the alert, no further alerts will be sent further for that incident.

As we see in the following screenshot, the alert is open and we can acknowledge the alert:

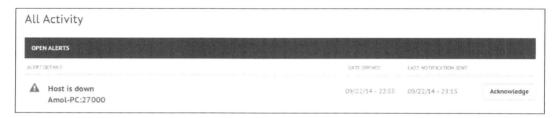

On clicking on **Acknowledge**, the following popup will let us choose the duration for which we will acknowledge:

This means that for this particular incident, no more alerts will be sent out until the selected time period elapses.

The Open alerts can be viewed by clicking on the **Activities** menu option on the left.

See also

▶ Visit the URL `http://www.mongodb.com/blog/post/five-mms-monitoring-alerts-keep-your-mongodb-deployment-track` for some of the important alerts that you should set up for your deployment

Back up and restore data in Mongo using out-of-the-box tools

In this recipe, we will look at some basic backup and restore operations using utilities such as `mongodump` and `mongorestore` to back up and restore files.

Getting ready

We will start a single instance of mongod. Refer to the recipe *Installing single node MongoDB* in *Chapter 1, Installing and Starting the Server*, to start a mongo instance and connect to it from a mongo shell. We will need some data to backup. If you already have some data in your test database, that will be fine. If not, create some from the `countries.geo.json` file available in the code bundle using the following command:

```
$ mongoimport  -c countries -d test --drop countries.geo.json
```

How to do it...

1. With the data in the `test` database, execute the following (assuming we want to export the data to a local directory called `dump` in the current directory):

   ```
   $ mongodump -o dump -oplog -h localhost -port 27017
   ```

   Verify that there is data in the `dump` directory. All files will be `.bson` files, one per collection in the respective database folder created.

2. Now let's import the data back into the mongo server using the following command. This is again with the assumption that we have the directory `dump` in the current directory with the required `.bson` files present in it:

   ```
   mongorestore --drop -h localhost -port 27017 dump -oplogReplay
   ```

How it works...

Just a couple of steps executed to export and restore the data. Let's now see what it exactly does and what the command-line options for this utility are. The `mongodump` utility is used to export the database into the `.bson` files, which can then be later used to restore the data in the database. The export utility exports one folder per database except local database, and then each of them will have one `.bson` file per collection. In our case, we used the `-oplog` option to export a part of the oplog too and the data will be exported to the `oplog.bson` file. Similarly, we import the data back into the database using the `mongorestore` utility. We explicitly ask the existing data to be dropped by providing the `--drop` option before the import and replay of the contents in the oplog if any.

The `mongodump` utility simply queries the collection and exports the contents to the files. The bigger the collection, the longer it will take to restore the contents. It is thus advisable to prevent write operations when the dump is being taken. In the case of sharded environments, the balancer should be turned off. If the dump is taken while the system is running, export with the `-oplog` option to export the contents of the oplog as well. This oplog can then be used to restore to the point in time data. The following table shows some of the important options available for the `mongodump` and `mongorestore` utility, first for `mongodump`:

Option	Description
`--help`	Shows all the possible, supported options and a brief description of these options.
`-h` or `--host`	The host to connect to. By default, it is localhost on port `27017`. If a standalone instance is to be connected to, we can set the hostname as `<hostname>:<port number>`. For a replica set, the format will be `<replica set name>/<hostname>:<port>,… .<hostname>:<port>` where the comma-separated list of hostnames and port is called the **seed list**. It can contain all or a subset of hostnames in a replica set.
`--port`	The port number of the target MongoDB instance. This is not really relevant if the port number is provided in the previous `-h` or `--host` option.
`-u` or `--username`	Provides the username of the user using which the data would be exported. Since the data is read from all databases, the user is at least expected to have read privileges in all databases.
`-p` or `--password`	The password used in conjunction with the username.
`--authenticationDatabase`	The database in which the user credentials are kept. If not specified, the database specified in the `--db` option is used.
`-d` or `--db`	The database to back up. If not specified, then all the databases are exported.

Option	Description
-c or --collection	The collection in the database to be exported.
-o or --out	The directory to which the files will be exported. By default, the utility will create a dump folder in the current directory and export the contents to that directory.
--dbpath	If we don't intend to connect to the database server and instead directly read from the database file. The value is the path of the directory where the database files will be found. The server should not be up and running while reading directly from the database files as the export locks the data files, which can't happen if a server is up and running. A lock file will be created in the directory while the lock is acquired.
--oplog	With the option enabled, the data from the oplog from the time the export process started is also exported. Without this option enabled, the data in the export will not represent a single point in time if writes are happening in parallel as the export process can take few hours and it simply is a query operation on all the collections. Exporting the oplog gives an option to restore to a point in time data. There is no need to specify this option if you are preventing write operations while the export is in progress.

Similarly, for the mongorestore utility, here are the options. The meaning of the options --help, -h, or --host, --port, -u, or --username, -p or --password, --authenticationDatabase, -d, or --db, -c or --collection.

Option	Description
--dbpath	If we don't intend to connect to the database server and instead directly write to the database file, use this option. The value is the path of the directory where the database files will be found. The server should not be up and running while writing directly to the database files as the restore operation locks the data files, which can't happen if a server is up and running. A lock file will be created in the directory while the lock is acquired.
--drop	Drop the existing data in the collection before restoring the data from the exported dumps.
--oplogReplay	If the data was exported while writes to the database were allowed and if the --oplog option was enabled during export, the oplog exported will be replayed on the data to bring all the data in the database to the same point in time.

Option	Description
`--oplogLimit`	The value of this parameter is a number representing the time in seconds. This option is used in conjunction with `oplogReplay` command line option, which is used to tell the restore utility to replay the oplog and stop just at the limit specified by this option.

You might think, *Why not copy the files and take a backup?* That works well but there are a few problems associated with it. First, you cannot get a point-in-time backup unless write operations are disabled. Secondly, the space used for backups is very high as the copy would also copy the 0 padded files of the database as against the `mongodump`, which exports just the data.

Having said that, filesystem snapshotting is a commonly used practice for backups. One thing to remember is while taking the snapshot the journal files and the data files need to come in the same snapshot for consistency.

If you were using **Amazon Web Services** (**AWS**), it would be highly recommended that you upload your database backups to AWS S3. As you may be aware, AWS offers extremely high data redundancy with a very low storage cost.

Download the script `generic_mongodb_backup.sh` from the Packt Publishing website and use it to automate your backup creation and upload to AWS S3.

Configuring MMS Backup service

MMS Backup is a relatively new offering by MongoDB for real-time incremental backup of your MongoDB instances, replica sets, and shards, and offers you point in time recovery of your instances. The service is available as on-premise (in your data center) or cloud. However, we will demonstrate the on-cloud service that is the only option for the Community and Basic subscription. For more details on the available options, you can visit different product offerings by MongoDB at `https://www.mongodb.com/products/subscriptions`.

Getting ready

Mongo MMS Backup service will work only on Mongo 2.0 and above. We will start a single server that we will backup. MMS backup relies on the oplog for continuous backup and since oplog is available only in replica sets, the server needs to be started as a replica set. Refer to the recipe *Connecting to a single node using a Python client* in *Chapter 1, Installing and Starting the Server* to learn more about how to install Python and PyMongo, the Python client of Mongo.

How to do it...

If you don't already have a MMS account, then log in to `https://mms.mongodb.com/` and sign up for an account. For screenshots, refer to the recipe *Signing up for MMS and setting up an MMS monitoring agent* in this chapter.

1. Start a single instance of Mongo and replace the value of the appropriate filesystem path on your machine:

    ```
    $ mongod --replSet testBackup --smallfiles --oplogSize 50 --dbpath
    /data/mongo/db
    ```

    Note that the `smallfiles` and `oplogSize` are options only set for testing purposes and are not to be used in production.

2. Start a shell, connect to the instance in step 1 and initiate the replica set as follows:

    ```
    > rs.initiate()
    ```

    The replica set will be up and running in some time.

3. Go back to the browser to `mms.mongodb.com`. Add a new host by clicking on the **+ Add Host** button. Set the type as replica set and the hostname as your hostname and the port as the default one `27017` in our case. Refer to the recipe *Signing up for MMS and setting up an MMS monitoring agent* for the screenshots of the **Add Host** process.

4. Once the host is successfully added, register for MMS backup by clicking on the **Backup** option the left and then **Begin Setup**.

5. An SMS or Google authenticator can be used for registration. If a smartphone is available with Android, iOS, or Blackberry OS, Google authenticator is a good option. For countries like India, Google Authenticator is the only option available.

6. Assuming Google Authenticator is not configured already and we are planning to use it, we would need the app to be installed on your smartphone. Go to the respective app store of your mobile OS platform and install the Google Authenticator software.

7.   With the software installed on the phone, come back to the browser. You should see the following screen on selecting the Google Authenticator:

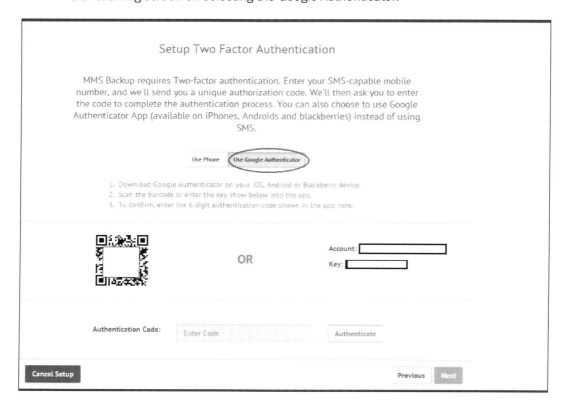

8.   Begin the setup for a new account by scanning the QR code from the Google Authenticator application. If barcode scanning is a problem, you may choose to manually enter the key given on the right side of the screen.

9. Once the scanning or the key is entered successfully, your smartphone should show a 6-digit number that changes every 30 seconds. Enter that number in the **Authentication Code** box given on the screen.

 It is important not to delete this account in Google Authenticator on your phone as this will be used in future whenever we wish to change any settings related to backup, such as stopping backup, changing exclusion list, and almost any operation in MMS backup. The QR code and key will not be visible again once the setup is done. You will have to contact MongoDB support to get the configuration reset.

10. Once the authentication is done, the next screen you should see is the billing address and billing details, such as the card you register. All charges below $5 are waived so you should be ok to try out a small test instance before being charged.

11. Once the credit card details are saved, we move ahead with the setup. We will have for installation a backup agent. This is a separate agent from the monitoring agent. Choose the appropriate platform and follow the instructions for its installation. Take a note of the location where the configuration files of the agent will be placed.

12. A new popup will contain the instruction/link to the archive/installer for the platform and the steps to install. It should also contain the `apiKey`. Take a note of the API key; we will need it in the next step.

13. Once the installation is complete, open the `local.config` file placed in the `config` directory of the agent installation (the location that was shown/modified during installation of the agent) and paste/type in the `apiKey` noted down in the previous step.

14. Once the agent is configured and started, click on the **Verify Agent** button.

15. Once the agent is successfully verified, we will start by adding a host to back up. The drop-down menu should show us all the replica sets and shards we have added. Select the appropriate one and set the **Sync source** as the primary instance, as that is the only one we have in our standalone instance. **Sync source** is only used for the initial sync process. Whenever we have a proper replica set with multiple instances, I prefer using a secondary as a sync process instance.

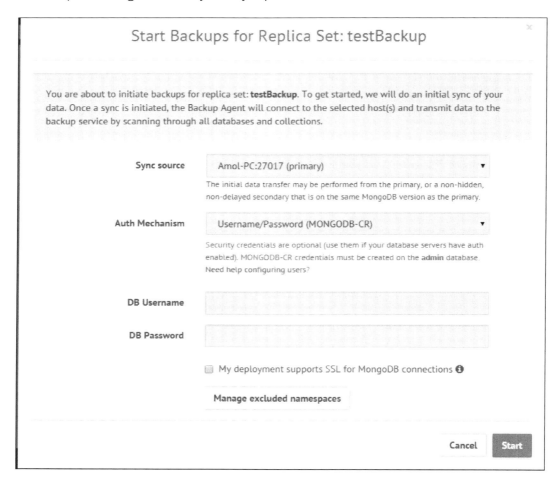

Since the instance is not started with security, leave the **DB Username** and **DB Password** fields blank.

If security is enabled on the mongod instance, a username and password need to be provided, which will be used by the MMS backup agent. The username and password are provided while setting up backup for the replica set, as in step 15. Since the agent needs to read the oplog, possibly all databases for the initial sync and write data to `admin` database the following roles are expected for the user: `readAnyDatabase`, `clusterAdmin`, `readWrite` on `admin` and `local` databases, and `userAdminAnyDatabase`. This is in case in version 2.4 and above. In versions prior to v2.4, we would expect the user to have read access on all the databases and read/write access to admin and local databases.

While setting up a replica set for backup you may get an error like, `Insufficient oplog size: The oplog window must be at least 1 hours over the last 24 hours for all active replica set members. Please increase the oplog..` While you may think this is always something to do with oplog size, it is also seen when the replica set has an instance that is in recovering state. This might feel misleading, so do look out for recovering nodes, if any, in the replica set while setting up a backup for a replica set. As per the MMS support too, it seems too restrictive to not set up a replica set for backup with some recovering nodes, and it might be fixed in the future.

Managing backups in MMS Backup service

In the previous recipe, we saw how to set up MMS backup service and a simple one member replica set was set up for backup. Though a single member replica set makes no sense at all, it was needed as a standalone instance cannot be set up for backup in MMS. In this recipe, we dive deeper and look at the operations we can perform on the server that is set up for backup, such as starting, stopping, or terminating a backup; managing exclusion lists; managing backup snapshots and retention; and restoring to point in time data.

Getting ready

The previous recipe is all that is needed for this recipe. The necessary setup is expected to be done as we are going to use the same server we had set up for backup in this recipe.

How to do it...

With the server up and running, let's import some data to it. It can be anything, but we chose to use the `countries.geo.json` file that was used in the last chapter. It should be available in the bundle downloaded from the Packt site.

Start by importing the data into a collection called `countries` in the `test` database. Use the following command to do it. The following import command was executed with the current directory having the `countries.geo.json` file:

```
$ mongoimport  -c countries -d test --drop countries.geo.json
```

We have already seen how to exclude namespaces when the replica set backup was being set up. We will now see how to exclude namespaces once the backup for a replica set is done. Click on the **Backup** menu option on the left and then the **Replica Set Status**, which opens by default when **Backup** is clicked. Click on the **Gear** button on the right side of the row where the replica set is shown. It should look like this:

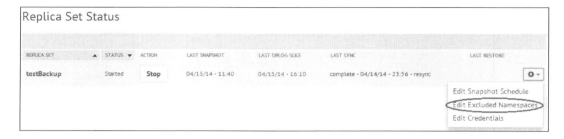

1. As we see in the preceding image, click on **Edit Excluded Namespaces** and type in the name of the collection that we want to exclude. Suppose we want to exclude the applicationLogs collection in test database, type in test.applicationLogs.

2. On saving, you will be asked to enter the token code that is currently displayed on your Google Authenticator.

3. On successful validation of the code, the namespace test.applicationLogs will be added to the list of namespaces excluded from being backed up.

4. We now shall see how to manage snapshot scheduling. A snapshot is the state of the database as of a particular point in time. To manage the snapshot frequency and retention policy, click on the **Gear** button shown in the previous screenshot and click on **Edit Snapshot Schedule**.

5. As we can see in the following image, we can set the times when the snapshots are taken and their retention period. We will discuss more on this in the next section. Any changes to it would need multifactor authentication to save the changes.

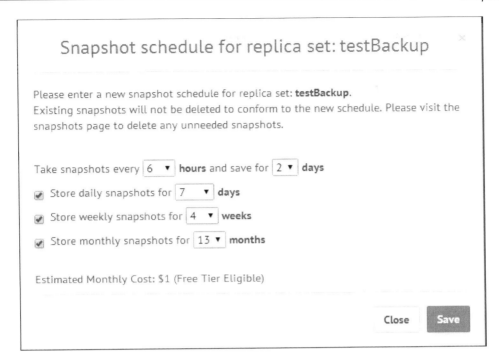

6. We will now see how we go about restoring the data using MMS backup. At any point in time whenever we want to restore the data, click on **Backup** and **Replica Set Status/Shard Cluster Status** click on **set/cluster name**.

On clicking it, we will see the snapshots that are saved against this set. It should look something like this:

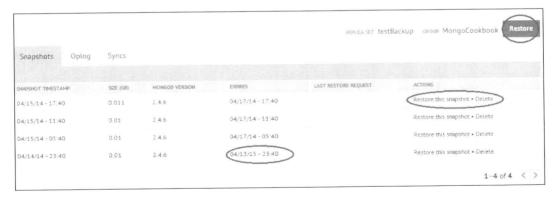

We have encircled some of the portions on the screen which we will see one by one.

7. To restore to the time when the snapshot was taken, click on the **Restore this snapshot** link in the **Actions** column of the grid.

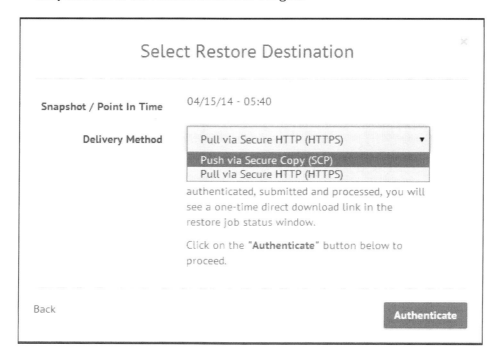

8. The preceding image shows us how we can export the data either over HTTPS or SCP. We select HTTPS for now, and click **Authenticate**. We will see about SCP in the next section.

9. Enter the token that is received either over SMS or seen on Google Authenticator and click **Finalize Request** on entering the auth code.

10. On successful authentication, click on **Restore Jobs**. This is a one-time download that will let you download the `tar.gz` archive. Click on the **download** link to download the `tar.gz` archive.

11. Once the archive is downloaded, extract it to get the database files within it.

12. Stop the mongod instance, replace the database files with the ones that are extracted, and restart the server to get the data as of the time when the snapshot was taken. Note that the database file will not contain data for the collection that was excluded from backup if all.

13. We will now see how to get point in time data using MMS backup.

14. Click on **Replica Set Status / Shard Cluster Status** and then the cluster/set which is to be restored.

    1. On the right-hand side of the screen, click on the **Restore** button.

    2. This should give a list of available snapshots or you may enter a custom time. Check **Use Custom Point In Time**. Click on the **Date** field and select a date and a time to which you want to restore the data in Hours and Minutes and click **Next**. Note that the **Point in Time** feature only restores to a point in last 24 Hours.

       Here, you will be asked to specify the format as HTTPS or SCP. The subsequent steps are similar to what we did on the previous occasion, from step 14 onwards.

How it works...

After setting up the backup for a replica set, we imported random data into the database. Backup for this database would be done by MMS and later on we will restore the database using this backup. We saw how to exclude namespaces from being backed up in steps 2-5.

Looking at the snapshot and retention policy settings, we can see we have the choice of the time interval in which the snapshots are to be taken and the number of days they are to be retained (step 9). We can see that by default snapshots are taken every 6 hours and they are saved for 2 days. The snapshot that is taken at the end of the day gets saved for a week. The snapshot taken at the end of the week and month are saved for 4 weeks and 13 months respectively. A snapshot can be taken once every 6, 8, 12, and 24 hours. However, you need to understand the flip side of taking snapshots after long time duration. Suppose the last snapshot is taken at 18 hours; getting the data as of that time for restore is very easy as it is stored on the MMS backup servers. However, we need the data as of 21:30 hours for restoration. Since MMS backup supports point in time backup, it would use the base snapshot at 18:00 hours and then just replay the changes on it after the snapshot is taken at 21:30 hours. This is similar to how an oplog would be replayed on the data. There is a cost for this replay and thus getting point in time backup is slightly more expensive than getting the data from a snapshot. Here, we had to replay the data for 3.5 hours, from 18:00 hours to 21:30 hours. Imagine if the snapshots were set to be taken after 12 hours and our first snapshot is taken at 00:00 hours, then we would have snapshots at 00:00 hours and 12:00 hours every day. To restore the data as of 21:30 hours with 12:00 hours as the last snapshot, we will have to replay 9.5 hours of data. This is much more expensive.

More frequent snapshots means more storage space usage but less time needed to restore a database to a given point in time. At the same time, less frequent snapshots require less storage but at the cost of more time to restore the data to a point in time. You need to decide and have a trade-off between these two, space and time of restoration. For the daily snapshot, we can choose retention of between 3 to 180 days. Similarly, for the weekly and monthly snapshots, the retention period can be chosen between 1 to 52 weeks and 1 to 36 months, respectively.

The screenshot in step 9 has a column for the expiry of the snapshot. This, for the first snapshot taken, is 1 year, whereas others expire in 2 days. The expiration is as per what we discussed in the last paragraph. On changing the expiration values, the old snapshots are not affected or adjusted as per the changed times. However, the new snapshots taken will be as per the modified settings for the retention and frequency.

We saw how to download the dump (step 10 onwards) and then use it to restore the data in the database. It was pretty straightforward and doesn't need a lot of explanation except a couple of things. First, if the data is for a shard, there will be multiple folders—one for each shard and each of them will have the database files as against what we saw here in case of a replica set where we have a single folder with database files in it. Finally, let's look at the screen when we choose SCP as the option:

SCP is short for secure copy. The files will be copied over a secure channel to a machine's filesystem. The host that is given needs to have a public IP which will be used to SCP. This makes a lot of sense when we want the data from MMS to be delivered to a machine running on Unix OS on the cloud, for example, one of the AWS virtual instances. Rather than getting the file using HTTPS on our local machine and then reuploading it to the server on the cloud, you can specify the location on which the data needs to be copied in the Target Directory block, the hostname, and the credentials. There are a couple of ways of authentication too. A password is an easy way with an additional option to SSH key pair. If you have to configure host's firewalls on the cloud to allow incoming traffic over the SSH port, the public IP addresses are given at the bottom of the screen (`64.70.114.115/32` or `4.71.186.0/24` in our screenshot). You should whitelist them to allow incoming secure copy requests over port `22`.

See also

We have seen running backups using MMS which uses oplogs for this purpose. There is a recipe called *Implementing triggers in Mongo using oplog* in *Chapter 5, Advanced Operations*, which uses oplog to implement trigger-like functionalities. This concept is the backbone of the real-time backup used by MMS backup service.

7
Deploying MongoDB on the Cloud

In this chapter, we will cover the following recipes:

- ▶ Setting up and managing the MongoLab account
- ▶ Setting up a sandbox MongoDB instance on MongoLab
- ▶ Performing operations on MongoDB from MongoLab GUI
- ▶ Setting up MongoDB on Amazon EC2 without AMI
- ▶ Setting up MongoDB using the Docker containers

Introduction

Though explaining cloud computing is not in the scope for this book, I will explain it in just one paragraph. Any business, big or small, needs hardware infrastructure with different software installed on it. An operating system is the basic software needed along with different servers (from the software perspective) for storage, mail, web, database, DNS, and so on. The list of software frameworks/platforms that are needed would end up being large. The point of interest here is that the initial budget for this hardware and software platform is high, and so we are not even considering the real estate needed to host it. This is where cloud computing providers such as Amazon, Rackspace, Google, and Microsoft come into play. They have hosted the high-end hardware and software in different data centers across the globe and let us choose from different configurations to start an instance. This is then accessed remotely over the public network for management purposes. Literally, all our setting up is done in the cloud provider's data center and we just pay as we use. Shut down the instance and you stop paying for it. Not only small start-ups, but large enterprises often temporarily fall back to cloud servers for temporary rise in the computing resource demands. The prices offered by the providers are very competitive too, particularly AWS, and its popularity says it all.

The wiki page, `http://en.wikipedia.org/wiki/Cloud_computing`, has a lot of details, perhaps a bit too much for someone new to the concept, but is a good read nevertheless. The article at `http://computer.howstuffworks.com/cloud-computing/cloud-computing.htm` is pretty good and also recommended for you to read if you are not aware of the concept of cloud computing.

In this chapter, we will set up MongoDB instances on the cloud using MongoDB service providers and then by ourselves on **Amazon Web Service** (**AWS**).

Setting up and managing the MongoLab account

In this recipe, we will evaluate one of the vendors, MongoLab, that provides MongoDB as a service. This introductory recipe will introduce to you what MongoDB as a service is and then will demonstrate how to set up and manage an account in MongoLab (`https://mongolab.com/`).

In all the recipes in the book so far, we have covered setting up, administering, monitoring, and developing the instances of MongoDB in the organizational/personal premises. This not only needs manpower with the appropriate skill set to manage the deployments, but also appropriate hardware to install and run Mongo servers. This needs large investments up front that might not be a viable solution for start-ups or even organizations who are not clear on adopting or migrating to this technology. They might want to evaluate it and see how it goes before moving full-fledged to this solution. What would be ideal is to have a service provider who takes care of hosting the MongoDB deployments, managing and monitoring the deployments, and providing support. The organizations opting for these services need not invest up front to set up the servers or recruit or outsource to consultants for the administration and monitoring of the instances. All that one needs to do is choose the hardware and software platforms and configurations and an appropriate MongoDB version, and then set up an environment from a user-friendly GUI. It even gives you an option to use your existing cloud provider's servers.

We saw in brief what these vendor hosting services do and why they are needed; we will start this recipe by setting up an account with MongoLab and see some basic user and account management. MongoLab is by no means the only hosting provider for MongoDB. You can also look at `http://www.mongohq.com/` and `http://www.objectrocket.com/`. At the time of writing this book, MongoDB themselves started providing MongoDB as a service on the Azure cloud and is currently in the beta phase.

How to do it...

1. Visit `https://mongolab.com/signup/` to sign up if you don't have an account created; just fill in the relevant details and create one account.

2. Once the account has been created, click on the **Account** link in the top right corner:

3. Click on the **Account Users** tab at the top; it should be selected by default:

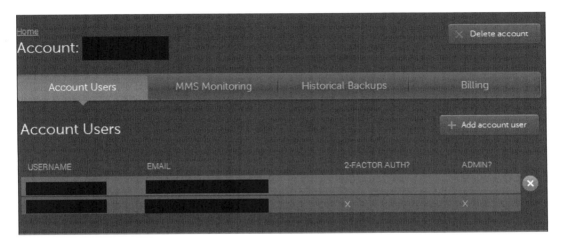

4. To add a new account, click on the **+ Add account user** button. One pop-up window will ask for the username, e-mail ID, and password. Enter the relevant details and click on the **Add** button.

5. Click on the user, and you should be navigated to a page where you can change the username, e-mail ID, and password. You can transfer the administrative rights to the user by clicking on the **Change to admin** button on this screen.

6. Similarly, by clicking on your own user details, you have the option to change the username, e-mail ID, and password.

7. Click on the **Set up two-factor authentication** button to activate the multifactor authentication using Google Authenticator. You need to have the Google Authenticator installed on your Android, iOS, or BlackBerry phone to proceed with the setting up of multifactor authentication.

8. On clicking the button, we should see the QR code that can be scanned using Google Authenticator or, if scanning is not possible, click on the URL underneath the QR code, which should show the code. Set up a time-based account in the Google Authenticator manually. There are two types of Google Authenticator accounts, time-based and counter-based.

Refer to `http://en.wikipedia.org/wiki/` `Google_Authenticator` for more details.

9. Similarly, you can delete users from the accounts page by clicking on the cross next to the user's row in **Account Users**.

How it works...

There is not much to explain in this section. The setup process and user administration is pretty simple. Note that the users that we added here are not database users. These are the users that have access to the MongoLab account. **Account** can be the name of the organization and can be seen at the top of the screen. The multifactor authentication account setup in the Google Authenticator software on the handheld device should not be deleted as whenever the user logs in to the MongoLab account from the browser, he will be asked to enter the Google Authenticator account to continue.

Setting up a sandbox MongoDB instance on MongoLab

In the previous recipe, we saw how to set up an account on MongoLab and add users to the account. We still haven't seen how to fire up an instance on the cloud and use it to perform some simple operations. In this recipe, this is exactly what we will do.

Getting ready

Refer to the previous recipe, *Setting up and managing MongoLab account*, to set up an account with MongoLab. We will set up a free sandbox instance. We will require some way to connect to this started `mongo` instance and thus will need a mongo shell that comes only with the complete mongo installation or you can choose to use a programming language of your choice in order to connect to the started `mongo` instance. Refer to *Chapter 3, Programming Language Drivers* for recipes on connecting and performing operations using a Java or Python client.

How to do it...

1. Go to the home page, `https://mongolab.com/home`, and click on the **Create new** button.

2. Select a cloud provider, for this example, we choose Amazon Web Services (AWS):

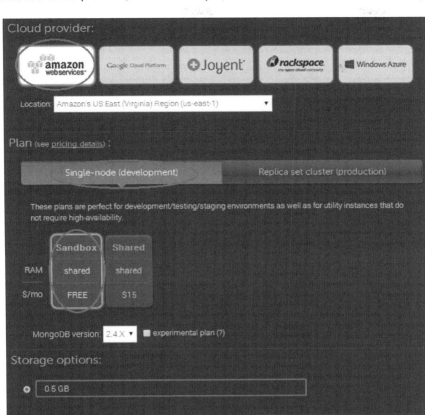

3. Click on the **Single-node (development)** and then, the **Sandbox** options. Do not change the location of the cloud server as the free sandbox instance is not available in all data centers. As this is a sandbox, we are okay with any location.

4. Add any name for your database; the name that I chose is `mongolab-test`. Click on **Create new MongoDB deployment** after entering the name.

5. This should take you to the home page, and the database should now be visible. Click on the instance name. The page here shows the details of the MongoDB instance selected. The instruction to connect in the shell or programming language is given at the top of the page along with the public hostname of the started instance.

6. Click on the **Users** tab and then the **Add database user** button. In the pop-up window, add the username and password as `testUser` and `testUser`, respectively (or any of your choice).

7. With the user added, start the mongo shell as follows, assuming that the name of the database is `mongolab-test` and the username and password is `testUser`:

    ```
    $ mongo <host-name>/mongolab-test -u testUser -p testUser
    ```

    On connecting, execute the following in the shell and check whether the database name is `mongolab-test`:

    ```
    > db
    ```

8. Insert one document in a collection as follows:

    ```
    > db.messages.insert({_id:1, message:'Hello mongolab'})
    ```

9. Query the collection as follows:

    ```
    > db.messages.findOne()
    ```

How it works...

The steps executed are very simple, and we created one shared sandbox instance in the cloud. MongoLab themselves do not host the instances but use one of the cloud providers to do the hosting. MongoLab does not support sandbox instances for all providers. The storage with the sandbox instance is 0.5 GB and is shared with other instances on the same machine. Shared instances are cheaper than running on a dedicated instance but the price is paid in performance. The CPU and IO is shared with other instances and thus the performance of our shared instance is not necessarily in our control. For a production use case, a shared instance is not a recommended option. Similarly, we need to set up a replica set when running in production. If we look at the image in step 2, then we see another tab next to the **Single-node (development)** option. This is where you can choose the configuration for the machine in terms of RAM and disk capacity (and the price as well) and set up a replica set.

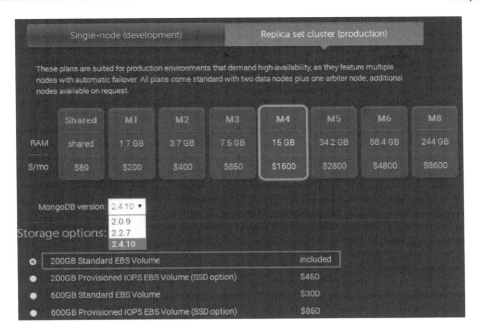

As you can see, you get to choose the version of MongoDB to use. Even if a new version of MongoDB gets released, MongoLab will not start supporting it immediately as they usually wait for a few minor versions to be rolled out before supporting them for production users. Additionally, when we choose a configuration, the default available option is two data nodes and one arbiter, which is sufficient for a majority of use cases.

The RAM and disk chosen depend completely on the nature of the data and how query-intensive or write-intensive it is. This sizing is something that we do irrespective of whether we are deploying on our own infrastructure or the cloud. The working set is something that is important to be known before we choose the RAM of the hardware. Proofing of concepts and experiments are done to deal with a subset of data and then the estimation can be done for the entire dataset. If IO activity is high and low IO latency is desired, you can even opt for SSD, as shown in the preceding image. Standalone instances are as good as replica sets in terms of scalability except for availability. Thus, we can choose standalone instances for such estimation and development purposes. Shared instances, both free and paid, are good candidates for development purposes. Note that shared instances cannot be restarted on demand as we can for dedicated instances.

What cloud provider do we choose? If you already have your application servers deployed in the cloud, then obviously it has to be the same vendor as your existing vendor. It is recommended that you use the same cloud vendor for the application server and database, and see that they are both deployed on the same location in order to minimize latency and improve on performance. If you are starting fresh, then invest some time in choosing the cloud provider. Look at all the other services that the application would need, such as the storage, compute, other services such as mail, notification services, and so on. All this analysis is outside the scope of this book, but once you are done with this and finalized with a provider, you can choose the provider to use accordingly in MongoLab. As far as the pricing goes, all the leading providers offer competitive pricing.

Performing operations on MongoDB from MongoLab GUI

In the previous recipe, we saw how to set up a simple sandbox instance for MongoDB in the cloud using MongoLab. In this recipe, we build on it and see what services MongoLab provides you with, from the management, administrative, monitoring, and backups perspectives.

Getting ready

Refer to the previous recipe, *Setting up a sandbox MongoDB instance on MongoLab*, on how to set up a sandbox instance in the cloud using MongoLab.

How to do it...

1. Go to `https://mongolab.com/home`; you should see the list of databases, servers, and clusters. If you have followed the last recipe, you should see one standalone database, `mongolab-test` (or whatever name you chose for the database). Click on the database name, which should take you to the database details page.

2. After clicking on the **Collections** tab, which should be selected by default, we should see the list of collections present in the database. If the previous recipe was executed before this one, you should see one collection, messages, in the database.

3. Click on the name of the collection and we should get navigated to the collection details page as follows:

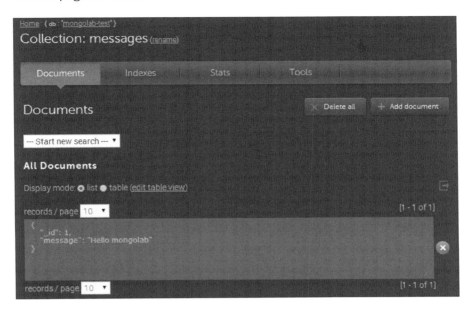

4. Click on the **Stats** option to view the stats of the collection.

5. In the **Documents** tab, we can query the collection. By default, we see all the documents with 10 documents shown per page, which can be changed from the records/page drop-down menu. A maximum value of 100 can be chosen.

6. There is another way to view the documents, as a table. Click on the **table** radio button in the **Display** mode and click on the link to create/edit table view. In the popup that is shown, enter the following document for the messages collection and click on **Submit**:

```
{
    "id": "_id",
    "Message Text": "message"
}
```

On doing this, the display will change as follows:

7. From the **–Start new search–** dropdown, select the **[new search]** option, as shown in the following image:

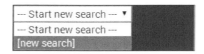

8. With the new query, we see the following fields that let us enter the query string, sort order, and projections. Enter the query as `{"_id":1}` and fields as `{"message":1, "_id":0}`:

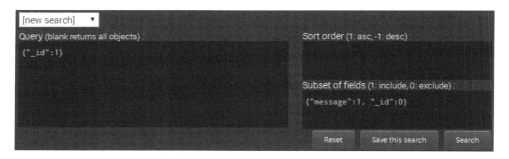

9. You can choose to save the query by clicking on the **Save this search** button and giving a name to the query to be saved.

10. Individual documents can be deleted by clicking on the cross next to each record. Similarly, the **Delete all** button at the top will delete all the contents of the collection.

11. Similarly, clicking on **+ Add document** will pop up an editor to type in the document that would be inserted into the collection. As MongoDB is schemaless, the document need not have a fixed set of fields; the application should make sense out of it.

12. Go to `https://mongolab.com/databases/<your database name>` (`mongolab-test`, in this case), which can also be reached by clicking on the database name from the home page.

13. Click on the **Stats** tab next to the **Users** tab. The content shown here in the table is the result of the `db.stats()` command.

14. Similarly, click on the **Backups** tab at the top next to the **Stats** tab. Here, we have options to take a recurring or one-time backup.

15. When you click on **Schedule recurring backup**, you get a pop-up window that lets you enter the details of the scheduling, such as the frequency of the backup, time of the day when the backup needs to be taken, and the number of backups to keep.

16. The backup location can be chosen as either MongoLab's own S3 bucket or the Rackspace cloud file. You can choose to use your own account's storage, in which case you will have to share the AWS access key/secret key or UserID/API key in case of Rackspace.

How it works...

Steps 1 to 5 are pretty straightforward. In step 6, we provided a JSON document to show the results in a tabular format. The format of the document is as follows:

```
{
    <display column 1> : <name of the field in the JSON document> ,
    <display column 2> : <name of the field in the JSON document> ,

    <display column n> : <name of the field in the JSON document>
}
```

The key is the name of the column to display and the value of the name of the field in the actual document whose value will be shown as the value of this column. To get a clear understanding, look at the document defined for the messages collection, and then take a look at the displayed tabular data. The following is the JSON document that we provided, which states the name of the column as the value of the key and the actual field in the document as the value of the column:

```
{
    "id": "_id",
    "Message Text": "message"
}
```

Note that the field name and values of the JSON documents here are enclosed in quotes. The Mongo shell is lenient in this sense, where it allows us to give field names without quotes.

If we visit step 16 about backups, we see that the backups are stored either in MongoLab's AWS S3/Rackspace cloud file or your custom AWS S3 bucket /Rackspace cloud files. In the latter cases, you need to share your AWS/Rackspace credentials with MongoLab. If this is a concern and the credentials can potentially be used to access other resources, it is recommended that you create a separate account and use it for backup purposes from MongoLab. You can also use the backup created to create a new MongoDB server instance from MongoLab. Needless to say, if you have used your own AWS S3 bucket/Rackspace cloud files, storage charges are additional as they are not a part of MongoLab's charges.

There are some important points worth mentioning. MongoLab provides a REST API for various operations. The REST API can be used in place of the standard drivers to perform CRUD operations; however, using MongoDB client libraries is the recommended approach. One good reason to use the REST API right now over a language driver is if the client is connecting to the MongoDB server over a public network. The shell that we started on our local machine connecting to the MongoDB server on the cloud sends unencrypted data to the server, which makes it vulnerable. On the other hand, if REST APIs are used, the traffic is sent over a secure channel as HTTPS is used. MongoLab plans to support a secure channel for the communication between the client and server in future, but as of the writing of this book, this is not available. If the application and database are in the same data center of the cloud provider, you are safe and can depend on the security provided by the cloud provider for their local network, which generally is not a concern. However, there is nothing that you can do for secure communication other than ensuring that your data doesn't go over public networks.

One more scenario where MongoLab doesn't work is when you want the instances to be running on your own instance of a virtual machine rather than one chosen by MongoLab or we want the application to be in a virtual private cloud. Cloud providers do provide services such as Amazon VPC, where part of the AWS cloud can be treated as a part of your network. If you intend to deploy your MongoDB instance in such an environment, MongoLab cannot be used.

Setting up MongoDB on Amazon EC2 manually

In the previous few recipes, we saw how to start MongoDB in the cloud using a hosted service provided by MongoLab that gave an alternative to set up MongoDB on all the leading cloud vendors. However, if we plan to host and monitor the instance ourselves for greater control or set up within our own virtual private cloud, we can do it ourselves. Though the procedure varies from cloud provider to provider, we will be demonstrating it using AWS. There are a couple of ways to do it, but in this recipe, we will use **Amazon Machine Image** (**AMI**). AMI is a template containing details such as the operating system, software that would be available on the started virtual machine, and so on. All this information would be used while booting up a new virtual machine instance on the cloud. To know more about AMI, refer to `http://en.wikipedia.org/wiki/Amazon_Machine_Image`.

Talking about AWS EC2, which stands for Elastic Cloud Compute, it is a service that lets you create, start, and stop servers of different configurations in the cloud running on operating systems of your choice. (The prices differ accordingly.) Similarly, Amazon **Elastic Block Store** (**EBS**) is a service that provides persistent block storage with high availability and low latency. Initially, each instance has a store known as an ephemeral store attached to it. This is a temporary store and the data might be lost when the instance restarts. The EBS block storage is thus attached to the EC2 instance to maintain persistence even when the instance is stopped and then restarted. Standard EBS does not provide guaranteed minimum **IO operations per second** (**IOPS**). For a moderate workload, the default of about 100 IOPS is okay. However, for a high performance IO, EBS blocks with guaranteed IOPS are also available. The pricing is more as compared to the standard EBS block but is a good option to opt for if a low IO rate can be a bottleneck in the performance of the system.

In this recipe, we will set up a small micro instance that is good enough as a sandbox instance with one EBS block volume attached.

Getting ready

The first thing that you need to do is sign up for an AWS account. Visit `http://aws.amazon.com/` and click on **Sign up**. Log in if you have an Amazon account, or else, create a new one. You will have to give your credit card details although the recipes that we have here will use the free micro instance unless we explicitly mention otherwise. We will connect to the instance on the cloud using Putty. You can download Putty and install it on your machine if it is not already installed. It can be downloaded from `http://www.putty.org/`.

For this specific recipe for the installation using AMI, we cannot use the micro instance and will have to use the Standard Large. You can get more details about the pricing of the EC2 instances in different regions at `https://aws.amazon.com/ec2/pricing/`. Choose the appropriate region based on the geographical and financial factors.

1. The first thing that you need to do is create a key pair in case you have not created one already. The following steps from 1 to 5 are only to create the key pair. This key pair will be used to log in to the Unix instance started in the cloud from the Putty client. Skip to step 6 if the key pair has already been created and the `.pem` file is available for you.

2. Go to `https://console.aws.amazon.com/ec2/` and make sure that the region you have on the top right (as shown in the following image) is the same as the one in which you are planning to set up the instance.

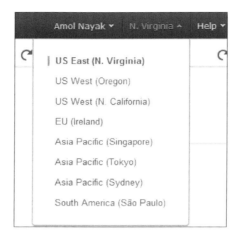

3. Once the region is selected, the page with the **Resources** heading will show you all the instances, key pairs, IP addresses, and so on for this region. Click on the **Key Pairs** link, which should direct you to the page where all the existing key pairs will be shown and you can create new ones.

4. Click on the **Create Key Pair** button, and in the pop-up window, type any name of your choice. Let's say that we call it `EC2 Test Key Pair`, and then click on **Create**.

5. Once created, a `.pem` file will be generated. Ensure that the file is saved as this would be needed for subsequent access to the machine.

6. We will next convert this `.pem` file to a `.ppk` file to be used with Putty.

7. Start puttygen; if it is not available already, it can be downloaded from `http://www.chiark.greenend.org.uk/~sgtatham/putty/download.html`.

   You should see the following on the screen:

8. Select the **SSH-2 RSA** option and click on the **Load** button. In the file dialog, select **All files** and then select the `.pem` file that was downloaded with the key pair, which was generated in the EC2 console.

9. Once the `.pem` file is imported, click the **Save private key** option and save the file with any name; the file this time is a `.ppk` file. Save this file for future logging in to the EC2 instance from putty.

 If you are using Mac OS X or Linux, you can use the `ssh-keygen` utility to generate the SSH keys.

How to do it...

1. Go to `https://console.aws.amazon.com/ec2/` and click on the **Instances** option on the left and then the **Launch Instance** button:

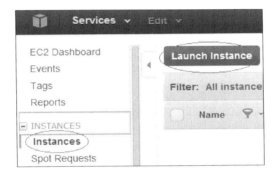

2. As we want to start a free micro instance, check the **Free tier only** checkbox on the left. On the right-hand side, select the instance that we want to set up. We choose to use the **Ubuntu server**. Click on **Select** to navigate to the next window.

3. Choose the micro instance and click on **Review and Launch**. Ignore the security warning; the default security group that you will have is the one that will accept connections over port 22 from all the hosts on a public network.

4. Without editing any default settings, click on **Launch**. Upon launch, a popup will appear that lets you choose an existing key pair. If you proceed without a key pair, you will need the password or need to create a new key pair. In the previous recipe, we already created a key pair, which is what we will use here.

5. Click on **Launch Instance** to start the new micro instance.

6. Refer to steps 9 to 12 in the previous recipe on how to connect to the started instance using Putty. Note that we will be using the Ubuntu user instead of `ec2-user`, which we used in the last recipe, as this time, we are using Ubuntu instead of Amazon Linux.

7. Before we add a MongoDB repository, we need to import the MongoDB public key as follows:

```
$ sudo apt-key adv --keyserver hkp://keyserver.ubuntu.com:80
--recv 7F0CEB10
```

8. Execute the following command in the operating system shell:

```
$ echo "deb http://repo.mongodb.org/apt/ubuntu trusty/mongodb-
org/3.0 multiverse" | sudo tee /etc/apt/sources.list.d/mongodb-
org-3.0.list
```

9. Load the local database by executing the following command:

```
$ sudo apt-get install mongodb-org
```

10. Execute the following command to create the required directories:

```
$ sudo mkdir /data /log
```

11. Start the mongod process as follows:

```
$ sudo mongod --dbpath /data --logpath /log/mongodb.log
--smallfiles --oplogsize 50 –fork
```

To ensure that the server process is up and running, execute the following command in the shell and we should see the following in the log:

```
$ tail /log/mongodb.log
```

```
2015-05-04T13:41:16.533+0000 [initandlisten] journal dir=/data/
journal
```

```
2015-05-04T13:41:16.534+0000 [initandlisten] recover : no journal
files present, no recovery needed
```

```
2015-05-04T13:41:16.628+0000 [initandlisten] waiting for
connections on port 27017
```

12. Start the mongo shell as follows and execute the following command:

```
$ mongo
> db.ec2Test.insert({_id: 1, message: 'Hello World !'})
> db.ec2Test.findOne()
```

How it works...

A lot of steps are self-explanatory. It is recommended that you at least go through the previous recipe as a lot of concepts are explained there. Most concepts explained in the preceding recipe apply here. A few things that are different are explained in this section. For the installation, we chose Ubuntu as against Amazon Linux, which is the standard when you set up the server using AMI. Different operating systems have different steps for installation. Refer to `http://docs.mongodb.org/manual/installation/` for steps on how to install MongoDB on different platforms. Steps 7 to 9 in this recipe are specific for the installation of MongoDB on Ubuntu. Refer to `https://help.ubuntu.com/12.04/serverguide/apt-get.html` for more details on the `apt-get` command that we executed here to install MongoDB.

In our case, we chose to have the data, journal, and log folder on the same EBS volume. This is because what we set up is a `dev` instance. In case of a `prod` instance, there are different EBS volumes with provisioned IOPS for optimum performance. This setup allows us to gain advantage of the fact that these different volumes have different controllers and thus concurrent write operations are possible. EBS volumes with provisioned volumes are backed by the SSD drives. The production deployment notes at `http://docs.mongodb.org/manual/administration/production-notes/` states that MongoDB deployment should be backed by the RAID-10 disks. When deploying on AWS, prefer PIOPS over RAID-10. For instance, if 4000 IOPS is desired, then choose an EBS volume with 4000 IOPS rather than a RAID-10 setup with a 2 X 2000 IOPS or 4 X 1000 IOPS setup. This not only eliminates unnecessary complexity, but also makes snapshotting a single disk possible as against dealing with multiple disks in a RAID-10 setup. Speaking of snapshotting, the journal log and data are written to separate volumes in majority of the production deployments. This is the scenario where snapshotting doesn't work. We need to flush the DB writes, lock the data for further writes until the backup is complete, and then release the lock. Refer to `http://docs.mongodb.org/manual/tutorial/backup-with-filesystem-snapshots/` for more details on snapshotiing and backups.

Refer to `http://docs.mongodb.org/ecosystem/platforms/` for more details on deployment on different cloud providers. There is a section specifically for backups on the Amazon EC2 instances. Prefer using AMIs to set up the MongoDB instances for production deployments as demonstrated in the previous recipe over manually setting up the instances. A manual setup is okay for small development purposes, where a large instance with EBS volumes with provisioned IOPS is an overkill.

See also

▶ Cloud formation is a way where you can define templates and automate your instance creation for the EC2 instances. You can know more what cloud formation is at `https://aws.amazon.com/cloudformation/` and refer to `https://mongodb-documentation.readthedocs.org/en/latest/ecosystem/tutorial/automate-deployment-with-cloudformation.html`.

▶ Another alternative is using Mongo's cloud service: `https://docs.cloud.mongodb.com/tutorial/nav/add-servers-through-aws-integration/`.

▶ You can know more on RAID by referring to these two URLs on Wikipedia: `http://en.wikipedia.org/wiki/Standard_RAID_levels` and `http://en.wikipedia.org/wiki/Nested_RAID_levels`. The description given here is quite comprehensive.

Setting up MongoDB using the Docker containers

The container movement, as I like to call it, has touched almost all the aspects of information technology. Docker, being the tool of choice, is integral to the creating and managing of containers.

In this recipe, we will install Docker on the Ubuntu (14.04) server and run MongoDB in a container.

Getting ready

1. First, we need to install Docker on our Ubuntu server, which can be done by running this command:

   ```
   $ wget -qO- https://get.docker.com/ | sh
   ```

2. Start the Docker service:

   ```
   $ service docker start
   > docker start/running, process 24369
   ```

3. Confirm that Docker is running as follows:

   ```
   $ docker info
   > Containers: 40
   > Images: 311
   > Storage Driver: aufs
   >   Root Dir: /var/lib/docker/aufs
   ```

> Dirs: 395

> Execution Driver: native-0.2

> Kernel Version: 3.13.0-37-generic

> Operating System: Ubuntu 14.04.2 LTS

> WARNING: No swap limit support

How to do it...

1. Fetch the default MongoDB image from Docker Hub as follows:

   ```
   $ docker pull mongo
   ```

2. Let's confirm that the images are installed with the following command:

   ```
   $ docker images | grep mongo
   ```

3. Start the MongoDB server:

   ```
   $ docker run -d  --name mongo-server-1 mongo
   > dfe7684dbc057f2d075450e3c6c96871dea98ff6b78abe72944360f4c239a72e
   ```

   Alternately, you can also run the docker ps command to check the list of running containers.

4. Fetch the IP of this container:

   ```
   $ docker inspect mongo-server-1 | grep IPAddress
   > "IPAddress": "172.17.0.3",
   ```

5. Connect to our new container using the mongo client:

   ```
   $ mongo  172.17.0.3
   >MongoDB shell version: 3.0.4
   > connecting to: 172.17.0.3/test
   >
   ```

6. Create a directory on the server:

   ```
   $ mkdir -p /data/db2
   ```

7. Start a new MongoDB container:

   ```
   $ docker run -d --name mongo-server-2 -v /data/db1:/data/db mongo
   ```

8. Fetch the IP of this new container as mentioned in Step 4, and connect using the Mongo client:

   ```
   $ docker inspect mongo-server-2 | grep IPAddress
   > "IPAddress": "172.17.0.4",
   $ mongo  172.17.0.4
   ```

```
>MongoDB shell version: 3.0.4
> connecting to: 172.17.0.4/test
>
```

9. Let's make another directory for our final container:

```
$ mkdir –p /data/db3
```

Start a new MongoDB container:

```
$ docker run -d --name mongo-server-3  -v /data/db3:/data/db -p
9999:27017 mongo
```

10. Let's connect to this container via localhost:

```
$ mongo localhost:9999
> MongoDB shell version: 3.0.4
> connecting to: localhost:9999/test
```

How it works...

We start by downloading the default MongoDB image from DockerHub (`https://hub.docker.com/_/mongo/`). A Docker image is a self-sustaining OS image that is customized for the application that it is supposed to run. All Docker containers are isolated executions of these images. This is very similar to how an OS template is used to create virtual machines.

The image download operation defaults to fetching the latest stable MongoDB image, but you can specify your version of choice by mentioning the tag, for example, `docker pull mongo:2.8`.

We verify that the image was downloaded by running the `docker images` command, which will list all the images installed on the server. In step 3, we start a container in the detached (`-d`) mode with the name, `mongo-server-1`, using our mongo image. Describing the container internals may be out of the scope of this cookbook, but, in short, we now have an isolated `docker pseudo-sever` running inside our Ubuntu machine.

By default, each Docker container gets an RFC 1918 (non-routable) IP address space assigned by the docker server. In order to connect to this container, we fetch the IP address in step 4 and connect to the `mongodb` instance in step 5.

However, each Docker container is ephemeral and hence, destroying the container would mean losing the data. In step 6, we create a local directory that can be used to store our mongo database. We start a new container in step 7; it is similar to our earlier command with the addition of the Volumes (`-v`) switch. In our example, we are exposing the `/data/db2` directory to the mongo container namespace as `/data/db`. This is similar to NFS-like file mounting but within the confines of the kernel namespace.

Finally, if we want external systems to connect to this container, we bind the container's ports to that of the host machine. In step 9, we use the Port (-p) switch to bind the TCP 9999 port on the Ubuntu server to TCP 27017 of this container. This ensures that any external systems connecting to the server's port 9999 will be routed to this particular container.

See also

You can also try to link two containers using the Link (-1) command line parameter of the docker command.

For more information visit http://docs.docker.com/userguide/dockerlinks/.

8
Integration with Hadoop

In this chapter, we will cover the following recipes:

- ▶ Executing our first sample MapReduce job using the mongo-hadoop connector
- ▶ Writing our first Hadoop MapReduce job
- ▶ Running MapReduce jobs on Hadoop using streaming
- ▶ Running a MapReduce job on Amazon EMR

Introduction

Hadoop is a well-known open source software to process large datasets. It also has an API for the MapReduce programming model, which is widely used. Nearly all the big data solutions have some sort of support to integrate them with Hadoop in order to use its MapReduce framework. MongoDB has a connector as well that integrates with Hadoop and lets us write MapReduce jobs using the Hadoop MapReduce API, process the data residing in the MongoDB/MongoDB dumps, and write the result to the MongoDB/MongoDB dump files. In this chapter, we will look at some recipes about the basic MongoDB and Hadoop integration.

Executing our first sample MapReduce job using the mongo-hadoop connector

In this recipe, we will see how to build the mongo-hadoop connector from the source and set up Hadoop just for the purpose of running the examples in the standalone mode. The connector is the backbone that runs Hadoop MapReduce jobs on Hadoop using the data in Mongo.

Getting ready

There are various distributions of Hadoop; however, we will use Apache Hadoop (http://hadoop.apache.org/). The installation will be done on Ubuntu Linux. Apache Hadoop always runs on the Linux environment for production, and Windows is not tested for production systems. For development purposes, Windows can be used. If you are a Windows user, I would recommend that you install a virtualization environment such as VirtualBox (https://www.virtualbox.org/), set up a Linux environment, and then install Hadoop on it. Setting up VirtualBox and Linux on it is not shown in this recipe, but this is not a tedious task. The prerequisite for this recipe is a machine with the Linux operating system on it and an Internet connection. The version that we will set up here is 2.4.0 of Apache Hadoop. At the time of writing of this book, the latest version of Apache Hadoop, which is supported by the mongo-hadoop connector, is 2.4.0.

A Git client is needed to clone the repository of the mongo-hadoop connector to the local filesystem. Refer to http://git-scm.com/book/en/Getting-Started-Installing-Git to install Git.

You will also need MongoDB to be installed on your operating system. Refer to http://docs.mongodb.org/manual/installation/ and install it accordingly. Start the mongod instance listening to port 27017. It is not expected for you to be an expert in Hadoop but some familiarity with it will be helpful. Knowing the concept of MapReduce is important and knowing the Hadoop MapReduce API will be an advantage. In this recipe, we will explain what is needed to get the work done. You can get more details on Hadoop and its MapReduce API from other sources. The wiki page at http://en.wikipedia.org/wiki/MapReduce gives some good information about the MapReduce programming.

How to do it...

1. We will first install Java, Hadoop, and the required packages. We will start with installing JDK on the operating system. Type the following on the command prompt of the operating system:

    ```
    $ javac –version
    ```

2. If the program doesn't execute and you are told about various packages that contain javac and program, then we need to install Java as follows:

   ```
   $ sudo apt-get install default-jdk
   ```

   This is all we need to do to install Java.

3. Download the current version of Hadoop from `http://www.apache.org/dyn/closer.cgi/hadoop/common/` and download version 2.4.0 (or the latest mongo-hadoop connector support).

4. After the `.tar.gz` file is downloaded, execute the following on the command prompt:

   ```
   $ tar -xvzf <name of the downloaded .tar.gz file>
   $ cd <extracted directory>
   ```

   Open the `etc/hadoop/hadoop-env.sh` file and replace export JAVA_HOME = ${JAVA_HOME} with export JAVA_HOME = /usr/lib/jvm/default-java.

   We will now get the mongo-hadoop connector code from GitHub on our local filesystem. Note that you don't need a GitHub account to clone a repository. Clone the Git project from the operating system command prompt as follows:

   ```
   $git clone https://github.com/mongodb/mongo-hadoop.git
   $cd mongo-hadoop
   ```

5. Create a soft link—the Hadoop installation directory is the same as the one that we extracted in step 3:

   ```
   $ln -s <hadoop installation directory> ~/hadoop-binaries
   ```

   For example, if Hadoop is extracted/installed in the home directory, then this is the command to be executed:

   ```
   $ln -s ~/hadoop-2.4.0 ~/hadoop-binaries
   ```

   By default, the mongo-hadoop connector will look for a Hadoop distribution under the `~/hadoop-binaries` folder. So, even if the Hadoop archive is extracted elsewhere, we can create a soft link to it. Once this link has been created, we should have the Hadoop binaries in the `~/hadoop-binaries/hadoop-2.4.0/bin` path.

6. We will now build the mongo-hadoop connector from the source for the Apache Hadoop version 2.4.0. The build-by-default builds for the latest version, so as of now, the `-Phadoop_version` parameter can be left out as 2.4 is the latest.

   ```
   $./gradlew jar -Phadoop_version='2.4'
   ```

   This build process will take some time to get completed.

7. Once the build completes successfully, we will be ready to execute our first MapReduce job. We will do this using a `treasuryYield` sample provided with the mongo-hadoop connector project. The first activity is to import the data to a collection in Mongo.

8. Assuming that the `mongod` instance is up and running and listening to port `27017` for connections and the current directory is the root of the mongo-hadoop connector code base, execute the following command:

```
$ mongoimport -c yield_historical.in -d mongo_hadoop --drop
examples/treasury_yield/src/main/resources/yield_historical_
in.json
```

9. Once the import action is successful, we are left with copying two jar files to the `lib` directory. Execute the following in the operating system shell:

```
$ wget http://repo1.maven.org/maven2/org/mongodb/mongo-java-
driver/2.12.0/mongo-java-driver-2.12.0.jar
```

```
$ cp core/build/libs/mongo-hadoop-core-1.2.1-SNAPSHOT-
hadoop_2.4.jar ~/hadoop-binaries/hadoop-2.4.0/lib/
```

```
$ mv mongo-java-driver-2.12.0.jar ~/hadoop-binaries/hadoop-2.4.0/
lib
```

> The JAR built for the mongo-hadoop core to be copied was named as shown in the preceding section for the trunk version of the code and built for Hadoop-2.4.0. Change the name of the JAR accordingly when you build it yourself for a different version of the connector and Hadoop. The Mongo driver can be the latest version. Version 2.12.0 is the latest version at the time of writing of this book.

10. Now, execute the following command on the command prompt of the operating system shell:

```
 ~/hadoop-binaries/hadoop-2.4.0/bin/hadoop     jar     examples/
treasury_yield/build/libs/treasury_yield-1.2.1-SNAPSHOT-
hadoop_2.4.jar  \
com.mongodb.hadoop.examples.treasury.TreasuryYieldXMLConfig  \
-Dmongo.input.split_size=8     -Dmongo.job.verbose=true  \
-Dmongo.input.uri=mongodb://localhost:27017/mongo_hadoop.yield_
historical.in  \
-Dmongo.output.uri=mongodb://localhost:27017/mongo_hadoop.yield_
historical.out
```

11. The output should print out a lot of things; however, the following line in the output tells us that the map reduce job is successful:

```
 14/05/11 21:38:54 INFO mapreduce.Job: Job job_
local1226390512_0001 completed successfully
```

12. Connect the `mongod` instance running on localhost from the mongo client and execute a find on the following collection:

```
$ mongo
> use mongo_hadoop
switched to db mongo_hadoop
> db.yield_historical.out.find()
```

How it works...

Installing Hadoop is not a trivial task and we don't need to get into this to try our samples for the hadoop-mongo connector. To learn about Hadoop, its installation, and other things, there are dedicated books and articles available. For the purpose of this chapter, we will simply download the archive and extract and run the MapReduce jobs in the standalone mode. This is the quickest way to get going with Hadoop. All the steps up to step 6 are needed to install Hadoop. In the next couple of steps, we will clone the mongo-hadoop connector recipe. You can also download a stable version for your version of Hadoop at `https://github.com/mongodb/mongo-hadoop/releases` if you prefer not to build from the source. We then build the connector for our version of Hadoop (2.4.0) till step 13. Step 14 onward is what we will do to run the actual MapReduce job to work on the data in MongoDB. We imported the data to the `yield_historical.in` collection, which will be used as an input for the MapReduce job. Go ahead and query the collection in the mongo shell using the `mongo_hadoop` database to see a document. Don't worry if you don't understand the contents; we want to see what we intend to do with this data in this example.

The next step was to invoke the MapReduce operation on the data. The Hadoop command was executed giving one jar's path, (`examples/treasury_yield/build/libs/treasury_yield-1.2.1-SNAPSHOT-hadoop_2.4.jar`). This is the jar that contains the classes implementing the sample MapReduce operation for the treasury yield. The `com.mongodb.hadoop.examples.treasury.TreasuryYieldXMLConfig` class in this JAR file is the Bootstrap class containing the main method. We will visit this class soon. There are lots of configurations supported by the connector. The complete list of configurations can be found at `https://github.com/mongodb/mongo-hadoop/`. For now, we will just remember that `mongo.input.uri` and `mongo.output.uri` are the collections for input and output for the map reduce operations.

With the project cloned, you can now import it to any Java IDE of your choice. We are particularly interested in the project at `/examples/treasury_yield` and core present in the root of the cloned repository.

Let's look at the `com.mongodb.hadoop.examples.treasury.`
`TreasuryYieldXMLConfig` class. This is the entry point for the MapReduce method
and has a main method in it. To write MapReduce jobs for mongo using the mongo-hadoop
connector, the main class always has to extend from `com.mongodb.hadoop.util.`
`MongoTool`. This class implements the `org.apache.hadoop.Tool` interface, which has
the run method and is implemented for us by the `MongoTool` class. All that the main method
needs to do is execute this class using the `org.apache.hadoop.util.ToolRunner` class
by invoking its static `run` method passing the instance of our main class (which is an instance
of `Tool`).

There is a static block that loads some configurations from two XML files, `hadoop-local.`
`xml` and `mongo-defaults.xml`. The format of these files (or any XML file) is as follows.
The root node of the file is the configuration node with multiple property nodes under it:

```
<configuration>
  <property>
    <name>{property name}</name>
    <value>{property value}</value>
  </property>
  ...
</configuration>
```

The property values that make sense in this context are all those that we mentioned in the
URL provided earlier. We instantiate `com.mongodb.hadoop.MongoConfig` wrapping
an instance of `org.apache.hadoop.conf.Configuration` in the constructor of the
bootstrap class, `TreasuryYieldXmlConfig`. The `MongoConfig` class provides sensible
defaults, which are enough to satisfy majority of the use cases. Some of the most important
things that we need to set in the `MongoConfig` instance are the output and input format,
`mapper` and `reducer` classes, output key and value of the mapper, and output key and
value of the reducer. The input format and output format will always be the `com.mongodb.`
`hadoop.MongoInputFormat` and `com.mongodb.hadoop.MongoOutputFormat`
classes, which are provided by the mongo-hadoop connector library. For the mapper and
reducer output key and value, we have any of the `org.apache.hadoop.io.Writable`
implementations. Refer to the Hadoop documentation for different types of the Writable
implementations in the `org.apache.hadoop.io` package. Apart from these, the mongo-
hadoop connector also provides us with some implementations in the `com.mongodb.`
`hadoop.io` package. For the treasury yield example, we used the `BSONWritable` instance.
These configurable values can either be provided in the XML file that we saw earlier or be
programmatically set. Finally, we have the option to provide them as `vm` arguments that we did
for `mongo.input.uri` and `mongo.output.uri`. These parameters can be provided either
in the XML or invoked directly from the code on the `MongoConfig` instance; the two methods
are `setInputURI` and `setOutputURI`, respectively.

We will now look at the `mapper` and `reducer` class implementations. We will copy the important portion of the class here in order to analyze. Refer to the cloned project for the entire implementation:

```
public class TreasuryYieldMapper
    extends Mapper<Object, BSONObject, IntWritable, DoubleWritable> {

    @Override
    public void map(final Object pKey,
                    final BSONObject pValue,
                    final Context pContext)
        throws IOException, InterruptedException {
        final int year = ((Date) pValue.get("_id")).getYear() + 1900;
        double bid10Year = ((Number) pValue.get("bc10Year")).
doubleValue();
        pContext.write(new IntWritable(year), new
DoubleWritable(bid10Year));
    }
}
```

Our mapper extends the `org.apache.hadoop.mapreduce.Mapper` class. The four generic parameters are the key class, type of the input value, type of the output key, and output value. The body of the map method reads the `_id` value from the input document, which is the date, and extracts the year out of it. Then, it gets the double value from the document for the `bc10Year` field and simply writes to the context key-value pair where key is the year and value of the double to the context key value pair. The implementation here doesn't rely on the value of the `pKey` parameter passed, which can be used as the key instead of hardcoding the `_id` value in the implementation. This value is basically the same field that would be set using the `mongo.input.key` property in the XML or the `MongoConfig.setInputKey` method. If none is set, `_id` is the default value.

Let's look at the reducer implementation (with the logging statements removed):

```
public class TreasuryYieldReducer
  extends Reducer<IntWritable, DoubleWritable, IntWritable,
    BSONWritable> {

    @Override
    public void reduce(final IntWritable pKey, final
      Iterable<DoubleWritable> pValues, final Context pContext)
        throws IOException, InterruptedException {
      int count = 0;
      double sum = 0;
      for (final DoubleWritable value : pValues) {
        sum += value.get();
        count++;
```

```
            }
            final double avg = sum / count;
            BasicBSONObject output = new BasicBSONObject();
            output.put("count", count);
            output.put("avg", avg);
            output.put("sum", sum);
            pContext.write(pKey, new BSONWritable(output));
        }
    }
```

This class extends from `org.apache.hadoop.mapreduce.Reducer` and has four generic parameters: the input key, input value, output key, and output value. The input to the reducer is the output from the mapper, and thus, if you notice carefully, the type of the first two generic parameters is the same as the last two generic parameters of the mapper that we saw earlier. The third and fourth parameters are the type of the key and value emitted from the reduce. The type of the value is `BSONDocument` and thus we have `BSONWritable` as the type.

We now have the reduce method that has two parameters: the first one is the key, which is the same as the key emitted from the map function, and the second parameter is `java.lang.Iterable` of the values emitted for the same key. This is how standard map reduce functions work. For instance, if the map function gave the following key value pairs, (1950, 10), (1960, 20), (1950, 20), (1950, 30), then reduce will be invoked with two unique keys, 1950 and 1960, and the values for the key 1950 will be `Iterable` with (10, 20, 30), whereas that of 1960 will be `Iterable` of a single element (20). The reducer's reduce function simply iterates though `Iterable` of the doubles, finds the sum and count of these numbers, and writes one key value pair where the key is the same as the incoming key and the output value is `BasicBSONObject` with the sum, count, and average for the computed values.

There are some good samples including the Enron dataset in the examples of the cloned mongo-hadoop connector. If you would like to play around a bit, I would recommend that you take a look at these example projects and run them.

There's more...

What we saw here is a readymade sample that we executed. There is nothing like writing one MapReduce job ourselves to clear our understanding. In the next recipe, we will write one sample MapReduce job using the Hadoop API in Java and see it in action.

See also...

If you're wondering what the `Writable` interface is all about and why you should not use plain old serialization instead, then refer to this URL that gives the explanation by the creator of Hadoop himself: `http://www.mail-archive.com/hadoop-user@lucene.apache.org/msg00378.html`.

Writing our first Hadoop MapReduce job

In this recipe, we will write our first MapReduce job using the Hadoop MapReduce API and run it using the mongo-hadoop connector getting the data from MongoDB. Refer to the *Executing MapReduce in Mongo using a Java client* recipe in *Chapter 3, Programming Language Drivers* to see how MapReduce is implemented using a Java client, test data creation, and problem statement.

Getting ready

Refer to the previous *Executing our first sample MapReduce job using the mongo-hadoop connector* recipe to set up the mongo-hadoop connector. The prerequisites of this recipe and the *Executing MapReduce in Mongo using a Java client* recipe from *Chapter 3, Programming Language Drivers* are all that we need for this recipe. This is a maven project and thus maven needs to be set up and installed. Refer to the *Connecting to the Single node from a Java client* recipe in *Chapter 1, Installing and Starting the Server* where we provided the steps to set up maven in Windows; this project is built on Ubuntu Linux and the following is the command that you need to execute in the operating system shell to get maven:

```
$ sudo apt-get install maven
```

How to do it...

1. We have a Java `mongo-hadoop-mapreduce-test` project, which can be downloaded from the Packt website. The project is targeted to achieve the same use case that we achieved in the recipes in *Chapter 3, Programming Language Drivers* where we used MongoDB's MapReduce framework. We had invoked that MapReduce job using the Python and Java client on previous occasions.

2. On the command prompt with the current directory in the root of the project, where the `pom.xml` file is present, execute the following command:

   ```
   $ mvn clean package
   ```

3. The JAR file, `mongo-hadoop-mapreduce-test-1.0.jar`, will be built and kept in the target directory.

4. With the assumption that the CSV file is already imported to the `postalCodes` collection, execute the following command with the current directory still in the root of the `mongo-hadoop-mapreduce-test` project that we just built:

   ```
   ~/hadoop-binaries/hadoop-2.4.0/bin/hadoop \
    jar target/mongo-hadoop-mapreduce-test-1.0.jar \
    com.packtpub.mongo.cookbook.TopStateMapReduceEntrypoint \
    -Dmongo.input.split_size=8 \
   -Dmongo.job.verbose=true \
   ```

```
-Dmongo.input.uri=mongodb://localhost:27017/test.postalCodes \
-Dmongo.output.uri=mongodb://localhost:27017/test.
postalCodesHadoopmrOut
```

5. Once the MapReduce job is completed, open the mongo shell by typing the following on the operating system command prompt and execute the following query in the shell:

```
$ mongo
> db.postalCodesHadoopmrOut.find().sort({count:-1}).limit(5)
```

6. Compare the output to the one that we got earlier when we executed the MapReduce jobs using mongo's map reduce framework (in *Chapter 3*, *Programming Language Drivers*).

How it works...

We have kept the classes very simple and with the bare minimum things that we need. We just have three classes in our project: `TopStateMapReduceEntrypoint`, `TopStateReducer`, and `TopStatesMapper`, all in the same `com.packtpub.mongo.cookbook` package. The mapper's `map` function just writes a key value pair to the context, where the key is the name of the state and value is an integer value, one. The following is the code snippet from the `mapper` function:

```
context.write(new Text((String)value.get("state")), new
IntWritable(1));
```

What the reducer gets is the same key that is the list of the states and Iterable of integer value, one. All that we do is write the same name of the state and sum of the iterables to the context. Now, as there is no size method in Iterable that can give the count in constant time, we are left with adding up all the ones that we get in linear time. The following is the code in the reducer method:

```
int sum = 0;
for(IntWritable value : values) {
  sum += value.get();
}
BSONObject object = new BasicBSONObject();
object.put("count", sum);
context.write(text, new BSONWritable(object));
```

We write the text string that is the key and value that is the JSON document containing the count to the context. The mongo-hadoop connector is then responsible for writing the `postalCodesHadoopmrOut` document to the output collection that we have, with the `_id` field the same as the key emitted. Thus, when we execute the following, we get the top five states with the most number of cities in our database:

```
> db. postalCodesHadoopmrOut.find().sort({count:-1}).limit(5)
{ "_id" : "Maharashtra", "count" : 6446 }
{ "_id" : "Kerala", "count" : 4684 }
{ "_id" : "Tamil Nadu", "count" : 3784 }
{ "_id" : "Andhra Pradesh", "count" : 3550 }
{ "_id" : "Karnataka", "count" : 3204 }
```

Finally, the main method of the main entry point class is as follows:

```
Configuration conf = new Configuration();
MongoConfig config = new MongoConfig(conf);
config.setInputFormat(MongoInputFormat.class);
config.setMapperOutputKey(Text.class);
config.setMapperOutputValue(IntWritable.class);
config.setMapper(TopStatesMapper.class);
config.setOutputFormat(MongoOutputFormat.class);
config.setOutputKey(Text.class);
config.setOutputValue(BSONWritable.class);
config.setReducer(TopStateReducer.class);
ToolRunner.run(conf, new TopStateMapReduceEntrypoint(), args);
```

All we do is wrap the `org.apache.hadoop.conf.Configuration` object with the `com.mongodb.hadoop.MongoConfig` instance to set various properties and then submit the MapReduce job for execution using ToolRunner.

See also

We executed a simple MapReduce job on Hadoop using the Hadoop API, sourcing the data from MongoDB, and writing the data to the MongoDB collection. What if we want to write the `map` and `reduce` functions in a different language? Fortunately, this is possible using a concept called Hadoop streaming where `stdout` is used as a means to communicate between the program and Hadoop MapReduce framework. In the next recipe, we will demonstrate how to use Python to implement the same use case that we did in this recipe using Hadoop streaming.

Running MapReduce jobs on Hadoop using streaming

In our previous recipe, we implemented a simple MapReduce job using the Java API of Hadoop. The use case was the same as what we did in the recipes in *Chapter 3*, *Programming Language Drivers* where we implemented MapReduce using the Mongo client APIs in Python and Java. In this recipe, we will use Hadoop streaming to implement MapReduce jobs.

The concept of streaming works on communication using `stdin` and `stdout`. You can get more information on Hadoop streaming and how it works at `http://hadoop.apache.org/docs/r1.2.1/streaming.html`.

Getting ready...

Refer to the *Executing our first sample MapReduce job using the mongo-hadoop connector* recipe in this chapter to see how to set up Hadoop for development purposes and build the mongo-hadoop project using Gradle. As far as the Python libraries are concerned, we will be installing the required library from the source; however, you can use `pip` (Python's package manager) to set up if you do not wish to build from the source. We will also see how to set up pymongo-hadoop using `pip`.

Refer to recipe *Connecting to a single node using a Python client*, in *Chapter 1*, *Installing and Starting the Server* on how to install PyMongo for your host operating system.

How it works...

1. We will first build pymongo–hadoop from the source. With the project cloned to the local filesystem, execute the following in the root of the cloned project:

    ```
    $ cd streaming/language_support/python
    $ sudo python setup.py install
    ```

2. After you enter the password, the setup will continue to be installed on pymongo-hadoop on your machine.

3. This is all we need to do to build pymongo-hadoop from the source. However, if you had chosen not to build from the source, you can execute the following command in the operating system shell:

    ```
    $ sudo pip install pymongo_hadoop
    ```

4. After installing pymongo-hadoop in either way, we will now implement our `mapper` and `reducer` function in Python. The `mapper` function is as follows:

    ```
    #!/usr/bin/env python

    import sys
    ```

```python
from pymongo_hadoop import BSONMapper
def mapper(documents):
  print >> sys.stderr, 'Starting mapper'
  for doc in documents:
    yield {'_id' : doc['state'], 'count' : 1}
  print >> sys.stderr, 'Mapper completed'

BSONMapper(mapper)
```

5. Now for the `reducer` function, which will look like the following:

```python
#!/usr/bin/env python

import sys
from pymongo_hadoop import BSONReducer
def reducer(key, documents):
  print >> sys.stderr, 'Invoked reducer for key "', key,
    '"'
  count = 0
  for doc in documents:
    count += 1
  return {'_id' : key, 'count' : count}



BSONReducer(reducer)
```

6. The environment variables, $HADOOP_HOME and $HADOOP_CONNECTOR_HOME, should point to the base directory of Hadoop and the mongo-hadoop connector project, respectively. Now, we will invoke the MapReduce function using the following command in the operating system shell. The code available with the book on the Packt website has the mapper, reduce Python script, and shell script that will be used to invoke the mapper and reducer function:

```
$HADOOP_HOME/bin/hadoop jar \
$HADOOP_HOME/share/hadoop/tools/lib/hadoop-streaming* \
-libjars $HADOOP_CONNECTOR_HOME/streaming/build/libs/mongo-hadoop-streaming-1.2.1-SNAPSHOT-hadoop_2.4.jar \
-input /tmp/in \
-output /tmp/out \
-inputformat com.mongodb.hadoop.mapred.MongoInputFormat \
-outputformat com.mongodb.hadoop.mapred.MongoOutputFormat \
-io mongodb \
-jobconf mongo.input.uri=mongodb://127.0.0.1:27017/test.postalCodes \
```

```
-jobconf mongo.output.uri=mongodb://127.0.0.1:27017/test.
pyMRStreamTest \

-jobconf stream.io.identifier.resolver.class=com.mongodb.hadoop.
streaming.io.MongoIdentifierResolver \

-mapper mapper.py \

-reducer reducer.py
```

The `mapper.py` and `reducer.py` files are present in the current directory when executing this command.

7. On executing the command, which should take some time for the successful execution of the MapReduce job, open the mongo shell by typing the following command on the operating system command prompt and execute the following query from the shell:

```
$ mongo

> db.pyMRStreamTest.find().sort({count:-1}).limit(5)
```

8. Compare the output to the one that we got earlier when we executed the MapReduce jobs using mongo's MapReduce framework in *Chapter 3*, *Programming Language Drivers*.

How to do it...

Let's look at steps 5 and 6 where we write the `mapper` and `reducer` functions. We define a `map` function that accepts a list of all the documents. We iterate through these and yield documents, where the `_id` field is the name of the key and the count value field has a value of one. There will be the same number of documents yielded as the total number of input documents.

We instantiate `BSONMapper` finally, which accepts the `mapper` function as the parameter. The function returns a generator object, which is then used by this `BSONMapper` class to feed the value to the MapReduce framework. All we need to remember is that the `mapper` function needs to return a generator (which is returned as we call yield in the loop) and then instantiate the `BSONMapper` class, which is provided to us by the `pymongo_hadoop` module. For the intrigued, you can choose to look at the source code under the project cloned on our local filesystem in the `streaming/language_support/python/pymongo_hadoop/mapper.py` file and see what it does. It is a small and simple-to-understand piece of code.

For the `reducer` function, we get the key and list of documents for this key as the value. The key is the same as the value of the `_id` field emitted from the document in the `map` function. We simply return a new document here with `_id` as the name of the state and count is the number of documents for this state. Remember that we return a document and not emit one as we did in map. Finally, we instantiate `BSONReducer` and pass the `reducer` function. The source code under the project cloned on our local filesystem in the `streaming/language_support/python/pymongo_hadoop/reducer.py` file has the implementation of the `BSONReducer` class.

We finally invoked the command in the shell to initiate the MapReduce job that uses streaming. A few things to note here are that we need two JAR files: one in `share/hadoop/tools/lib` of the Hadoop distribution and one in the mongo-hadoop connector, which is present in the `streaming/build/libs/` directory. The input and output formats are `com.mongodb.hadoop.mapred.MongoInputFormat` and `com.mongodb.hadoop.mapred.MongoOutputFormat`, respectively.

As we saw earlier, `sysout` and `sysin` forms the backbone of streaming. So, basically, we need to encode our BSON objects to write to `sysout`, and then, we should be able to read `sysin` to convert the content to the BSON objects again. For this purpose, the mongo-hadoop connector provides us with two framework classes, `com.mongodb.hadoop.streaming.io.MongoInputWriter` and `com.mongodb.hadoop.streaming.io.MongoOutputReader` to encode and decode from and to the BSON objects. These classes extend from `org.apache.hadoop.streaming.io.InputWriter` and `org.apache.hadoop.streaming.io.OutputReader`, respectively.

The value of the `stream.io.identifier.resolver.class` property is given as `com.mongodb.hadoop.streaming.io.MongoIdentifierResolver`. This class extends from `org.apache.hadoop.streaming.io.IdentifierResolver` and gives us a chance to register our implementations of `org.apache.hadoop.streaming.io.InputWriter` and `org.apache.hadoop.streaming.io.OutputReader` with the framework. We also register the output key and output value class using our custom `IdentifierResolver`. Just remember to use this resolver always in case you are using streaming with the mongo-hadoop connector.

We finally execute the `mapper` and `reducer` python functions, which we discussed earlier. An important thing to remember is that do not print out logs to `sysout` from the `mapper` and `reducer` functions. The `sysout` and `sysin` mapper and reducer are the means of communication, and writing logs to it can yield undesirable behavior. As we can see in the example, write either to standard error (`stderr`) or a log file.

 When using a multiline command in Unix, you continue the command on the next line using \. However, remember not to have spaces after \.

Running a MapReduce job on Amazon EMR

This recipe involves running the MapReduce job on the cloud using AWS. You will need an AWS account in order to proceed. Register with AWS at `http://aws.amazon.com/`. We will see how to run a MapReduce job on the cloud using **Amazon Elastic Map Reduce** (**Amazon EMR**). Amazon EMR is a managed MapReduce service provided by Amazon on the cloud. Refer to `https://aws.amazon.com/elasticmapreduce/` for more details. Amazon EMR consumes data, binaries/JARs, and so on from AWS S3 bucket, processes them and writes the results back to S3 bucket. **Amazon Simple Storage Service** (**Amazon S3**) is another service by AWS for data storage on the cloud. Refer to `http://aws.amazon.com/s3/` for more details on Amazon S3. Though we will use the mongo-hadoop connector, an interesting fact is that we won't require a MongoDB instance to be up and running. We will use the MongoDB data dump stored in an S3 bucket for our data analysis. The MapReduce program will run on the input BSON dump and generate the result BSON dump in the output bucket. The logs of the MapReduce program will be written to another bucket dedicated for logs. The following figure gives us an idea of how our setup would look at a high level:

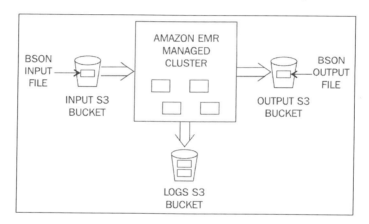

Getting ready

We will use the same Java sample as we did in the *Writing our first Hadoop MapReduce job* recipe for this recipe. To know more about the `mapper` and `reducer` class implementation, you can refer to the *How It works* section of the same recipe. We have a `mongo-hadoop-emr-test` project available with the code that can be downloaded from the Packt website, which is used to create a MapReduce job on the cloud using the AWS EMR APIs. To simplify things, we will upload just one JAR to the S3 bucket to execute the MapReduce job. This JAR will be assembled using a BAT file for Windows and a shell script on Unix-based operating systems. The `mongo-hadoop-emr-test` Java project has the `mongo-hadoop-emr-binaries` subdirectory containing the necessary binaries along with the scripts to assemble them in one JAR.

The assembled `mongo-hadoop-emr-assembly.jar` file is also provided in the subdirectory. Running the `.bat` or `.sh` file will delete this JAR and regenerate the assembled JAR, which is not mandatory. The already provided assembled JAR is good enough and will work just fine. The Java project contains subdirectory data with a `postalCodes.bson` file in it. This is the BSON dump generated out of the database containing the `postalCodes` collection. The `mongodump` utility provided with the mongo distribution is used to extract this dump.

How to do it...

1. The first step of this exercise is to create a bucket on S3. You can choose to use an existing bucket; however, for this recipe, I am creating a `com.packtpub.mongo.cookbook.emr-in` bucket. Remember that the name of the bucket has to be unique across all the S3 buckets and you will not be able to create a bucket with this very name. You will have to create one with a different name and use it in place of `com.packtpub.mongo.cookbook.emr-in` that is used in this recipe.

     Do not create bucket names with an underscore (_); instead, use a hyphen (-). The bucket creation with an underscore will not fail; however, the MapReduce job later will fail as it doesn't accept underscores in the bucket names.

2. We will upload the assembled JAR files and a `.bson` file for the data to the newly created (or existing) S3 bucket. To upload the files, we will use the AWS web console. Click on the **Upload** button and select the assembled JAR file and the `postalCodes.bson` file to be uploaded to the S3 bucket. After uploading, the contents of the bucket should look as follows:

3. The following steps are to initiate the EMR job from the AWS console without writing a single line of code. We will also see how to initiate this using AWS Java SDK. Follow steps 4 to 9 if you are looking to initiate the EMR job from the AWS console. Follow steps 10 and 11 to start the EMR job using the Java SDK.

4. We will first initiate a MapReduce job from the AWS console. Visit `https://console.aws.amazon.com/elasticmapreduce/` and click on the **Create Cluster** button. In the **Cluster Configuration** screen, enter the details as shown in the image, except for the logging bucket, which you need to select as your bucket to which the logs need to be written. You can also click on the folder icon next to the textbox for the bucket name and select the bucket present for your account to be used as the logging bucket.

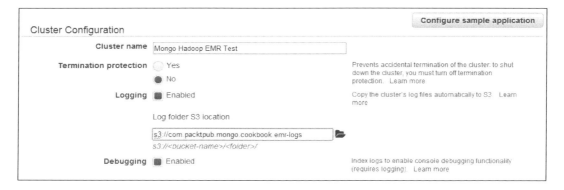

The termination protection option is set to **No** as this is a test instance. In case of any error, we would rather want the instances to terminate in order to avoid keeping them running and incurring charges.

5. In the **Software Configuration** section, select the **Hadoop version** as **2.4.0** and **AMI version** as **3.1.0 (hadoop 2.4.0)**. Remove the additional applications by clicking on the cross next to their names, as shown in the following image:

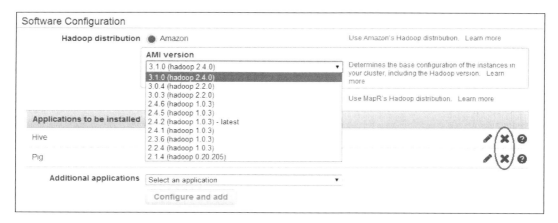

6. In the **Hardware Configuration** section, select the **EC2 instance type** as **m1.medium**. This is the minimum that we need to select for the Hadoop version 2.4.0. The number of instances for the slave and task instances is zero. The following image shows the configuration that is selected:

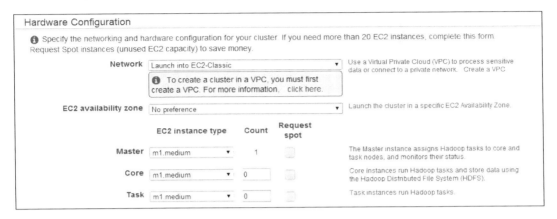

7. In the **Security and Access** section, leave all the default values. We also have no need for a **Bootstrap Action**, so leave this as well.

8. The final step is to set up **Steps** for the MapReduce job. In the **Add step** drop down, select the **Custom JAR** option, and then select the **Auto-terminate** option as **Yes**, as shown in the following image:

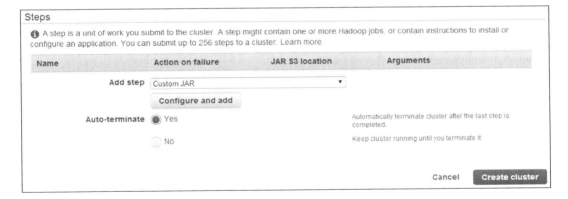

Now click on the **Configure** and **Add** button and enter the details.

The value of the **JAR S3 Location** is given as s3://com.packtpub.mongo. cookbook.emr-in/mongo-hadoop-emr-assembly.jar. This is the location in my input bucket; you need to change the input bucket as per your own input bucket. The name of the JAR file would be same.

Enter the following arguments in the **Arguments** text area; the name of the main class is the first in the list:

```
com.packtpub.mongo.cookbook.TopStateMapReduceEntrypoint

-Dmongo.job.input.format=com.mongodb.hadoop.BSONFileInputFormat

-Dmongo.job.mapper=com.packtpub.mongo.cookbook.TopStatesMapper

-Dmongo.job.reducer=com.packtpub.mongo.cookbook.TopStateReducer

-Dmongo.job.output=org.apache.hadoop.io.Text

-Dmongo.job.output.value=org.apache.hadoop.io.IntWritable

-Dmongo.job.output.value=org.apache.hadoop.io.IntWritable

-Dmongo.job.output.format=com.mongodb.hadoop.
BSONFileOutputFormat

-Dmapred.input.dir=s3://com.packtpub.mongo.cookbook.emr-in/
postalCodes.bson

-Dmapred.output.dir=s3://com.packtpub.mongo.cookbook.emr-out/
```

9. The value of the final two arguments contains the input and output bucket used for my MapReduce sample; this value will change according to your own input and output buckets. The value of Action on failure would be Terminate. The following image shows the values filled in; click on **Save** after all these details have been entered:

10. Now click on the **Create Cluster** button. This will take some time to provision and start the cluster.

11. In the following few steps, we will create a MapReduce job on EMR using the AWS Java API. Import the EMRTest project provided with the code samples to your favorite IDE. Once imported, open the `com.packtpub.mongo.cookbook.AWSElasticMapReduceEntrypoint` class.

12. There are five constants that need to be changed in the class. They are the Input, Output, and Log bucket that you will use for your example and the AWS access and secret key. The access key and secret key act as the username and password when you use AWS SDK. Change these values accordingly and run the program. On successful execution, it should give you a job ID for the newly initiated job.

13. Irrespective of how you initiated the EMR job, visit the EMR console at `https://console.aws.amazon.com/elasticmapreduce/` to see the status of your submitted ID. The Job ID that you can see in the second column of your initiated job will be same as the job ID printed to the console when you executed the Java program (if you initiated using the Java program). Click on the name of the job initiated, which should direct you to the job details page. The hardware provisioning will take some time, and then finally, your map reduce step will run. Once the job has been completed, the status of the job should look as follows on the Job details screen:

When expanded, the **Steps** section should look as follows:

14. Click on the stderr link below the Log files section to view all the logs' output for the MapReduce job.

15. Now that the MapReduce job is complete, our next step is to see the results of it. Visit the S3 console at `https://console.aws.amazon.com/s3` and visit the output bucket. In my case, the following is the content of the out bucket:

Name	Storage Class	Size	Last Modified
_SUCCESS	Standard	0 bytes	Fri May 30 13:34:28 GMT+530 2014
part-r-00000.bson	Standard	1.2 KB	Fri May 30 13:34:27 GMT+530 2014

All Buckets / com.packtpub.mongo.cookbook.emr-out

The `part-r-0000.bson` file is of our interest. This file contains the results of our MapReduce job.

16. Download the file to your local filesystem and import to a running mongo instance locally, using the mongorestore utility. Note that the restore utility for the following command expects a mongod instance to be up and running and listening to port 27017 with the `part-r-0000.bson` file in the current directory:

```
$ mongorestore part-r-00000.bson -d test -c mongoEMRResults
```

17. Now, connect to the `mongod` instance using the mongo shell and execute the following query:

```
> db.mongoEMRResults.find().sort({count:-1}).limit(5)
```

We will see the following results for the query:

```
{ "_id" : "Maharashtra", "count" : 6446 }
{ "_id" : "Kerala", "count" : 4684 }
{ "_id" : "Tamil Nadu", "count" : 3784 }
{ "_id" : "Andhra Pradesh", "count" : 3550 }
{ "_id" : "Karnataka", "count" : 3204 }
```

18. This is the expected result for the top five results. If we compare the results that we got in *Executing MapReduce in Mongo using a Java client* from *Chapter 3, Programming Language Drivers* using Mongo's MapReduce framework and the *Writing our first Hadoop MapReduce job* recipe in this chapter, we can see that the results are identical.

How it works...

Amazon EMR is a managed Hadoop service that takes care of the hardware provisioning and keeps you away from the hassle of setting up your own cluster. The concepts related to our MapReduce program have already been covered in the *Writing our first Hadoop MapReduce job* recipe and there is nothing more to mention. One thing that we did was to assemble the JARs that we need in one big fat JAR to execute our MapReduce job. This approach is okay for our small MapReduce job; in case of larger jobs where a lot of third-party JARs are needed, we will have to go for an approach where we will add the JARs to the `lib` directory of the Hadoop installation and execute in the same way as we did in our MapReduce job that we executed locally. Another thing that we did differently from our local setup was not to use a `mongid` instance to source the data and write the data to, but instead, we used the BSON dump files from the mongo database as an input and wrote the output to the BSON files. The output dump will then be imported to a mongo database locally and the results will be analyzed. It is pretty common to have the data dumps uploaded to S3 buckets, and running analytics jobs on this data that has been uploaded to S3 on the cloud using cloud infrastructure is a good option. The data accessed from the buckets by the EMR cluster need not have public access as the EMR job runs using our account's credentials; we are good to access our own buckets to read and write data/logs.

See also

After trying out this simple MapReduce job, it is highly recommended that you get to know about the Amazon EMR service and all its features. The developer's guide for EMR can be found at `http://docs.aws.amazon.com/ElasticMapReduce/latest/DeveloperGuide/`.

There is a sample MapReduce job in the Enron dataset given as part of the mongo-hadoop connector's examples. It can be found at `https://github.com/mongodb/mongo-hadoop/tree/master/examples/elastic-mapreduce`. You can choose to implement this example as well on Amazon EMR as per the given instructions.

9

Open Source and Proprietary Tools

In this chapter, we will cover some open source and proprietary tools. The following are the recipes that we will go through in this chapter:

- ▶ Developing using spring-data-mongodb
- ▶ Accessing MongoDB using JPA
- ▶ Accessing MongoDB over REST
- ▶ Installing a GUI-based client, MongoVUE, for MongoDB

Introduction

There is a vast array of tools/frameworks available to ease the development/administration process for software that uses MongoDB. We will look at some of these available frameworks and tools. For a developer's productivity (Java developers, in this case), we will look at spring-data-mongodb, which is a part of the popular spring data suite.

JPA is an ORM specification that is widely used, particularly with relational databases. (This was the objective of the ORM frameworks.) However, there are a few implementations that let us use it with NoSQL stores—MongoDB, in this case. We will look at a provider who provides this implementation and put it to the test with a simple use case.

We will use spring-data-rest to expose the CRUD repositories for MongoDB over a REST interface for clients to invoke various operations supported by the underlying spring-data-mongo repository.

Querying the database in the shell is okay, but it would be nice to have a good GUI to enable us to do all the administrative-related/development-related tasks from the GUI rather than execute the commands in the shell to perform these activities. We will look at one such tool in this chapter.

Developing using spring-data-mongodb

From a developer's perspective, when a program needs to interact with a MongoDB instance, they need to use the respective client APIs for their specific platforms. The trouble with doing this is that we need to write a lot of boilerplate code and it is not necessarily object-oriented. For instance, we have a class called `Person` with various attributes such as `name`, `age`, `address`, and so on. The corresponding JSON document shares a similar structure to this `person` class as follows:

```
{
  name:"…",
  age:..,
  address:{lineOne:"…", …}
}
```

However, to store this document, we need to convert the `Person` class to DBObject, which is a map with key and value pairs. What is really needed is to let us persist this `Person` class itself as an object in the database without having to convert it to DBObject.

Additionally, some of the operations such as searching by a particular field of a document, saving an entity, deleting an entity, searching by the ID, and so on are pretty common operations, and we tend to repeatedly write similar boilerplate code. In this recipe, we will see how spring-data-mongodb relieves us of these laborious and cumbersome tasks to reduce, not only the development effort, but also the possibility of introducing bugs in these commonly written functions.

Getting ready

The `SpringDataMongoTest` project, present in the bundle with the chapter, is a Maven project and has to be imported to any IDE of your choice. The required maven artifacts will automatically be downloaded. A single MongoDB instance is required to be up and running and listening to port `27017`. Refer to the *Installing single node MongoDB* recipe from *Chapter 1, Installing and Starting the Server*, for instructions on how to start a standalone instance.

For the aggregation example, we will use the postal codes data. Refer to the *Creating test data* recipe in *Chapter 2, Command-line Operations and Indexes*, for the creation of the test data.

How to do it...

1. We will explore the spring-data-mongodb's repository feature first. Open the test case's `com.packtpub.mongo.cookbook.MongoCrudRepositoryTest` class from your IDE and execute it. If all goes well and the MongoDB server instance is reachable, the test case will get executed successfully.

2. Another test case, `com.packtpub.mongo.cookbook.MongoCrudRepositoryTest2`, is used to explore more features of the repository support provided by spring-data-mongodb. This test case too should get executed successfully.

3. We will see how spring-data-mongodb's `MongoTemplate` can be used to perform CRUD operations and other common operations on MongoDB. Open the `com.packtpub.mongo.cookbook.MongoTemplateTest` class and execute it.

4. Alternatively, if an IDE is not used, all the tests can be executed using maven from the command prompt with the current directory being in the root of the `SpringDataMongoTest` project:

```
$ mvn clean test
```

How it works...

We will first look at what we did in `com.packtpub.mongo.cookbook.MongoCrudRepositoryTest`, where we saw the repository support provided by spring-data-mongodb. Just in case you didn't notice, we haven't written a single line of code for the repository. The magic of implementing the required code for us is done by the spring data project.

Let's start by looking at the relevant portions of the XML configuration file:

```
<mongo:repositories base-package="com.packtpub.mongo.cookbook" />
<mongo:mongo id="mongo" host="localhost" port="27017"/>
<mongo:db-factory id="factory" dbname="test" mongo-ref="mongo"/>
<mongo:template id="mongoTemplate" db-factory-ref="factory"/>
```

We first look at the last three lines, which are the spring-data-mongodb namespace declarations to instantiate `com.mongodb.Mongo`, a factory for the `com.mongodb.DB` instances from the client, and `template` instance, which is used to perform various operations on MongoDB, respectively. We will see `org.springframework.data.mongodb.core.MongoTemplate` in more detail later.

The first line is a namespace declaration for the base package of all the CRUD repositories that we have. In this package, we have an interface with the following body:

```
public interface PersonRepository extends PagingAndSortingRepository<P
erson, Integer>{

    /**
     *
     * @param lastName
     * @return
     */
    Person findByLastName(String lastName);
}
```

The `PagingAndSortingRepository` interface is from the `org.springframework.data.repository` package of the spring data core project and extends from `CrudRepository` in the same project. These interfaces give us some of the most common methods such as searching by the ID/primary key, deleting an entity, and inserting and updating an entity. The repository needs an object that it maps to the underlying data store. The spring data project supports a large number of data stores not just limited to SQL (using JDBC and JPA) or MongoDB, but also to other NoSQL stores such as Redis and Hadoop and search engines such as Solr and Elasticsearch. In case of spring-data-mongodb, the object is mapped to a document in the collection.

The `PagingAndSortingRepository<Person, Integer>` signature indicates that the first one is the entity that the CRUD repository is built for and the second is the type of the primary key/ID field.

We added just one `findByLastName` method, which accepts one string value for the last name as a parameter. This is an interesting operation that is specific to our repository and not even implemented by us, but it will still work just as expected. Person is a POJO where we annotated the `id` field with the `org.springframework.data.annotation.Id` annotation. Nothing else is really special about this class; it just has some plain getters and setters.

With all these small details, let's join these dots together by answering some questions that you'll have in mind. First, we will see which server, database, and collection our data goes to. If we look at the XML definition, `mongo:mongo`, for the configuration file, we can see that we instantiated the `com.mongodb.Mongo` class by connecting to localhost and port `27017`. The `mongo:db-factory` declaration is used to denote that the database to be used is `test`. One final question is: which collection? The simple name of our class is `Person`. The name of the collection is the simple name with the first character in lowercase, and thus, `Person` goes to person and something like `BillingAddress` would go to the `billingAddress` collection. These are the default values. However, if you need to override this value, you can annotate your class with the `org.springframework.data.mongodb.core.mapping.Document` annotation and use its collection attribute to give any name of your choice, as we will see in a later example.

To view the document in the collection, execute just one test case `saveAndQueryPerson` method from the `com.packtpub.mongo.cookbook.MongoCrudRepositoryTest` class. Now, connect to the MongoDB instance in the mongo shell and execute the following query:

```
> use test
> db.person.findOne({_id:1})
{
        "_id" : 1,
        "_class" : "com.packtpub.mongo.cookbook.domain.Person",
        "firstName" : "Steve",
        "lastName" : "Johnson",
        "age" : 20,
        "gender" : "Male"
    ...
}
```

As we can see in the preceding result, the contents of the document are similar to the object that we persisted using the CRUD repository. The names of the field in the document are the same as the names of the respective attributes in the Java object with two exceptions. The field annotated with `@Id` is now `_id`, irrespective of the name of the field in the Java class and an additional `_class` attribute is added to the document whose value is the fully qualified name of the Java class itself. This is not of any use to the application but is used by spring-data-mongodb as metadata.

Now it makes more sense and gives us an idea what spring-data-mongodb must be doing for all the basic CRUD methods. All the operations that we perform will use the `MongoTemplate` (`MongoOperations`, which is an interface that `MongoTemplate` implements) class from the spring-data-mongodb project. Using the primary key, it will invoke a find by the `_id` field on the collection derived using the `Person` entity class. The `save` method simply calls the `save` method on `MongoOperations`, which, in turn, calls the `save` method on the `com.mongodb.DBCollection` class.

We still haven't answered how the `findByLastName` method worked. How does spring know what query to invoke in order to return the data? These are the special types of methods that begin with `find`, `findBy`, `get`, or `getBy`. There are some rules that one needs to follow while naming a method, and the proxy object on the repository interface is able to correctly convert this method into an appropriate query on the collection. For instance, the `findByLastName` method in the repository for the `Person` class will execute a query on the `lastName` field in person's document. Hence, the `findByLastName(String lastName)` method will fire the `db.person.find({'lastName': lastName })` query on the database. Based on the return type of the method defined, it will return either `List` or the first result in the returned result from the database. We used `findBy` in our queries; however, anything that begins with find, has any text in between, and ends with `By`, works. For instance, `findPersonBy` is also the same as `findBy`.

To see more on these `findBy` methods, we have another test `MongoCrudRepositoryTest2` class. Open this class in your IDE where it can be read along with this text. We already executed this test case; now, let's see these `findBy` methods used and their behavior. This interface has seven `findBy` methods in it, with one of the methods being a variant of another method in the same interface. To get a clear idea of the queries, we will first look at one of the documents in the `personTwo` collection in the test database. Execute the following in the mongo shell connected to the MongoDB server running on localhost:

```
> use test
> db.personTwo.findOne({firstName:'Amit'})
{
        "_id" : 2,
        "_class" : "com.packtpub.mongo.cookbook.domain.Person2",
        "firstName" : "Amit",
        "lastName" : "Sharma",
        "age" : 25,
        "gender" : "Male",
        "residentialAddress" : {
                "addressLineOne" : "20, Central street",
                "city" : "Mumbai",
                "state" : "Maharashtra",
                "country" : "India",
                "zip" : "400101"
        }
}
```

Note that the repository uses the `Person2` class; however, the name of the collection used is `personTwo`. This was possible because we used the `@Document(collection="personTwo")` annotation on the top of the `Person2` class.

Getting back to the seven methods in the `com.packtpub.mongo.cookbook.`
`PersonRepositoryTwo` repository class, let's look at them one by one:

Method	Description
`findByAgeGreaterThanEqual`	This method will fire a query on the `personTwo` collection, `{'age':{'$gte':<age>}}`.
	The secret lies in the name of the method. If we break it up, what we have after `findBy` tells us what we want. The `age` property (with the first character in lowercase) is the field that would be queried on the document with the `$gte` operator because we have `GreaterThanEqual` in the name of the method. The value that would be used for the comparison would be the value of the parameter passed. The result is a collection of the `Person2` entities as we will have multiple matches.
`findByAgeBetween`	This method will again be queried on age but will be using a combination of `$gt` and `$lt` to find the matching result. The query, in this case, would be `{'age' : {'$gt' : from, '$lt' : to}}`. It is important to note that both the values from and to are exclusive in the range. There are two methods in the test case, `findByAgeBetween` and `findByAgeBetween2`. These methods demonstrate the behavior of the between query for different input values.
`findByAgeGreaterThan`	This method is a special method that also sorts the result because there are two parameters to the method: the first parameter is the value against which the age will be compared and the second parameter is the field of the `org.springframework.data.domain.Sort` type. For more details, refer to the Javadocs for spring-data-mongodb.

Method	Description
`findPeopleByLastNameLike`	This method is used to find results by the last name matching a pattern. Regular expressions are used for the matching purpose. For instance, in this case, the query fired will be `{'lastName' : <lastName as regex>}`. This method's name begins with `findPeopleBy` instead of `findBy`, which works the same as `findBy`. Thus, when we say `findBy` in all the descriptions, we actually mean `find...By`.
	The value provided as the parameter will be used to match the last name.
`findByResidentialAddressCountry`	This is an interesting method to look at. Here, we are searching by the country of the residential address. This is, in fact, a field in the `Address` class in the `residentialAddress` field of the person. Take a look at the document from the `personTwo` collection for how the query should be.
	When spring data finds the name as `ResidentialAddressCountry`, it will try to find various combinations using this string. For instance, it can look at the `residentialAddressCountry` field in the `Person` class or `residential.addressCountry`, `residentialAddress.country`, or `residential.address.country`. If there are no conflicting values as in our case the `residentialAddress`. The field 'country' is a part of the 'Person2' document and thus that would be used in the query.
	However, if there are conflicts, then underscores can be used to clearly specify what we are looking at. In this case, the method can be renamed `findByResidentialAddress_country` to clearly specify what we expect as the result. The test case `findByCountry2` method demonstrates this.

Method	Description
`findByFirstNameAndCountry`	This is an interesting method. We are not always able to use the method names to implement what we actually want to. The name of the method required for spring to automatically implement the query might be a bit awkward to use as is. For instance, `findByCountryOfResidence` sounds better than `findByResidentialAddressCountry`. However, we are stuck with the latter as that is how spring-data-mongodb would construct the query. Using `findByCountryOfResidence` gives no details on how to construct the query to spring data.
	There is a solution for this. You can choose to use the `@Query` annotation and specify the query to be executed when the method is invoked. The following is the annotation that we used:
	`@Query("{'firstName':?0, 'residentialAddress.country': ?1}")`
	We write the value as a query that would get executed and bind the parameters of the functions to the query as numbered parameters starting from zero. Thus, the first parameter of the method will be bound to `?0`, the second to `?1`, and so on.

We saw how the `findBy` or `getBy` methods are automatically translated to the queries for MongoDB. Similarly, we have the following prefixes for the methods. The `countBy` method returns the long number for the count for a given condition, which is derived from the rest of the method name similar to `findBy`. We can have `deleteBy` or `removeBy` to delete the documents by the derived condition. One thing to note about the `com.packtpub.mongo.cookbook.domain.Person2` class is that it does not have a no argument constructor or setter to set the values. Instead, spring will use reflection to instantiate this object.

A lot of the `findBy` methods are supported by spring-data-mongodb and all are not covered here. Refer to the spring-data-mongodb reference manual for more details. A lot of XML-based or Java-based configuration options are available and can be found in the reference manual. The URLs are given in the *See also* section later in this recipe.

We are not done yet; we have another test case, `com.packtpub.mongo.cookbook.MongoTemplateTest`, which uses `org.springframework.data.mongodb.core.MongoTemplate` to perform various operations. You can open the test case class and see what operations are performed and which methods of MongoTemplate are invoked.

Let's look at some of the important and frequently used methods of the MongoTemplate class:

Method	Description
`save`	This method is used to save (insert, if new; or else, update) an entity in MongoDB. The method takes one parameter, the entity, and finds the target collection based on its name or the `@Document` annotation present on it.
	There is an overloaded version of the save method that also accepts the second parameter, the name of the collection to which the data entity passed needs to be persisted.
`remove`	This method will be used to remove documents from the collection. It has some overloaded methods in this class. All of them accept either an entity to be deleted or the `org.springframework.data.mongodb.core.query.Query` instance, which is used to determine the document(s) to be deleted. The second parameter is the name of the collection from which the document has to be deleted. When an entity is provided, the name of the collection can be derived. With a `Query` instance provided, we have to give either the name of the collection or the entity class name, which, in turn, will be used to derive the name of the collection.
`updateMulti`	This is the function invoked to update multiple documents with one update call. The first parameter is the query that would be used to match the documents. The second parameter is the `org.springframework.data.mongodb.core.query.Update` instance. This is the update that would be executed on the documents selected using the first `Query` object. The next parameters are the entity class or collection name to execute the update on. Refer to the Javadocs for more details on the method and its various overloaded versions.
`updateFirst`	It is the opposite of the `updateMulti` method. This operation will update just the first matching document. We have not covered this method in our unit test case.

Method	Description
insert	We mentioned that the save method can perform insertion and updates. The insert method in the template calls the insert method of the underlying mongo client. If one entity or document is to be inserted, there is no difference in calling the insert or save method.
	However, as we can see in the insertMultiple method in the test case, we created a list of three Person instances and passed them to the insert method. All the three documents for the three Person instances will go to the server as part of one call. The behavior on what happens whenever an insert fails is determined by the continue on error parameter of the Write Concern. It will determine whether the bulk insert fails at the first failure or continues even after errors while reporting the last error. The URL, http://docs.mongodb.org/manual/core/bulk-inserts/, gives more details on bulk inserts and various write concern parameters that can alter the behavior.
findAndRemove/ findAllAndRemove	Both these operations are used to find and then remove the document(s). The first one finds one and then returns the deleted document. This operation is atomic. The latter, however, finds all the documents and removes them before returning the list of all the entities of all the documents deleted.
findAndModify	This method is functionally similar to findAndModify that we have with the mongo client library. It will atomically find and modify the document. If the query matches more than one document, only the first match will be updated. The first two parameters of this method are the query and update to execute. The next few parameters are either the entity class or collection name to execute the operation on. Additionally, there is a special org.springframework.data.mongodb.core.FindAndModifyOptions class, which makes sense only for the findAndModify operation. This instance tells us whether we are looking for the new instance or old instance after the operation is performed and whether upsert is to be performed. It is relevant only if the document with the matching query doesn't exist. There is an additional Boolean flag to tell the client whether this is a findAndRemove operation. In fact, the findAndRemove operation that we saw earlier is just a convenient function that delegates findAndModify with this remove flag set.

In the preceding table, we mentioned the `Query` and `Update` classes when talking about update. These are special convenient classes in spring-data-mongodb, which let us build MongoDB queries using a syntax that is easy to understand with improved readability. For instance, the query to check whether `lastName` is `Johnson` in mongo is `{'lastName':'Johnson'}`. The same query can be constructed in spring-data-mongodb as follows:

```
new Query(Criteria.where("lastName").is("Johnson"))
```

This syntax looks neat compared to giving the query in JSON. Let's take another example where we want to find all the females under 30 years in our database. The query would now be built as follows:

```
new Query(Criteria.where("age").lt(30).and("gender").is("Female"))
```

Similarly, for update, we want to set a Boolean flag, `youngCustomer`, to `true` for some of the customers based on some conditions. To set this flag in the document, the MongoDB format would be as follows:

```
{'$set' : {'youngCustomer' : true}}
```

In spring-data-mongodb, this would be achieved in the following way:

```
new Update().set("youngCustomer", true)
```

Refer to the Javadocs for all the possible methods that are available to build the query and updates in spring-data-mongodb to be used with `MongoTemplate`.

These methods are by no means the only ones available in the `MongoTemplate` class. There are a lot of other methods for geospatial indexes, convenient methods to get the count of the documents in a collection, aggregation and MapReduce support, and so on. Refer to the Javadocs of `MongoTemplate` for more details and methods.

Speaking of aggregation, we also have a test case `aggregationTest` method to perform the aggregation operation on the collection. We have a `postalCodes` collection in MongoDB that contains the postal code details of various cities. An example document in the collection is as follows:

```
{
        "_id" : ObjectId("539743b26412fd18f3510f1b"),
        "postOfficeName" : "A S D Mello Road Fuller Marg",
        "pincode" : 400001,
        "districtsName" : "Mumbai",
        "city" : "Mumbai",
        "state" : "Maharashtra"
}
```

Our aggregation operation intends to find the top five states by the number of documents in the collection. In mongo, the aggregation pipeline would look as follows:

```
[
{'$project':{'state':1, '_id':0}},
{'$group':{'_id':'$state', 'count':{'$sum':1}}}
{'$sort':{'count':-1}},
{'$limit':5}
]
```

In spring-data-mongodb, we invoked the aggregation operation using `MongoTemplate`:

```
Aggregation aggregation = newAggregation(

    project("state", "_id"),
    group("state").count().as("count"),
    sort(Direction.DESC, "count"),
    limit(5)
);

AggregationResults<DBObject> results = mongoTemplate.aggregate(
    aggregation,
    "postalCodes",
    DBObject.class);
```

The key is in creating the instance of the `org.springframework.data.mongodb.core.aggregation.Aggregation` class. The `newAggregation` method is statically imported from the same class and accepts `varargs` for different instances of the `org.springframework.data.mongodb.core.aggregation.AggregationOperation` instances corresponding to the one operation in the chain. The `Aggregation` class has various static methods to create the instances of `AggregationOperation`. We have used a few of them such as `project`, `group`, `sort`, and `limit`. Refer to the Javadocs for more details and available methods. The `aggregate` method in `MongoTemplate` takes three arguments. The first one is the instance of the `Aggregation` class, the second one is the name of the collection, and the third one is the return type of the aggregation result. Refer to the aggregation operation test case for more details.

See also

- Refer to the Javadocs at `http://docs.spring.io/spring-data/mongodb/docs/current/api/` for more details and API documentation
- The reference manual for the spring-data-mongodb project can be found at `http://docs.spring.io/spring-data/data-mongodb/docs/current/reference/`

Accessing MongoDB using JPA

In this recipe, we will use a JPA provider that allows us to use JPA entities to achieve object-to-document mapping with MongoDB.

Getting ready

Start the standalone server instance listening to port 27017. This is a Java project using JPA. Familiarity with JPA and its annotations is expected, though what we will be looking at is fairly basic. Refer to the *Connecting to the single node using a Java client* recipe in *Chapter 1, Installing and Starting the Server*, to see how to set up maven if you are not aware of it. Download the DataNucleusMongoJPA project from the bundle provided with this book. Though we will be executing the test cases from the command prompt, you can import the project to your favorite IDE to view the source code.

How to do it...

1. Go to the root directory of the DataNucleusMongoJPA project and execute the following in the shell:

    ```
    $ mvn clean test
    ```

2. This should download the necessary artifacts needed to build and run the project and execute the test cases successfully.

3. Once the test cases get executed, open a mongo shell and connect to the local instance.

4. Execute the following query in the shell:

    ```
    > use test
    > db.personJPA.find().pretty()
    ```

How it works...

First, let's look at a sample document that was created in the personJPA collection:

```
{
        "_id" : NumberLong(2),
        "residentialAddress" : {
                "residentialAddress_zipCode" : "400101",
                "residentialAddress_state" : "Maharashtra",
                "residentialAddress_country" : "India",
                "residentialAddress_city" : "Mumbai",
                "residentialAddress_addressLineOne" : "20, Central
street"
```

```
    },
    "lastName" : "Sharma",
    "gender" : "Male",
    "firstName" : "Amit",
    "age" : 25
}
```

The steps that we executed are pretty simple; let's look at the classes that are used one by one. We start with the `com.packtpub.mongo.cookbook.domain.Person` class. On the top of the class (after the package and imports), we have the following:

```
@Entity
@Table(name="personJPA")
public class Person {
```

This denotes that the `Person` class is an entity and the collection to which it would persist is `personJPA`. Note that JPA was designed primarily as an **Object Relational Mapping (ORM)** tool and, so, the terminologies used are more for a relational database. A table in RDBMS is synonymous to a collection in MongoDB. The rest of the class contains the attributes of person and the columns annotated with `@Column` and `@Id` for a primary key. These are simple JPA annotations. What is interesting to look at is the `com.packtpub.mongo.cookbook.domain.ResidentialAddress` class, which is stored as a `residentialAddress` variable in the `Person` class. If we look at the person document that we gave earlier, all the values given in the `@Column` annotation are the names of the keys for person; also notice how `Enum` gets converted to a string value as well. The `residentialAddress` field is the name of the variable in the `Person` class against which the address instance is stored. If we look at the `ResidentialAddress` class, we can see the `@Embeddable` annotation at the top above the class name. This is again a JPA annotation that denotes that this instance is not an entity itself, but is embedded in another `Entity` or `Embeddable` class. Note the names of the fields in the document; in this case, they have the following format: `<name of the variable in person class>_<value of the variable name in ResidentialAddress class>`.

There is one problem here. The names of the fields are too long, consuming unnecessary space. The solution is to have a shorter value in the `@Column` annotation. For instance, the `@Column(name="ln")` annotation instead of `@Column(name="lastName")`, will create the key with a `ln` name in the document. Unfortunately, this doesn't work with the embedded `ResidentialAddress` class; in which case, you will have to deal with shorter variable names. Now that we have seen the entity classes, let's see `persistence.xml`:

```
<persistence-unit name="DataNucleusMongo">
  <class>com.packtpub.mongo.cookbook.domain.Person</class>
  <properties>
    <property name="javax.persistence.jdbc.url"
      value="mongodb:localhost:27017/test"/>
  </properties>
</persistence-unit>
```

We have got just the persistence-unit definition here with the name as `DataNucleusMongo`. There is one class node that is the entity that we will use. Note that the embedded address class is not mentioned here as it is not an independent entity. In the properties, we mentioned the URL of the data store to connect to. In this case, we connect to the instance on localhost, port `27017`, and database test.

Now, let's look at the class that queries and inserts the data. This is our `com.packtpub.mongo.cookbook.DataNucleusJPATest` test class. We create `javax.persistence.EntityManagerFactory` as `Persistence.createEntityManagerFactory("DataNucleusMongo")`. This is a thread-safe class and its instance is shared across threads; the string argument is also the same as the name of the persistence unit that we used in `persistence.xml`. All the other invocations on `javax.persistence.EntityManager` to persist or query the collection require us to create an instance using `EntityManagerFactory`—use it and then close it once the operation is completed. All the operations performed are as per the JPA specifications. The test case class persists entities and also queries them.

Finally, we look at `pom.xml`, particularly the enhancer plugin that we used, which is as follows:

```xml
<plugin>
  <groupId>org.datanucleus</groupId>
  <artifactId>datanucleus-maven-plugin</artifactId>
  <version>4.0.0-release</version>
  <configuration>
    <log4jConfiguration>${basedir}/src/main/resources/log4j.properties</log4jConfiguration>
    <verbose>true</verbose>
  </configuration>
  <executions>
    <execution>
      <phase>process-classes</phase>
      <goals>
        <goal>enhance</goal>
      </goals>
    </execution>
  </executions>
</plugin>
```

The entities that we have written need to be enhanced in order to be used as JPA entities using data nucleus. The preceding plugin will be attached to the process-class phase and then call the plugin's enhance.

▸ There are various ways to enhance JPA entities using a data nucleus enhancer. Refer to `http://www.datanucleus.org/products/datanucleus/jdo/enhancer.html` for possible options. There is even a plugin for Eclipse to allow entity classes to be enhanced/instrumented for data nucleus.

▸ The JPA 2.1 specification can be found at `https://www.jcp.org/aboutJava/communityprocess/final/jsr338/index.html`.

Accessing MongoDB over REST

In this recipe, we will see how to access MongoDB and perform CRUD operations using REST APIs. We will use spring-data-rest for REST access and spring-data-mongodb to perform the CRUD operations. Before you continue with this recipe, it is important to know how to implement the CRUD repositories using spring-data-mongodb. Refer to the *Developing using spring-data-mongodb* recipe in this chapter to know how to use this framework.

The question one must be having is, why is a REST API needed? There are scenarios where there is a database that is being shared by many applications and is possibly written in different languages. Writing JPA DAO or using spring-data-mongodb is good enough for Java clients but not for clients in other languages. Having APIs locally with the application doesn't even give us a centralized way to access the database. This is where REST APIs come into play. We can develop the server-side data access layer and the CRUD repository in Java—spring-data-mongodb to be precise—and then expose it over a REST interface for a client written in any language to invoke them. We not only invoke our API in a platform-independent way, but also provide a single point of entry into our database.

Getting ready

Apart from the prerequisites of the spring-data-mongodb recipe, we have a few more requirements for this recipe. The first thing is to download the `SpringDataRestTest` project from the Packt website and import it to your IDE as a maven project. Alternatively, if you do not wish to import to the IDE, you can run the server servicing the requests from the command prompt, which we will see in the next section. There is no specific client application used to perform the CRUD operations over REST. I will be demonstrating the concepts using the Chrome browser and a special plugin of the Advanced REST Client browser to send HTTP POST requests to the server. The tools can be found under the **Developer Tools** section of the Chrome web store.

How to do it...

1. If you have imported the project in your IDE as a maven project, execute the `com. packtpub.mongo.cookbook.rest.RestServer` class, which is the bootstrap class and starts the server locally that would accept client connections.

2. If the project is to be executed from the command prompt as a maven project, go to the root directory of the project and run the following:

```
mvn spring-boot:run
```

3. The following line on the command will be seen on the command prompt if all goes well and the server has been started:

```
[INFO] Attaching agents: []
```

4. After starting the server in either way, enter `http://localhost:8080/people` in the browser's address bar and we should see the following JSON response. This response is seen because the underlying person collection is empty.

```
{
  "_links" : {
    "self" : {
      "href" : "http://localhost:8080/people{?page,size,sort}",
      "templated" : true
    },
    "search" : {
      "href" : "http://localhost:8080/people/search"
    }
  },
  "page" : {
    "size" : 20,
    "totalElements" : 0,
    "totalPages" : 0,
    "number" : 0
  }
}
```

5. We will now insert a new document in the person collection using an HTTP POST request to `http://localhost:8080/people`. We will be sending a POST request to the server using the Advanced REST Client Chrome extension. The document posted is:

```
{"lastName":"Cruise", "firstName":"Tom", "age":52, "id":1}.
```

The request's content type is `application/json`.

The following image shows the POST request sent to the server and the response from the server:

6. We will now query this document from the browser using the `_id` field, which is `1` in this case. Enter `http://localhost:8080/people/1` in the browser's address bar. You should see the document that we inserted in step 3.

7. Now that we have one document in the collection, (you can try to insert more documents for people with different names and, more importantly, a unique ID.) we will query the document using the last name. First, type the following URL in the browser's address bar to view the entire search options available: `http://localhost:8080/people/search`. We should see one `search` method, `findByLastName`, that accepts a command line parameter, `lastName`.

8. To search by the last name, Cruise in our case, enter the following URL in the browser's address bar: `http://localhost:8080/people/search/findByLastName?lastName=Cruise`.

9. We will now update the last name and age of the person with the ID 1, Tom Cruise for now. Let's update the last name to Hanks and the age to 58. To do this, we will be using the HTTP PATCH request and the request will be sent to `http://localhost:8080/people/1`, which uniquely identifies the document to update. The body of the HTTP PATCH request is `{"lastName":"Hanks", "age":58}`. Refer to the following image for the request that we sent out for an update:

10. To validate whether our update went through successfully or not (we know it did as we got a response status 204 after the PATCH request), enter `http://localhost:8080/people/1` again in the browser's address bar.

11. Finally, we delete the document. This is straightforward, and we simply send a DELETE request to `http://localhost:8080/people/1`. Once the DELETE request is successful, send an HTTP GET request from the browser to `http://localhost:8080/people/1` and we should not get any document in return.

How it works...

We will not be reiterating the spring-data-mongodb concepts again in this recipe, but will look at some of the annotations that we added specifically for the REST interface to the repository class. The first one is on the top of the class name, as follows:

```
@RepositoryRestResource(path="people")
public interface PersonRepository extends PagingAndSortingRepository<Person, Integer> {
```

This is used to instruct the server that this CRUD repository can be accessed using the people resource. This is the reason why we always make HTTP GET and POST requests on `http://localhost:8080/people/`.

The second annotation is in the `findByLastName` method. We have the following method signature:

```
Person findByLastName(@Param("lastName") String lastName);
```

Here, the method's `lastName` parameter is annotated with the `@Param` annotation, which is used to annotate the name of the parameter that will have the value of the `lastName` parameter that will be passed while invoking this method on the repository. If we look at step 6 in the previous section, we can see that `findByLastName` is invoked using an HTTP GET request, and the value of the URL `lastName` parameter is used as the string value passed while invoking the repository method.

Our example here is pretty simple with just one parameter used for the search operation. We can have multiple parameters for the repository method and an equal number of parameters in the HTTP request that will be mapped to these parameters for the method to be invoked on the CRUD repository. For some types, such as dates to be sent out, use the `@DateTimeFormat` annotation, which will be used to specify the date and time format. Refer to the spring Javadocs at `http://docs.spring.io/spring/docs/current/javadoc-api/` for more information on this annotation and its usage.

This was all about the GET request that we made to the REST interface to query and search data. We initially created a document data sending an HTTP POST request to the server. To create new documents, we would always be sending a POST request—with the document to be created as the body of the request—to the URL identifying the REST endpoint, in our case, `http://localhost:8080/people/`. All documents posted to this collection would be making use of `PersonRepository` to persist `Person` in the corresponding collection.

Our final two steps were to update person and delete person. The HTTP request types to perform these operations are PATCH and DELETE, respectively. In step 7, we updated the document for the person Tom Cruise and updated his last name and age. To achieve this, our PATCH request is sent to a URL identifying a specific person instance, which is `http://localhost:8080/people/1`. Note that in case of creating a new person, our POST request was always sent to `http://localhost:8080/people`, as against the PATCH and DELETE requests, where we sent the HTTP request to a URL representing the specific person that we want to update or delete. In the case of update, the body of the PATCH request is JSON whose provided fields would replace the corresponding fields in the target document to update. All the other fields would be left as is. In our case, `lastName` and the age of the target document were updated and `firstName` was left untouched. In case of delete, the message body was not empty, and the DELETE request itself indicates that the target to which the request was sent should be deleted.

You can also send a PUT request instead of PATCH to a URL, identifying a specific person; in which case, the entire document in the collection would get updated or replaced with the document provided as part of the PUT request.

See also

The spring-data-rest home is at `http://projects.spring.io/spring-data-rest/`, where you can find links to its Git repository, reference manual, and Javadocs URL.

Installing a GUI-based client, MongoVUE, for MongoDB

In this recipe, we will look at a GUI-based client for MongoDB. Throughout the book, we have used the mongo shell to perform various operations that we need. Its advantages are as follows:

- It comes packaged with the MongoDB installation
- Being lightweight, you don't need to worry about it taking up your system's resources
- On servers where GUI-based interfaces are not present, shell is the only option to connect, query, and administer the server instance

Having said this, if you are not on a server and want to connect to a database instance to query, view the plan of a query, administer, and so on, it is nice to have a GUI with these features to let you do things in the click of a button. As a developer, we always query our relational database with a GUI-based thick client, so why not for MongoDB?

In this recipe, we will see how to install some features of a MongoDB client, MongoVUE. This client is available only for Windows machines. This product has both a paid version (with various levels of licensing per number of users) and free version that has some limitations. For this recipe, we'll be looking at the free version.

Getting ready

For this recipe, the following steps are necessary:

1. Start a single instance of MongoDB server. The port on which the connections are accepted will be the default one, `27017`.

2. Import the following two collections from the command prompt after the mongod server has started:

   ```
   $ mongoimport --type json personTwo.json -c personTwo -d test -
   drop
   ```

   ```
   $ mongoimport --type csv -c postalCodes -d test pincodes.csv
   --headerline -drop
   ```

How to do it...

1. Download the installer ZIP for the MongoVUE from `http://www.mongovue.com/downloads/`. Once downloaded, it is a matter of a few clicks and the software gets installed.

2. Open the installed application; as this is a free version, we will have all the features available for the first 14 days, after which, some of the features will not be available. The details of this can be seen at `http://www.mongovue.com/purchase/`.

3. The first thing that we will do is add a database connection:

    ❏   Once the following window has opened, click on the (**+**) button to add a new connection:

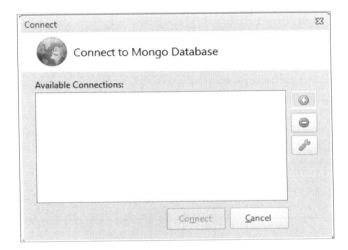

❑ Once opened, we will get another window in which we will fill in the server connection details. Fill in the following details in the new window and click on **Test**. This should succeed if the connection works; finally, click on **Save**.

❑ Once added, connect to the instance.

4. In the left navigation panel, we will see the instances added and the databases in them, as shown in the following image:

As we can see in the preceding image, hovering the mouse over the name of the collection shows us the size and count of the documents in the collection.

5. Let's see how to query a collection and get all the documents. We will use the `postalCodes` collection for our `test`. Right-click on the collection name, and click on **View**. We will see the contents of the collection shown as either a Tree View, where we can expand and see the contents, Table View, which shows the contents in a tabular grid, and Text View, which shows the contents as normal JSON text.

6. Let's see what happens when we query a collection with nested documents; `personTwo` is a collection with the following sample document in it:

```
{
  "_id" : 1,
  "_class" : "com.packtpub.mongo.cookbook.domain.Person2",
  "firstName" : "Steve",
  "lastName" : "Johnson",
  "age" : 30,
  "gender" : "Male",
  "residentialAddress" : {
    "addressLineOne" : "20, Central street",
    "city" : "Sydney",
    "state" : "NSW",
    "country" : "Australia"
  }
}
```

When we query to see all the documents in the collection, we see the following image:

3 Documents (0 to 2)							
_id	_class	firstName	lastName	age	gender	residentialAddress	
1	com.packtpub...	Steve	Johnson	30	Male	{4 Keys}	⇨
2	com.packtpub...	Amit	Sharma	25	Male	{5 Keys}	⇨
3	com.packtpub...	Neha	Sharma	27	Female	{5 Keys}	⇨

The `residentialAddress` column shows that the value is a nested document with the given number of fields present in it. Hovering your mouse over it shows the nested document; alternatively, you can click on the column to show the contents in this document again as a grid. Once the nested documents are shown, you can click on the top of the grid to come back one level.

7. Let's see how to write queries to retrieve selected documents:

❑ Right-click on the **postalCodes** collection, and click on **Find**. We will type the following query in the **{Find}** textbox and the **{Sort}** field, and click on the **Find** button to the right:

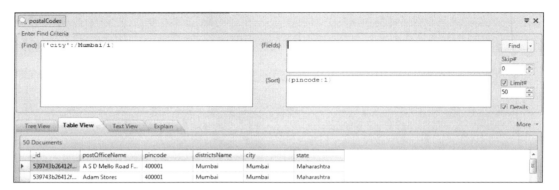

❑ We can choose the type of view that we want from the tab, which is a **Tree View**, **Table View**, or **Text View**. The plan of the query is also shown. Whenever any operation is run, the Learn shell at the bottom shows the actual Mongo query executed. In this case, we see the following:

```
[ 11:17:07 PM ]
db.postalCodes.find({ "city" : /Mumbai/i }).limit(50);
db.postalCodes.find({ "city" : /Mumbai/i }).limit(50).
explain();
```

❑ The plan of a query is also shown every time, and, as of the current version 1.6.9.0, there is no way to disable the showing of the query plan with the query.

8. In **Tree View**, right-clicking on a document will give you more options, such as expand it, copy the JSON contents, add keys to this document, remove the document, and so on. Try to remove a document from this collection using a right-click, and try adding any additional keys to the document. You can choose to restore the documents by reimporting the data from the postalCodes collection.

9. To insert a document in the collection, perform the following. We will be inserting a document in the `personTwo` collection:

   ❑ Right-click on the **personTwo** collection name, and click on **Insert/Import Documents...**, as shown in the following screenshot:

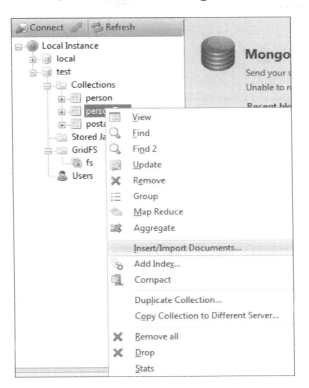

   ❑ Another pop-up window will appear, where you can choose to enter a single JSON document or valid text file with the JSON documents to be imported. We imported the following document by importing a single document:

```
{
  "_id" : 4,
  "firstName" : "Jack",
  "lastName" : "Jones",
 "age" : 35,
 "gender" : "Male"
}
```

   ❑ Query the collection once the document has been imported successfully; we will view the newly imported document along with the old ones.

10. Let's see how to update the document:

❑ You can either right-click on the collection name to the left and click **Update**, or select the **Update** option at the top. In either case, we will see the following window. Here, we will be updating the age of the person that we inserted in the previous step:

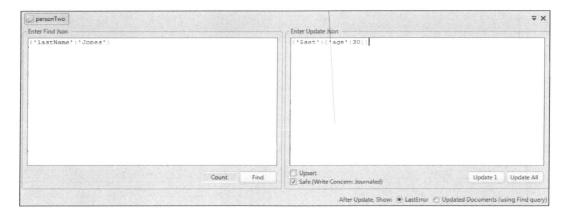

❑ Some things to note in this GUI are the query textbox on the left-hand side to find the document to be updated and the update JSON on the right-hand side, which will be applied to the selected document(s).

❑ Before you update, you can choose to hit the **Count** button to see the number of documents that can be updated (in this case, one). Clicking on **Find** will show you the documents in the Tree form. On the right-hand side, below the update JSON text, we have the option to update one document and multiple documents by clicking on **Update 1** or **Update All**.

❑ You can choose an **Upsert** operation in case the documents for the given **Find** condition are not found.

❑ The radio buttons on the bottom right of the preceding screen shows either the output of the getLastError operation or the result after the update, in which case, a query will be executed to find the document(s) updated.

❑ The find query, however, is not foolproof and might return different results than those truly updated as a separate query, the same as in the **Find** textbox. The update and find operations are not atomic.

11. We have queried on small collections so far. As the size of the collection increases, queries performing full collection scans are not acceptable and we need to create indexes as follows:

❑ To create an index by lastName in ascending order and age in descending order, we will invoke db.personTwo.ensureIndex({'lastName':1, 'age':-1}).

- Using MongoVUE, there is a way to visually create the same index by right-clicking on the collection name on the left-hand side of the screen and selecting **Add Index....**

- In the new pop-up window, enter the name of the index and select the **Visual** tab as shown. Select the **lastName** and **age** fields with ascending and descending values, respectively:

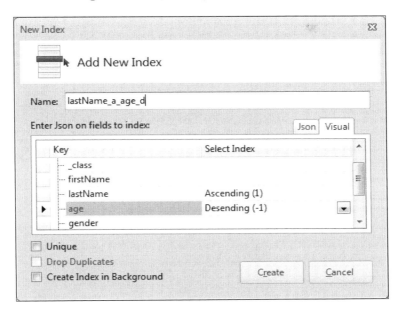

- Once these details are filled in, click on **Create**. This should create the index for us by firing the `ensureIndex` command.

- You can choose the index to be **Unique** and **Drop Duplicates** (which will be enabled when unique is selected), or even create big, long, and running index creations in the background.

- Note the **Json** tab next to the **Visual** tab. This is the place where you can type the `ensureIndex` command as you do in the shell in order to create the index.

12. We will see how to drop an index:

- Simply expand the tree on the left-hand side (as shown in the screen shot in step 9)

- On expanding the collection, we will see all the indexes created on it

- ❑ Except for the default index on the `_id` field, all the other indexes can be dropped

- ❑ Simply right-click on the name and select **Drop index** to drop or click on **Properties** to view its properties

13. After seeing how to do the basic CRUD operations and creating an index, let's look at how to execute the aggregation operations:

- ❑ There are no visual tools as in the index creation for aggregation but simply a text area where we enter our aggregation pipeline

- ❑ In the following sample, we perform aggregation on the `postalCodes` collection to find the top five states by the number of times they appear in the collection

- ❑ We will have the following aggregation pipeline entered:

    ```
    {'$project' : {'state':1, '_id':0}},
    {'$group': {'_id':'$state', 'count':{'$sum':1}}},
    {'$sort':{'count':-1}},
    {'$limit':5}
    ```

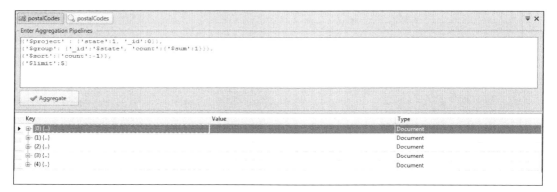

- ❑ Once the pipeline is entered, hit the **Aggregate** button to get the aggregation results

14. Executing MapReduce is even cooler. The use case that we will be executing is similar to the preceding one, but we will see how to implement a MapReduce operation using MongoVUE:

- ❑ To execute a map reduce job, right-click on the collection name in the left-hand side menu, and click on **Map Reduce**.

- ❑ This option is right above the **Aggregation** option that we saw in the previous image. This gives us a pretty neat GUI to enter the **Map**, **Reduce**, **Finalize** and the **In & Out**, as shown in the following image:

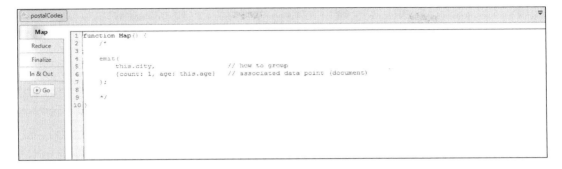

- ❑ The Map function is simply the following:

```
function Map() {
    emit(this.state, 1)
}
```

- ❑ The Reduce function is the following:

```
function Reduce(key, values) {
    return Array.sum(values)
}
```

- ❑ Leave the Finalize method unimplemented, and in the **In & Out** section, fill in the following details:

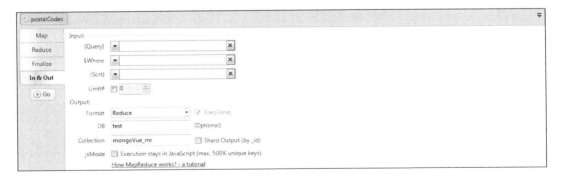

- ❑ Click on **Go** to start executing the MapReduce job.

❏ We will print the output to the `mongoVue_mr` collection. Query the `mongoVue_mr` collection using the following query:

```
db.mongoVue_mr.find().sort({value:-1}).limit(5)
```

❏ Check the results against those that we got using aggregation.

❏ The format of map reduce was chosen as **Reduce**. For more options and their behavior, visit `http://docs.mongodb.org/manual/reference/command/mapReduce/#mapreduce-out-cmd`.

15. Monitoring the server instances is now possible using `MongoVUE`:

❏ To monitor an instance, click on **Tools** | **Monitoring** in the top menu.

❏ By default, no server will be added, and we will have to click on **+ Add Server** to add a server instance.

❏ Select the Local Instance added or any server that you want to monitor, and click on **Connect**.

❏ We will see quite a lot of monitoring details. MongoVUE uses the `db.serverStatus` command to serve these stats and limit the frequency at which we execute this command on busy server instances, we can choose the **Refresh Interval** at the top of the screen, as shown in the following image:

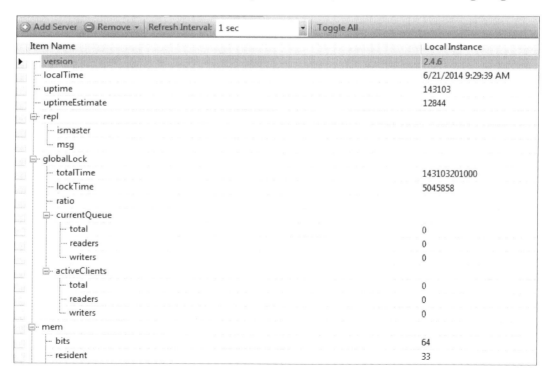

How it works...

What we covered in the previous sections was pretty straightforward for us to perform the majority of our activities as a developer and administrator.

There's more...

Refer to *Chapter 4, Administration* and *Chapter 6, Monitoring and Backups,* for recipes on the administration and monitoring of the MongoDB instances.

See also

▸   Refer to `http://www.mongovue.com/tutorials/` for various tutorials on MongoVUE

 While writing this book, MongoDB was planning to release a similar data visualisation and manipulation product called **Compass**. You should check it out `https://www.mongodb.com/products/compass`.

Concepts for Reference

This appendix contains some additional information that will help you understand the recipes better. We will discuss write concern and read preference in as much detail as possible.

Write concern and its significance

Write concern is the minimum guarantee that the MongoDB server provides with respect to the write operation done by the client. There are various levels of write concern that are set by the client application, to get a guarantee from the server that a certain stage will be reached in the write process on the server side.

The stronger the requirement for a guarantee, the greater the time taken (potentially) to get a response from the server. With write concern, we don't always need to get an acknowledgement from the server about the write operation being completely successful. For some less crucial data such as logs, we might be more interested in sending more writes per second over a connection. On the other hand, when we are looking to update sensitive information, such as customer details, we want to be sure of the write being successful (consistent and durable); data integrity is crucial and takes precedence over the speed of the writes.

An extremely useful feature of write concern is the ability to compromise between one of the factors: the speed of write operations and the consistency of the data written, on a case-to-case basis. However, it needs a deep understanding of the implications of setting up a particular write concern. The following diagram runs from the left and goes to the right, and shows the increasing level of write guarantees:

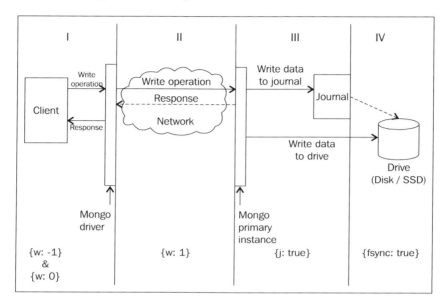

As we move from **I** to **IV**, the guarantee for the performed write gets stronger and stronger, but the time taken to execute the write operation is longer from a client's perspective. All write concerns are expressed here as JSON objects, using three different keys, namely, w, j, and fsync. Additionally, another key called wtimeout is used to provide timeout values for the write operation. Let's see the three keys in detail:

- ▶ w: This is used to indicate whether to wait for the server's acknowledgement or not, whether to report write errors due to data issues or not, and about the data being replicated to secondary. Its value is usually a number and a special case where the value can be majority, which we will see later.

- ▶ j: This is related to journaling and its value can be a Boolean (true/false or 1/0).

- ▶ fsync: This is a Boolean value and is related to whether the write should wait till the data is flushed to disk or not before responding.

- ▶ wtimeout: This specifies the timeout for write operations, whereby the driver throws an exception to the client if the server doesn't respond back in seconds within the provided time. We will see the option in some detail soon.

In part **I**, which we have demarcated till driver, we have two write concerns, namely, {w:-1} and {w:0}. Both these write concerns are common, in a sense that they neither wait for the server's acknowledgement upon receiving the write operation, nor do they report any exception on the server side caused by unique index violation. The client will get an ok response and will discover the write failure only when they query the database at some later point of time and find the data missing. The difference is in the way both these respond on the network error. When we set {w:-1}, the operation doesn't fail and a write response is received by the user. However, it will contain a response stating that a network error prevented the write operation from succeeding and no retries for write must be attempted. On the other hand, with {w:0}, if a network error occurs, the driver might choose to retry the operation and throw an exception to the client if the write fails due to network error. Both these write concerns give a quick response back to the invoking client at the cost of data consistency. These write concerns are ok for use cases such as logging, where occasional log write misses are fine. In older versions of MongoDB, {w:0} was the default write concern if none was mentioned by the invoking client. At the time of writing this book, this has changed to {w:1} by default and the option {w:0} is deprecated.

In part **II** of the diagram, which falls between the driver and the server, the write concern we are talking about is {w:1}. The driver waits for an acknowledgement from the server for the write operation to complete. Note that the server responding doesn't mean that the write operation was made durable. It means that the change just got updated into the memory, all the constraints were checked, and any exception will be reported to the client, unlike the previous two write concerns we saw. This is a relatively safe write concern mode, which will be fast, but there is still a slim chance of the data being lost if it crashes in those few milliseconds when the data was written to the journal from the memory. For most use cases, this is a good option to set. Hence, this is the default write concern mode.

Moving on, we come to part **III** of the diagram, which is from the entry point into the server as far as the journal. The write concern we are looking for here is at {j:1} or {j:true}. This write concern ensures a response to the invoking client only when the write operation is written to the journal. What is a journal though? This is something that we saw in depth in *Chapter 4, Administration*, but for now, we will just look at a mechanism that ensures that the writes are made durable and the data on the disk doesn't get corrupted in the event of server crashes.

Finally, let's come to part **IV** of the diagram; the write concern we are talking about is {fsync:true}. This requires that the data be flushed to disk to get before sending the response back to the client. In my opinion, when journaling is enabled, this operation doesn't really add any value, as journaling ensures data persistence even on server crash. Only when journaling is disabled does this option ensure that the write operation is successful when the client receives a success response. If the data is really important, journaling should never be disabled in the first place as it also ensures that the data on the disk doesn't get corrupted.

We have seen some basic write concerns for a single-node server or those relevant to the primary node only in a replica set.

An interesting thing to discuss is, what if we have a write concern such as {w:0, j:true}? We do not wait for the server's acknowledgement and also ensure that the write has been made to the journal. In this case, journaling flag takes precedence and the client waits for the acknowledgement of the write operation. One should avoid setting such ambiguous write concerns to avoid unpleasant surprises.

We will now talk about write concern when it involves secondary nodes of a replica set as well. Let's take a look at the following diagram:

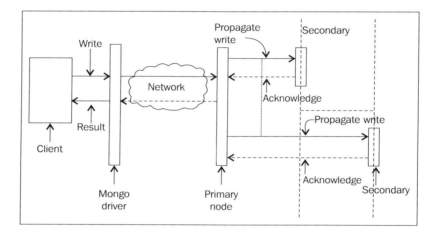

Any write concern with a w value greater than one indicates that secondary nodes too need to acknowledge before sending a response back. As seen in the preceding diagram, when a primary node gets a write operation, it propagates that operation to all secondary nodes. As soon as it gets a response from a predetermined number of secondary nodes, it acknowledges the client that the write has been successful. For example, when we have a write concern {w:3}, it means that the client should be sent a response only when three nodes in the cluster acknowledge the write. These three nodes include the primary node. Hence, it is now down to two secondary nodes to respond back for a successful write operation.

However, there is a problem with providing a number for the write concern. We need to know the number of nodes in the cluster and accordingly set the value of w. A low value will send an acknowledgement to a few nodes replicating the data. A value too high may unnecessarily slow the response back to the client, or in some cases, might not send a response at all. Suppose you have a three-node replica set and we have {w:4} as the write concern, the server will not send an acknowledgement till the data is replicated to three secondary nodes, which do not exist as we have just two secondary nodes. Thus, the client waits for a very long time to hear from the server about the write operation. There are a couple of ways to address this problem:

- ▶ Use the wtimeout key and specify the timeout for the write concern. This will ensure that a write operation will not block for longer than the time specified (in milliseconds) for the wtimeout field of the write concern. For example, {w:3, wtimeout:10000} ensures that the write operation will not block more than 10 seconds (10,000 ms), after which an exception will be thrown to the client. In the case of Java, a WriteConcernException will be thrown with the root cause message stating the reason as timeout. Note that this exception does not rollback the write operation. It just informs the client that the operation did not get completed in the specified amount of time. It might later be completed on the server side, some time after the client receives the timeout exception. It is up to the application program to deal with the exception and programmatically take the corrective steps. The message for the timeout exception does convey some interesting details, which we will see on executing the test program for the write concern.

- ▶ A better way to specify the value of w, in the case of replica sets, is by specifying the value as majority. This write concern automatically identifies the number of nodes in a replica set and sends an acknowledgement back to the client when the data is replicated to a majority of nodes. For example, if the write concern is {w:"majority"} and the number of nodes in a replica set is three, then majority will be 2. Whereas, at the later point in time, when we change the number of nodes to five, the majority will be 3 nodes. The number of nodes to form a majority automatically gets computed when the write concern's value is given as majority.

Now, let us put the concepts we discussed into use and execute a test program that will demonstrate some of the concepts we just saw.

Setting up a replica set

To set up a replica set, you should know how to start the basic replica set with three nodes. Refer to the *Starting multiple instances as part of a replica set* recipe in *Chapter 1, Installing and Starting the Server*. This recipe is built on that recipe because it needs an additional configuration while starting the replica set, which we will discuss in the next section. Note that the replica used here has a slight change in configuration to the one you have used earlier.

Here, we will use a Java program to demonstrate various write concerns and their behavior. The *Connecting to a single node using a Java client* recipe in *Chapter 1, Installing and Starting the Server*, should be visited until Maven is set up. This can be a bit inconvenient if you are coming from a non-Java background.

> The Java project named `Mongo Java` is available for download at the book's website. If the setup is complete, you can test the project just by executing the following command:
>
> ```
> mvn compile exec:java
> -Dexec.mainClass=com.packtpub.mongo.cookbook.
> FirstMongoClient
> ```
>
> The code for this project is available for download at the book's website. Download the project named `WriteConcernTest` and keep it on a local drive ready for execution.

So, let's get started:

1. Prepare the following configuration file for the replica set. This is identical to the config file that we saw in the *Starting multiple instances as part of a replica set* recipe in *Chapter 1, Installing and Starting the Server*, where we set up the replica set, as follows, with just one difference, `slaveDelay:5, priority:0`:

    ```
    cfg = {
      _id:'repSetTest',
      members:[
          {_id:0, host:'localhost:27000'},
          {_id:1, host:'localhost:27001'},
          {_id:2, host:'localhost:27002', slaveDelay:5, priority:0}
      ]
    }
    ```

2. Use this config to start a three-node replica set, with one node listening to port `27000`. The others can be any ports of your choice, but stick to `27001` and `27002` if possible (we need to update the config accordingly if we decide to use a different port number). Also, remember to set the name of the replica set as `replSetTest` for the `replSet` command-line option while starting the replica set. Give some time to the replica set to come up before going ahead with next step.

3. At this point, the replica set with the earlier mentioned specifications should be up and running. We will now execute the test code provided in Java, to observe some interesting facts and behaviors of different write concerns. Note that this program also tries to connect to a port where no Mongo process is listening for connections. The port chosen is `20000`; ensure that before running the code, no server is up and running and listening to port `20000`.

4. Go to the root directory of the `WriteConcernTest` project and execute the following command:

```
mvn compile exec:java
-Dexec.mainClass=com.packtpub.mongo.cookbook.WriteConcernTests
```

It should take some time to execute completely, depending on your hardware configuration. Roughly around 35 to 40 seconds were taken on my machine, which has a spinning disk drive with a 7200 RPM.

Before we continue analyzing the logs, let us see what those two additional fields added to the config file to set up the replica were. The `slaveDelay` field indicates that the particular slave (the one listening on port `27002` in this case) will lag behind the primary by 5 seconds. That is, the data being replicated currently on this replica node will be the one that was added on to the primary 5 seconds ago. Secondly, this node can never be a primary and hence, the `priority` field has to be added with the value `0`. We have already seen this in detail in *Chapter 4, Administration*.

Let us now analyze the output from the preceding command's execution. The Java class provided need not be looked at here; the output on the console is sufficient. Some of the relevant portions of the output console are as follows:

```
[INFO] --- exec-maven-plugin:1.2.1:java (default-cli) @ mongo-cookbook-
wctest ---
Trying to connect to server running on port 20000
Trying to write data in the collection with write concern {w:-1}
Error returned in the WriteResult is NETWORK ERROR
Trying to write data in the collection with write concern {w:0}
Caught MongoException.Network trying to write to collection, message is
Write operation to server localhost/127.0.0.1:20000 failed on database
test
Connected to replica set with one node listening on port 27000 locally


Inserting duplicate keys with {w:0}
No exception caught while inserting data with duplicate _id
Now inserting the same data with {w:1}
Caught Duplicate Exception, exception message is { "serverUsed" :
"localhost/127.0.0.1:27000" , "err" : "E11000 duplicate key error index:
test.writeConcernTest.$_id_  dup key: { : \"a\" }" , "code" : 11000 , "n"
: 0 , "lastOp" : { "$ts" :1386009990 , "$inc" : 2} , "connectionId" : 157
, "ok" : 1.0}
Average running time with WriteConcern {w:1, fsync:false, j:false} is 0 ms
Average running time with WriteConcern {w:2, fsync:false, j:false} is 12
ms
Average running time with WriteConcern {w:1, fsync:false, j:true} is 40 ms
```

```
Average running time with WriteConcern {w:1, fsync:true, j:false} is 44 ms
Average running time with WriteConcern {w:3, fsync:false, j:false} is 5128
ms
Caught WriteConcern exception for {w:5}, with following message {
"serverUsed" : "localhost/127.0.0.1:27000" , "n" : 0 , "lastOp" : {
"$ts" : 1386009991 , "$inc" : 18} , "connectionId" : 157 , "wtimeout"
: true , "waited" : 1004 , "writtenTo" : [ { "_id" : 0 , "host" :
"localhost:27000"} , { "_id" : 1 , "host" : "localhost:27001"}] , "err" :
"timeout" , "ok" : 1.0}
 [INFO] ------------------------------------------------------------------
------
[INFO] BUILD SUCCESS
[INFO] ------------------------------------------------------------------
-----
[INFO] Total time: 36.671s
[INFO] Finished at: Tue Dec 03 00:16:57 IST 2013
[INFO] Final Memory: 13M/33M
[INFO] ------------------------------------------------------------------
-----
```

The first statement in the log states that we try to connect to a Mongo process listening on port 20000. As there should not be a Mongo server running and listening to this port for client connections, all our write operations to this server should not succeed, and this will now give us a chance to see what happens when we use the write concerns {w:-1} and {w:0} and write to this nonexistent server.

The next two lines in the output show that when we have the write concern {w:-1}, we do get a write result back, but it contains the error flag set to indicate a network error. However, no exception is thrown. In the case of the write concern {w:0}, we do get an exception in the client application for any network errors. Of course, all other write concerns ensuring a strict guarantee will throw an exception in this case too.

Now we come to the portion of the code that connects to the replica set where one of the nodes is listening to port 27000 (if not, the code will show the error on the console and terminate). Now, we attempt to insert a document with a duplicate _id field ({'_id':'a'}) into a collection, once with the write concern {w:0} and once with {w:1}. As we see in the console, the former ({w:0}) didn't throw an exception and the insert went through successfully from the client's perspective, whereas the latter ({w:1}) threw an exception to the client, indicating a duplicate key. The exception contains a lot of information about the server's hostname and port, at the time when the exception occurred: the field for which the unique constraint failed; the client connection ID; error code; and the value that was not unique and caused the exception. The fact is that, even when the insert was performed using {w:0} as the write concern, it failed. However, as the driver didn't wait for the server's acknowledgement, it was never communicated about the failure.

Moving on, we now try to compute the time taken for the write operation to complete. The time shown here is the average of the time taken to execute the same operation with a given write concern five times. Note that these times will vary on different instances of execution of the program, and this method is just meant to give some rough estimates for our study. We can conclude from the output that the time taken for the write concern {w:1} is less than that of {w:2} (asking for an acknowledgement from one secondary node) and the time taken for {w:2} is less than {j:true}, which in turn is less than {fsync:true}. The next line of the output shows us that the average time taken for the write operation to complete is roughly 5 seconds when the write concern is {w:3}. Any guesses on why that is the case? Why does it take so long? The reason is, when w is 3, we send an acknowledgement to the client only when two secondary nodes acknowledge the write operation. In our case, one of the nodes is delayed from the primary by about 5 seconds, and thus, it can acknowledge the write only after 5 seconds, and hence, the client receives a response from the server in roughly 5 seconds.

Let us do a quick exercise here. What do you'll think would be the approximate response time when we have the write concern as {w:'majority'}? The hint here is, for a replica set of three nodes, two is the majority.

Finally we see a timeout exception. Timeout is set using the wtimeout field of the document and is specified in milliseconds. In our case, we gave a timeout of 1000 ms, that is 1 second, and the number of nodes in the replica set to get an acknowledgement from before sending the response back to the client is 5 (four secondary instances). Thus, we have the write concern as {w:5, wtimeout:1000}. As our maximum number of nodes is three, the operation with the value of w set to 5 will wait for a very long time until two more secondary instances are added to the cluster. With the timeout set, the client returns and throws an error to the client, conveying some interesting details. The following is the JSON sent as an exception message:

```
{ "serverUsed" : "localhost/127.0.0.1:27000" , "n" : 0 , "lastOp" : {
"$ts" : 1386015030 , "$inc" : 1} , "connectionId" : 507 , "wtimeout"
: true , "waited" : 1000 , "writtenTo" : [ { "_id" : 0 , "host" :
"localhost:27000"} , { "_id" : 1 , "host" : "localhost:27001"}] , "err" :
"timeout" , "ok" : 1.0}
```

Let us look at the interesting fields. We start with the n field. This indicates the number of documents updated. As in this case it is an insert and not an update, it stays 0. The wtimeout and waited fields tell us whether the transaction did timeout and the amount of time for which the client waited for a response; in this case 1000 ms. The most interesting field is writtenTo. In this case, the insert was successful on these two nodes of the replica set when the operation timed out, and hence, it is seen in the array. The third node has a slaveDelay value of 5 seconds and, hence, the data is still not written to it. This proves that the timeout doesn't roll back the insert and it does go through successfully. In fact, the node with slaveDelay will also have the data after 5 seconds, even if the operation times out, and this makes perfect sense as it keeps the primary and secondary instances in sync. It is the responsibility of the application to detect such timeouts and handle them.

Read preference for querying

In the previous section, we saw what a write concern is and how it affects the write operations (insert, update, and delete). In this section, we will see what a read preference is and how it affects query operations. We'll discuss how to use a read preference in separate recipes, to use specific programming language drivers.

When connected to an individual node, query operations will be allowed by default when connected to a primary, and in case if it is connected to a secondary node, we need to explicitly state that it is ok to query from secondary instances by executing `rs.slaveOk()` from the shell.

However, consider connecting to a Mongo replica set from an application. It will connect to the replica set and not a single instance from the application. Depending on the nature of the application, it might always want to connect to a primary; always to a secondary; prefer connecting to a primary node but would be ok to connect to a secondary node in some scenarios and vice versa and finally, it might connect to the instance geographically close to it (well, most of the time).

Thus, the read preference plays an important role when connected to a replica set and not to a single instance. In the following table, we will see the various read preferences that are available and what their behavior is in terms of querying a replica set. There are five of them and the names are self-explanatory:

Read preference	Description
`primary`	This is the default mode and it allows queries to be executed only on primary instances. It is the only mode that guarantees the most recent data, as all writes have to go through a primary instance. Read operations however will fail if no primary is available, which happens for a few moments when a primary goes down and continues till a new primary is chosen.
`primaryPreferred`	This is identical to the preceding primary read preference, except that during a failover, when no primary is available, it will read data from the secondary and those are the times when it possibly doesn't read the most recent data.
`secondary`	This is exactly the opposite to the default primary read preference. This mode ensures that read operations never go to a primary and a secondary is chosen always. The chances of reading inconsistent data that is not updated to the latest write operation are maximal in this mode. It, however, is ok (in fact, preferred) for applications that do not face end users and are used for some instances to get hourly statistics and analytics jobs used for in-house monitoring, where the accuracy of the data is least important, but not adding a load to the primary instance is key. If no secondary instance is available or reachable, and only a primary instance is, the read operation will fail.

Read preference	Description
secondaryPreferred	This is similar to the preceding secondary read preference, in all aspects except that if no secondary is available, the read operations will go to the primary instance.
nearest	This, unlike all the preceding read preferences, can connect either to a primary or a secondary. The primary objective for this read preference is minimum latency between the client and an instance of a replica set. In the majority of the cases, owing to the network latency and with a similar network between the client and all instances, the instance chosen will be one that is geographically close.

Similar to how write concerns can be coupled with shard tags, read preferences can also be used along with shard tags. As the concept of tags has already been introduced in *Chapter 4, Administration*, you can refer to it for more details.

We just saw what the different types of read preferences are (except for those using tags) but the question is, how do we use them? We have covered Python and Java clients in this book and will see how to use them in their respective recipes. We can set read preferences at various levels: at the client level, collection level, and query level, with the one specified at the query level overriding any other read preference set previously.

Let us see what the nearest read preference means. Conceptually, it can be visualized as something like the following diagram:

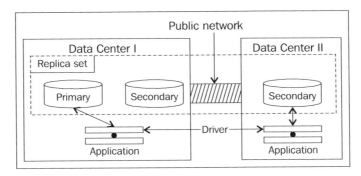

A Mongo replica set is set up with one secondary, which can never be a primary, in a separate data center and two (one primary and a secondary) in another data center. An identical application deployed in both the data centers, with a primary read preference, will always connect to the primary instance in **Data Center I**. This means, for the application in **Data Center II**, the traffic goes over the public network, which will have high latency. However, if the application is ok with slightly stale data, it can set the read preference as the nearest, which will automatically let the application in **Data Center I** connect to an instance in **Data Center I** and will allow an application in **Data Center II** to connect to the secondary instance in **Data Center II**.

But then the next question is, how does the driver know which one is the nearest? The term "geographically close" is misleading; it is actually the one with the minimum network latency. The instance we query might be geographically further than another instance in the replica set, but it can be chosen just because it has an acceptable response time. Generally, better response time means geographically closer.

The following section is for those interested in internal details from the driver on how the nearest node is chosen. If you are happy with just the concepts and not the internal details, you can safely skip the rest of the contents.

Knowing the internals

Let us see some pieces of code from a Java client (driver 2.11.3 is used for this purpose) and make some sense out of it. If we look at the `com.mongodb.TaggableReadPreference.NearestReadPreference.getNode` method, we see the following implementation:

```
@Override
ReplicaSetStatus.ReplicaSetNode getNode(ReplicaSetStatus.ReplicaSet
set) {
  if (_tags.isEmpty())
    return set.getAMember();

  for (DBObject curTagSet : _tags) {
    List<ReplicaSetStatus.Tag> tagList = getTagListFromDBObject(curTa
gSet);
    ReplicaSetStatus.ReplicaSetNode node = set.getAMember(tagList);
    if (node != null) {
      return node;
    }
  }
  return null;
}
```

For now, if we ignore the contents where tags are specified, all it does is execute `set.getAMember()`.

The name of this method tells us that there is a set of replica set members and we returned one of them randomly. Then what decides whether the set contains a member or not? If we dig a bit further into this method, we see the following lines of code in the `com.mongodb.ReplicaSetStatus.ReplicaSet` class:

```
public ReplicaSetNode getAMember() {

  checkStatus();

  if (acceptableMembers.isEmpty()) {

    return null;

  }

  return acceptableMembers.get(random.nextInt(acceptableMembers.
size()));

}
```

Ok, so all it does is pick one from a list of replica set nodes maintained internally. Now, the random pick can be a secondary, even if a primary can be chosen (because it is present in the list). Thus, we can now say that when the nearest is chosen as a read preference, and even if a primary is in the list of contenders, it might not necessarily be chosen randomly.

The question now is, how is the `acceptableMembers` list initialized? We see it is done in the constructor of the `com.mongodb.ReplicaSetStatus.ReplicaSet` class as follows:

```
this.acceptableMembers =
  Collections.unmodifiableList(calculateGoodMembers(all,
    calculateBestPingTime(all, true),
      acceptableLatencyMS, true));
```

The `calculateBestPingTime` line just finds the best ping time of all (we will see what this ping time is later).

Another parameter worth mentioning is `acceptableLatencyMS`. This gets initialized in `com.mongodb.ReplicaSetStatus.Updater` (this is actually a background thread that updates the status of the replica set continuously), and the value for `acceptableLatencyMS` is initialized as follows:

```
slaveAcceptableLatencyMS = Integer.parseInt(System.getProperty("com.
mongodb.slaveAcceptableLatencyMS", "15"));
```

As we can see, this code searches for the system variable called `com.mongodb.slaveAcceptableLatencyMS`, and if none is found, it initializes to the value `15`, which is 15 ms.

This `com.mongodb.ReplicaSetStatus.Updater` class also has a `run` method that periodically updates the replica set stats. Without getting too much into it, we can see that it calls `updateAll`, which eventually reaches the `update` method in `com.mongodb.ConnectionStatus.UpdatableNode`:

```
long start = System.nanoTime();
CommandResult res = _port.runCommand(_mongo.getDB("admin"),
isMasterCmd);
long end = System.nanoTime()
```

All it does is execute the `{isMaster:1}` command and record the response time in nanoseconds. This response time is converted to milliseconds and stored as the ping time. So, coming back to the `com.mongodb.ReplicaSetStatus.ReplicaSet` class it stores, all `calculateGoodMembers` does is find and add the members of a replica set that are no more than `acceptableLatencyMS` milliseconds more than the best ping time found in the replica set.

For example, in a replica set with three nodes, the ping times from the client to the three nodes (node 1, node 2, and node 3) are 2 ms, 5 ms, and 150 ms respectively. As we see, the best time is 2 ms and hence, node 1 goes into the set of good members. Now, from the remaining nodes, all those with a latency that is no more than `acceptableLatencyMS` more than the best, which is *2 + 15 ms = 17 ms*, as 15 ms is the default that will be considered. Thus, node 2 is also a contender, leaving out node 3. We now have two nodes in the list of good members (good in terms of latency).

Now, putting together all that we saw on how it would work for the scenario we saw in the preceding diagram, the least response time will be from one of the instances in the same data center (from the programming language driver's perspective in these two data centers), as the instance(s) in other data centers might not respond within 15 ms (the default acceptable value) more than the best response time due to public network latency. Thus, the acceptable nodes in **Data Center I** will be two of the replica set nodes in that data center, and one of them will be chosen at random, and for **Data Center II**, only one instance is present and is the only option. Hence, it will be chosen by the application running in that data center.

Index

Symbols

$text operator
reference link 201
@DateTimeFormat annotation
reference link 313
using 313

A

aggregation
implementing, with Java client 88, 89
implementing, with PyMongo 76, 77
alerts
setting up, on MMS 217-226
Amazon EC2
MongoDB, setting up 258-264
URL 259
Amazon Elastic Map Reduce (Amazon EMR)
about 284
MapReduce job, running 284-290
URL 284
Amazon Machine Image (AMI)
about 258
URL 258
Amazon Simple Storage Service (Amazon S3)
URL 284
Amazon Web Services (AWS)
about 232, 248
URL 259
Apache Hadoop
URL 270

atomic counters
implementing 162, 163
atomic find operation
performing 160-162
atomic modify operation
performing 160-162

B

background index
creating 51-54
binary data
storing 171, 172
built-in user roles
URL 124

C

capped collection
cursors, creating 166-168
cursors, tailing 166-168
normal collection, converting 169, 170
cloud computing
reference link 248
collection
manual splitting 152, 153
migrating 152, 153
modifying, collMod command used 127, 128
renaming 94-96
stats, viewing 96-99
command-line options
--config or -f 4
--configsvr 5

M

Thank you for buying
MongoDB Cookbook
Second Edition

About Packt Publishing

Packt, pronounced 'packed', published its first book, *Mastering phpMyAdmin for Effective MySQL Management*, in April 2004, and subsequently continued to specialize in publishing highly focused books on specific technologies and solutions.

Our books and publications share the experiences of your fellow IT professionals in adapting and customizing today's systems, applications, and frameworks. Our solution-based books give you the knowledge and power to customize the software and technologies you're using to get the job done. Packt books are more specific and less general than the IT books you have seen in the past. Our unique business model allows us to bring you more focused information, giving you more of what you need to know, and less of what you don't.

Packt is a modern yet unique publishing company that focuses on producing quality, cutting-edge books for communities of developers, administrators, and newbies alike. For more information, please visit our website at www.packtpub.com.

About Packt Open Source

In 2010, Packt launched two new brands, Packt Open Source and Packt Enterprise, in order to continue its focus on specialization. This book is part of the Packt open source brand, home to books published on software built around open source licenses, and offering information to anybody from advanced developers to budding web designers. The Open Source brand also runs Packt's open source Royalty Scheme, by which Packt gives a royalty to each open source project about whose software a book is sold.

Writing for Packt

We welcome all inquiries from people who are interested in authoring. Book proposals should be sent to author@packtpub.com. If your book idea is still at an early stage and you would like to discuss it first before writing a formal book proposal, then please contact us; one of our commissioning editors will get in touch with you.

We're not just looking for published authors; if you have strong technical skills but no writing experience, our experienced editors can help you develop a writing career, or simply get some additional reward for your expertise.

Web Development with MongoDB and NodeJS

Second Edition

ISBN: 978-1-78528-752-7   Paperback: 300 pages

Build an interactive and full-featured web application from scratch using Node.js and MongoDB

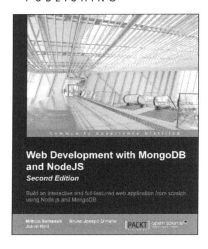

1. Configure your development environment to use Node.js and MongoDB.

2. Use Node.js to connect to a MongoDB database and perform data manipulations.

3. A practical guide with clear instructions to design and develop a complete web application from start to finish.

MongoDB for Java Developers

ISBN: 978-1-78528-027-6   Paperback: 192 pages

Design, build, and deliver efficient Java applications using the most advanced NoSQL database

1. Reuse the skills you have acquired through Hibernate or Spring to promote your applications to use NoSQL storage.

2. Explore the list of libraries that are already available to assist you in developing Java EE applications with MongoDB.

3. A step-by-step tutorial to create leaner and faster applications using MongoDB.

Please check **www.PacktPub.com** for information on our titles

MongoDB Data Modeling

ISBN: 978-1-78217-534-6   Paperback: 202 pages

Focus on data usage and better design schemas with the help of MongoDB

1. Create reliable, scalable data models with MongoDB.

2. Optimize the schema design process to support applications of all kinds.

3. Use this comprehensive guide to implement advanced schema designs.

Learning MongoDB [Video]

ISBN: 978-1-78398-392-6   Duration: 03:26 hours

A comprehensive guide to using MongoDB for ultra-fast, fault tolerant management of big data, including advanced data analysis

1. Master MapReduce and the MongoDB aggregation framework for sophisticated manipulation of large sets of data.

2. Manage databases and collections, including backup, recovery, and security.

3. Discover how to secure your data using SSL, both from the client and via programming languages.

Please check **www.PacktPub.com** for information on our titles

17145055R00205

Printed in Great Britain
by Amazon